PC GUIDE™
Introduction To
Computers

The Easiest Way To Master Your PC

Inter Trade Corporation
ITC Publishing Group
Norcross, Georgia 30092

Foreword

By: Bill Goodhew
President & CEO
Peachtree Software, Inc.

Owning a personal computer ten years ago was a luxury that most homes and small businesses couldn't afford. But today, thanks to a dramatic decrease in both hardware and software prices, the PC is an important part of our lives, often becoming a necessity to many users.

We use our PCs to shop, to pay our bills, to balance our checkbooks, to run our businesses, to play games, and to communicate with others across the country and across the world.

But while we have seen tremendous strides in development since the PC was first introduced in 1981, we are now at the threshold of what promises to be an immense explosion of technology.

On the horizon are even faster, more powerful PCs and intuitive, easier-to-use software. And beyond that is a future of interactive communications speeding along electronic highways that link communities worldwide and allow PCs to communicate and to interact. As cable operators and telephone companies become part of the PC revolution, we'll use their technology to download programs right from our telephone lines or from our cable channels on television directly to our PCs.

At Peachtree, we've been creating and selling software since the PC was first introduced. In fact, we were one of the first three software programs written for the PC. While we've seen the industry change, we've noted that one thing has remained constant: the importance of knowing how to use your personal computer.

That's why PC GUIDE is so important for PC users. You need to get the most out of your personal computer. If you want to keep pace in the PC revolution, both today and tomorrow, then you must know how to use a computer and how to use it effectively.

Acknowledgments

Special thanks to the following for their participation in the development and production of the "PC GUIDE Introduction To Computers" book, video, CD-ROM, and software tutorial.

Sol Rezai	Mark Sirull	Buddy Booker
Helene Erb	Fred Huff	Mike Sharafat
Jonathan Beacher	Tim King	

The staff of the reference library at the Georgia Institute of Technology

Trademarks

IBM, IBM PC, IBM XT, IBM AT, OS/2, PS/1, PS/2, Micro Channel are registered trademarks of International Business Machines

Intel is a registered trademark of Intel Corporation

Apple, Macintosh are registered trademarks of Apple Computer, Inc.

HP, HP DeskJet, HP LaserJet are registered trademarks of Hewlett Packard Corporation

MS-DOS, MS Windows, Word for Windows, MS Works, Excel are registered trademarks of Microsoft Corporation

1-2-3, Lotus are registered trademarks of Lotus Development Corporation

DR-DOS is a registered trademark of Digital Research Corporation

PageMaker is a registered trademark of Aldus Corporation

Peachtree Accounting, Peachtree Accounting for Windows are registered trademarks of Peachtree Software, Inc.

Prodigy is a registered trademark of Prodigy Services Company

Postscript is a registered trademark of Adobe Systems, Inc.

Hayes is a registered trademark of Hayes Microcomputer Products, Inc.

Quicken is a registered trademark of Intuit Corporation

PC Tools is a trademark of Central Point Software, Inc.

Desk Top Set is a registered trademark of Okna Corporation

Corel Draw is a registered trademark of Corel Corporation

All other products, product names and services identified throughout this book, video and software are trademarks or registered trademarks of their respective companies. They are used throughout this product for demonstration purposes only. No such demonstrations or uses, including display or use of any trade name in this product is intended to imply any affiliation or endorsement of the product, service, or trade name.

About This Book

Welcome to the wonderful world of personal computers! Your PC will assist you, amaze you, entertain you and at times frustrate you. But your life will be changed forever.

This book will be your handy companion as you learn to master your PC. It will walk you through a brief history of computers, then it will teach you what computers do and how they work. Finally, you'll learn to use your PC like it is meant to be used.

As you read this book keep reminding yourself that it's not a novel! It's not intended to be read from cover-to-cover. Only read the parts that interest you. If a section sounds confusing or appears to offer information that you feel you don't need at that moment, simply skip over it. You can always go back and review it again. Use the "Table of Contents" and the "Index" to find what you are looking for. You'll notice that as you read each chapter, you'll become progressively more knowledgeable about your PC.

Chapter 1 walks you through a brief history of computers.

Chapter 2 explains what your PC can do for you. You'll also learn about the variety of things that your PC is capable of doing.

Chapter 3 gives you a non-technical look at your PC and its various parts. You'll also learn about different computer programs.

Chapter 4 gives you an intimate look at your PC, the various parts inside it and other gizmos that work with it.

Chapter 5 covers everything you need to know about software without putting you to sleep! You'll learn about DOS, Windows, Word Processing and so on.

Chapter 6 teaches you how to choose the right PC (if you don't have one), or upgrade the one you have. Learn the important factors you should consider in your selection process.

Chapter 7 will help you determine the best places to buy your PC or the various parts that go with it. You can skip this chapter until you are ready to buy something.

Chapter 8 helps you create the right working environment for you and your PC. It also shows you the proper way everything needs to be connected together and ways to setup your PC for best performance. You'll also learn the proper way DOS, Windows and other programs need to be installed on your computer.

Chapter 9 shows you the best ways to simplify your work and enjoy using your PC. You'll learn about batch files, automatic saving, using shortcut keys, on-line services, bulletin boards, games and so on.

Chapter 10 teaches you the simple things you need to know about DOS. It will eliminate your fears of DOS forever!

Chapter 11 will make you familiar with Windows and helps you enjoy this wonderful tool. Once you learn to use Windows, you'll be hooked!

Chapter 12 is the icing on the cake! It's chock full of hints and tips you can use. You'll learn to optimize your system and create shortcuts. You'll also learn to open up your PC, troubleshoot, do simple maintenance, add or replace parts and so on.

Appendix contains a list of PC user groups, PC magazines and national service providers.

Glossary of Terms at the end of the book has a complete list of all the related terms that you can look up when and if you need an explanation. Use it as a reference guide.

Index is where you look for the location of specific topics or words. It's simply a road map of where all the key topics can be found.

**Your feedback is very important and helps us improve the PC GUIDE series.
Please complete and mail the Registration Card at the end of this book.
Thank you. We value your input.**

What Do You Have?

(This information is for your own use)

As you read this book, you'll come across certain topics that require you to have some knowledge of your own PC. Take a couple of minutes to complete this page. If you don't know the answer to some questions, ask a friend who is familiar with PCs.

Don't forget to take this page with you when you go shopping for software and other PC related products. This information will be very valuable to you.

What is the manufacturer's name on your:
PC:_____   Monitor:_____   Printer:_____

What is your microprocessor? 486___   486-SX___   386___   386-SX___   286___

How much memory do you have? 1 MB___   2 MB___   4 MB___   8 MB___

What size hard disk do you have? 40 MB___   80 MB___   120 MB ___   200 MB___

What size floppy drive(s) do you have? 3-1/2"_____   5-1/4"_____   Both_____

What type of video card do you have? Super VGA___   VGA___   EGA___

What type of monitor do you have? Color_____   Monochrome_____

What type of printer do you have? Laser___   Dot Matrix___   Ink Jet___

What type of pointing device do you have? Mouse_____   Trackball_____

What type of modem do you have? 2400 BPS___   9600 BPS___   14,400 BPS___

What version of DOS do you have? 6.2___   5.0___   4.0___   3.3___

What version of Windows do you have? 3.1___   3.0___

Table of Contents

Chapter 4. Get To Know Your PC Intimately

Chapter 5. Software You Can Use

Chapter 6. Best Way To Choose Or Upgrade Your PC

Chapter 7. How And Where To Buy PC Products

Chapter 8. Setting Up And Fine Tuning Your PC

Chapter 11. Using Windows

Chapter 12. Hints and Tips You Can Use

Appendix

Glossary of Terms

Index

Introduction

For many of us PCs have become an indispensable tool. Over seventy million PCs are now being used throughout the United States. Every year, ordinary people, businesses, governments, and other organizations buy twelve to fifteen million more PCs. Today, one out of every five people owns or uses a PC. That number will be one out of every two in the next five years. The rapid growth and acceptance of the PC by our society is very similar to our experience with color TVs and VCRs. The main difference is that TVs and VCRs just entertain us but PCs help us do things more quickly and efficiently. Pretty soon, anyone who is computer illiterate will be at a great disadvantage.

Ten years ago, a complete computer system with a printer and a few programs cost over $5,000 - almost as much as a small car. That was a major investment for most people and even small businesses. Today, a similarly packaged PC with ten times the power and speed can be purchased for under $1,500. More affordable PCs are within the means of most people and have opened the door to virtually unlimited uses.

In 1981, when IBM introduced the original PC, many people wondered what they could do with a computer. Since then, millions of people have discovered that they can use their PCs for hundreds of applications, such as writing letters, keeping appointments, balancing budgets, managing a business, keeping records, playing games, sending and receiving messages and even faxes, designing works of art, publishing newsletters, checking airline schedules and purchasing tickets, storing gourmet recipes, etc. As our society embraces the use of PCs in virtually every aspect of life, computer literacy becomes as essential as knowing how to drive a car. Industry experts predict that by the year 2000, every workplace will be equipped with some type of PC. They also predict that almost every household will have a PC that controls the heating/cooling system, lights, alarm system, cable/satellite TV, as well as telephone hookup to outside sources for banking, shopping, electronic mail, information sources, etc.

Today anyone can easily buy a PC from any of thousands of suppliers. These include computer dealers, computer super stores, mail order companies, office supply stores, warehouse membership clubs, discount stores, department stores and electronic specialty stores. The wide variety of PC types, the choices in power and performance levels, and the nonstop advances in technology confuse many PC owners or potential buyers.

If you already own a PC or use one at work or school, you are way ahead of millions of others. By learning more about your PC and learning how to use it properly, you will be even further ahead of everyone else. Millions of ordinary folks and businesspeople are still just thinking about buying a PC, but hesitate to do so. For them, making the right choice becomes more difficult every day. The biggest concern of many hesitant PC buyers is that something better, cheaper, and more powerful will be introduced shortly after they buy their system. They're right! But if they wait for improvements to stop, they'll have to wait a very long time for their PC. If that describes you, then you'd better read this book carefully.

We have specifically designed PC Guide to help you get the most from your computer. Specifically, we will show you what PCs do, how they work, and if you don't own one we will help you buy a suitable PC, and then teach you ways to use and enjoy your computer. This book walks you through the various phases without losing your interest or overwhelming you with computer jargon. We don't want to turn you into a computer "Nerd!" Instead, we want you to learn to use your PC like it is intended to be used.

PC Golden Rules: There are only two rules to remember about PCs.

RULE #1: Don't be afraid of your PC! It won't bite and it won't explode!

RULE #2: If you do something dumb and panic, look up rule #1.

Remember when you first learned to drive? Your biggest fear then was hitting someone or something and causing damage and injury to others. The good news is that while learning to use your PC, there is nothing that you can do which will harm your computer.

There is no best way to read this book. It all depends on you. If you know nothing or very little about PCs, we recommend that you start reading from the beginning. If you get to sections that sound too technical, simply skip over them. Some of that information you may never need, the others you can go back to read later. If, on the other hand you are pretty comfortable using your PC now, you can use this book as a reference guide. Simply look up the topic that interests you from the table of contents or from the index. If you get in trouble or get stuck, you can find the help you need in this book.

Have fun and enjoy your PC.

Chapter 1. The Way It Was!

If you want to understand your PC, you'll need to know a little about where it came from. Computers have one of the richest and best-documented histories among man-made products. During the last decade, PCs have gone through a dramatic increase in power, as well as significant reductions in their size and price. By comparison, if automobiles had gone through the same advancements, a car would now cost about a quarter, be the size of a match box, and get thousands of miles per gallon! Thousands of pioneers, many of them in their teens and twenties, propelled us into the so-called "information age." People that we jokingly refer to as nerds, because they seem to have a hard time fitting among ordinary people, have helped develop computers and programs that the average person like us can use with relative ease.

1.1. Cave Man's Computer

Thousands of years ago, man began computing by using pebbles for counting and communicating numbers to each other. Gradually, over hundreds of years, man learned to simulate the physical count by drawing the quantities on stone tablets, on animal skins, and finally, on paper. To ancient man, the invention of the abacus was as important as the invention of the wheel. Ancient scholars and scientists were content with using an abacus to calculate and pen and paper to record information.

1.2. Computers That Used Wheels and Sticks

For centuries, the abacus was state of the art. By the middle of the 19th century, Charles Babbage, an English mathematician, invented the first mechanical adding machine. After that, every few years, newer machines were invented that were a little faster, smaller, and easier to use than previous versions. By then, businesses, banks, governments, military forces, and other organizations were using these machines quite extensively. The average machine used to cost about ten times the annual salary of a bookkeeper.

1.3. The Grand Daddy of PCs

In 1935, Professor John Atanasoff of Iowa State University invented the first electro-mechanical computer that could be programmed to do simple mathematical calculations and store numbers. During that period, the main element of the computer was the vacuum tube, which was also used in radios and other electrical products. The key discovery that led to using electricity in computers was the realization that, like the Morse code used in telegraphs, anything could be expressed in terms of a predetermined series of "ON's" and "OFF's." For example, the number one could be described by "ON-OFF," the number two could be "ON-ON," the number three could be "ON-OFF-ON," and so forth. Letters of the alphabet could also be described the same way. The computer could then be told to relate the series of "ON" and "OFF" switches to a predetermined set of characters and numbers.

1.4. Mainframe Computers: The Giants

The first full-scale computer was developed during World War II. Introduced in 1945, it was called ENIAC, and it used over 18,000 vacuum tubes. It weighed nearly 30 tons, occupied about 15,000 square feet of space, stood two stories high, and cost over $45 million to make. By comparison, today, only 50 years later, a handheld calculator weighs less than 8 ounces, costs less than $50 and has more power than the ENIAC.

Because of their enormous size and operating requirements, these machines were called mainframe computers. In the 1940's and 50's, they were used mainly by the government and large corporations. Mainframe computers required specially designed and chilled computer rooms, the size of a football field. They also needed constant monitoring by groups of engineers, technicians, and programmers.

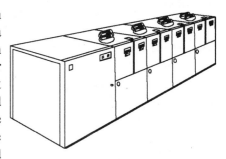

Mainframe computers performed all their activities in the central computer room. All calculations, data storage and data retrieval were performed by the main unit and the peripherals attached to it in that room. For example, the person in the accounting department sat in front of a video monitor and keyboard (called terminal), and sent information back and forth to the mainframe through special cables directly linking the terminal to the mainframe. This method of centralized data processing and data storage was the only way to take advantage of computers until the 1980's.

In 1957, a young inventor named Robert N. Noyce created the Integrated Circuit (IC) and helped propel the young computer industry into a new orbit. ICs replaced thousands of miles of wires and thousands of transistors, resistors, capacitors, and diodes in the mainframe computers. They helped make computers faster, smaller, and significantly more reliable. The same ICs are now standard in various electronic household appliances such as toasters, refrigerators, TVs, VCRs and radios as well as toys and automobiles.

1.5. Mini Computers: The Baby Giants

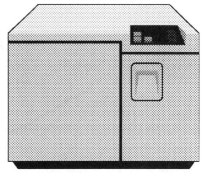

In the 1960's, smaller and less expensive versions of the mainframe were introduced. Called mini computers, they were used by organizations and departments that did not need the full power of mainframes. Also, because of their scaled-down power, they required less care and were easier and less expensive to maintain. They did, however, still use central processing and data storage.

1.6. PCs: Computers For The Masses

In 1971, Intel Corporation located in Sunnyvale, CA, invented the first microprocessor chip. That led to the creation of the handheld calculator. It was the size of a silver dollar. In a computer, the microprocessor chip could perform the function of thousands of the "ON" and "OFF" switches that were previously performed by vacuum tubes and transistors. Shortly after that invention, some people realized that the new chips would allow them to make a computer small enough to fit on a person's desk.

In 1974, Intel introduced a microprocessor called the 8080. In the same year, the first personal computer called Altair was sold in kit form through small ads in technical magazines. In 1975, two PC models, the Altair 8800 and the IMSAI 8080 computers based on the Intel 8080 microprocessor were rapidly becoming popular among hobbyists. Today, about twenty years later, there are thousands of brands and models to choose from. In those days, people had to write their own programs to make the computer do simple things. The PC industry and the rest of us owe a tremendous debt to Gary Kildall, who, in 1976, developed a special program called CP/M (Control Program/Monitor) to operate small computers based on the new microprocessors.

Suddenly, the area around Stanford University between San Francisco and San Jose became the hotbed of the new personal computer industry. The heavy usage of silicon to manufacture microprocessors and memory chips earned that area the nickname of "Silicon Valley." Hundreds of bright and talented young men and women ventured into this new field and started computer companies in that area.

In the early days the most famous PC was the Apple II computer, created in 1977 by nineteen-year-olds Steven Jobs and Steve Wozniack in their garage in Silicon Valley. During that period, a large number of companies started making personal computers. Names like Apple,

Commodore, Eagle, Kaypro, Morrow, Osborne, Radio Shack, Texas Instruments and Victor were suddenly appearing on small computers of various shapes and sizes.

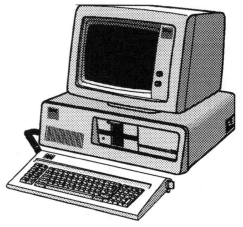

In 1980, the top management at IBM, the world's largest computer company, decided to enter the personal computer field. Their primary motivation was to make sure that their existing mainframe and mini computer customers remained loyal to the IBM brand. At that time the IBM PC team, led by the late Philip "Don" Estridge, estimated that they could sell as many as 250,000 PCs over a five year period. That was a very large number back then. They slightly underestimated the popularity of their computers! Since 1981, IBM alone has sold over sixteen million PCs.

In August 1981, the original IBM PC was introduced. It was made primarily from standard, off-the-shelf parts and components. The IBM logo on the front of the PC gave the infant industry a respectable standard backed by a giant corporation. Shortly after that, IBM compatibility became a standard, and hundreds of companies started making PCs for an insatiable market. Well, the rest is history! The flood gates were opened. In the thirteen years since the introduction of the IBM PC, over seventy million PCs have been sold in the United States alone. Industry sources estimate that in 1994, over twelve million PCs will be sold in this country. As costs continue to decline, and the power and ease of use of newer PCs increase, it is only natural that more individuals and businesses will buy PCs. During the last decade, businesses alone spent nearly a quarter of a trillion dollars on personal computers.

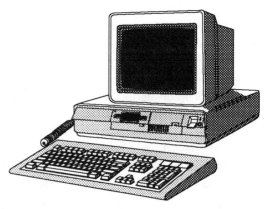

In 1971, there were about 51,000 computers throughout the world. Today, a little over twenty years later, over 55,000 computers are sold every day. This is the legacy of personal computers, and the real beginning of the information age. Now our world is interconnected economically and culturally. Our news media use PCs among other things to bring us the world in an instant. Information that used to take months or weeks to travel between two places, is now transmitted, analyzed, and interpreted in an instant.

Chapter 2. PCs That Do Everything

Do you ever wonder how different your life might be without a car or access to public transportation? Pretty grim thought isn't it? Computers have also become an essential part of our daily lives. In the early days when only a few people knew how to use computers, we paid them a lot of money and they took care of our data processing needs. These days when one out of five people are using PCs, we can't afford to stay in the dark. PCs are a new phenomenon. They were initially available only in small quantities and at high prices in the mid 1970's. Only in the last few years have PCs begun invading American homes, businesses, and schools in the millions. A lot of people are apprehensive about using PCs, because they fear ignorance when it comes to this magical little box. After all, most of us learned to ride bicycles when we were five to ten years old. We learned to drive cars when we were teenagers. Making mistakes while learning did not seem as embarrassing when everyone else was in the same boat.

When it comes to PCs, people older than thirty may be at a greater disadvantage, because most were not exposed to PCs at school or in college. A lot of people are reluctant to take advantage of one of the best service tools man has ever created. As our society becomes more dependent on computers, computer illiterate people will be at a greater disadvantage. Other nations are rapidly expanding the role of PCs in their personal and business lives. France and Singapore have a PC in almost every home. They are connected together through the phone lines. A greater number of their people will be able to work from home and perform higher paying and higher skilled work.

If you ever wonder about the role of PCs in our society just look at some statistics. According to the U.S. Census Bureau, about one out of every six American adults uses a personal computer. About half of the college-educated population have home computers. One out of every three workers currently uses a computer at work. Forty-six percent of students use computers at school.

2.1. What Are PCs Made To Do?

Think of a PC as your own secretary, bookkeeper, tax accountant, art editor, printer, music teacher, and entertainer, all rolled into one obedient, 24-hours-a-day servant. Once you buy the PC that is right for you, then you can do a wide variety of things on your computer. The only limitation is your imagination. The following are the most frequently used functions of computers and PCs.

Number Crunching

Calculating the U. S. Census numbers was the main reason that led to the creation of the first generation of computers. Crunching massive amounts of repetitive numbers was well suited for computers. It is very likely that you have used a calculator sometime in your life. A PC can do everything a calculator can do, and a lot more. The advantage of a PC is that it can be told to perform certain repetitive calculations automatically. For example, if you decide to put your checkbook into the computer, every time you write a check and tell the computer the amount of the check, it automatically calculates your new balance. Or, if your business uses budgets for various income and expense items, you can set up a method to take the previous years' numbers and automatically adjust each item for inflation and other factors.

Analyzing Numbers and Playing With Words

Computers convert numbers and letters of the alphabet to a series of simple "ON" and "OFF" signals. Then it can easily manipulate either, or a combination of both, to do whatever you want. Anything you can write, sketch, or draw on a piece of paper, the computer can do for you. Unlike the rest of us, the computer is capable of incredible accuracy. You can be sure that if the information you feed into the PC is correct, you will get an accurate answer. In computer terms it's called "garbage in, garbage out."

Storing Information

Another major function of a PC is to store information in a well-organized manner, and retrieve that information whenever you want it. The main technique for storing information is magnetic, very similar to a cassette tape. Therefore, you are also able to store information on something that can be carried around to other computers, allowing you to share data between your PC and other PCs. This is how companies who write software are able to sell their products throughout the world.

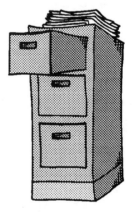

2.2. What Do Most People Use PCs For?

If you already own a PC or use one at work or school, then you probably have some idea of what they can do. On the other hand, if you don't already have a PC at home or at work, then you belong to one of two groups of people: The people in the first group simply ignore what is happening around them and believe that by totally avoiding PCs they may be immune to their influence. The second group is made up of people who know that PCs are rapidly becoming part of their lives, but hesitate to take the first step. These people are still not sure of what they should do. If you belong to these groups, the fact that you are reading this book is a step in the right direction.

Computers can be used for so many different things that no one book can contain a complete list. Following are some of the most common uses for a PC:

Writing Letters, Reports and other Documents

Typing letters, memos, reports and books account for about 80% of what we use a PC. The software that helps us type on a PC is called a "word processor." Word processing software convert the PC to a super-charged typewriter with many other capabilities.

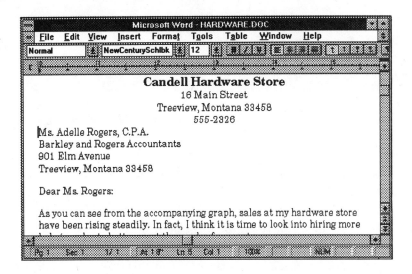

A sample word processing screen that shows a letter with different size characters.

When you use a word processor on a PC, you type on the keyboard and see what you have typed on the screen of the monitor. With most programs, you can not only check your spelling but also search for better words from a thesaurus. Some programs even help you improve the grammar of your document. If you make mistakes, you can easily go back and correct them on the screen. With very little effort, you can remove a section, add a new section, or move a paragraph. All of these revisions are done before anything is put on paper.

Organizing Information and Maintaining Lists

Another major use for PCs is the storage of information. That information can be just about anything you choose: names, addresses, and birthdays of friends and relatives; lists of your household goods; recipes, wine lists, etc. This information is maintained by using database management programs.

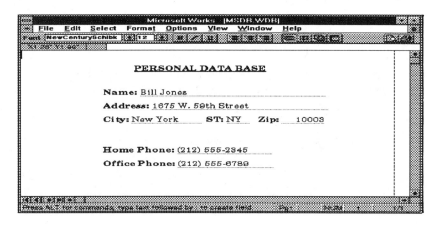

A sample database management screen that shows a name and address file.

These programs let you create your lists any way you wish, just like you do on a sheet of paper. The computer stores that information so it can be retrieved, added to, or modified whenever you need.

Number Crunching, Analysis, and Budgeting

People, and especially businesses, can use mathematically oriented programs called spreadsheets for calculation and manipulation of numbers. Family budgets, as well as investment calculations can be performed on a spreadsheet with greater ease and speed than by using a calculator and a paper ledger.

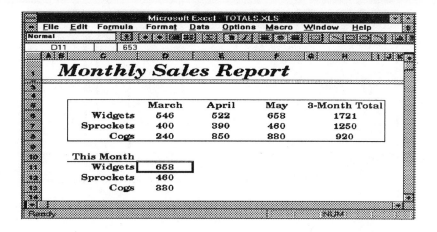

A sample spreadsheet screen that shows monthly sales data and totals.

Businesses use spreadsheets for practically all aspects of tracking and manipulating numbers. For example, a manager can track the performance of salespeople by region, salesperson, or product type.

Data Communication and Information Exchange

Your PC can connect you to other computers through the telephone lines using a device called modem. An increasing use for PCs in the 1990's, is the ability to communicate with other computers. We can use our PCs at home to access computer services and hundreds of information sources like encyclopedias, Wall Street stock reports, entertainment, airline schedules and reservations, banks, mail order catalogs, etc. Businesspeople can connect their home or portable PCs to their work computers to send or receive information.

Sample phone dialer screen.

Personal Finance and Income Taxes

PCs are an excellent tool for keeping track of your finances, budgeting your expenditures, and even organizing your information for income tax preparation. Some programs help you prepare your income tax forms and even help you with tax saving advice.

Date	Num	Description / Memo	Category	Payment	C	Deposit	Balance
2/1 1992	3032	Stephanie Castor	Gifts	144|76			-1,018|99
2/15 1992	480	American Home Mortgage Corp.	{mortgage}	165|06			-1,179|05
2/29 1992	481	M.J. Latterell-Baker	– Splits –	88|00			-1,264|05
3/26 1992							

Save   Restore   Open Splits   Ending Balance $ -1,264.05

Sample checking account register showing check information and account balance.

Business Accounting

Large companies have been using computers for accounting purposes since the 1950's. Smaller businesses have been turning to PCs for accounting and other financial uses since the 1980's.

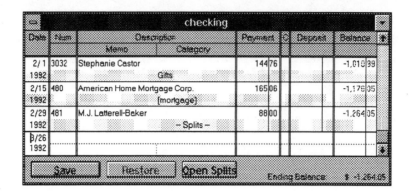

American Business Corporation, Ltd.

American Business Corporation, Ltd.
(Includes unrealized gains)

SAMPLE-All Accounts

Acct	Balance
Cash and Bank Accounts	
cash	36.55
checking	-1,264.05
savings	4,500.00
Total Cash and Bank Accounts	3,272.50
Other Assets	
house	153,375.17
Total Other Assets	153,375.17
Investments	
IRA	13,941.39
Total Investments	13,941.39
TOTAL ASSETS	170,589.06

A sample balance sheet that shows a summary of assets and liabilities.

Programs that help run all the accounting functions of a business such as order entry, inventory, payroll, accounts payable, accounts receivable, sales analysis, and financial reporting are available with various power levels and prices ranging from under $100 to several thousand dollars.

Creating Newsletters, Flyers and Books

If you like to print newsletters, pamphlets, books, or articles, the PC is a perfect tool for organizing the information on the screen exactly the way you want it to look. It's then easy to print the finished product. Most newspapers and magazines now compose their pages on PCs. Schools, churches, and other organizations are using PCs for designing and printing their own publications.

Many entrepreneurs are using their PCs to produce newsletters on topics ranging from stock market advice, to neighborhood news or real estate flyers. Others operate small design firms out of their homes.

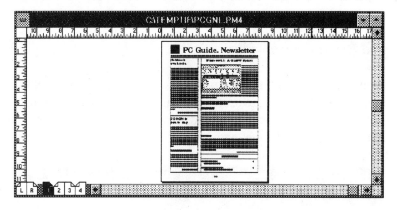

A sample desktop publishing screen that shows page layout for a newsletter.

Education

Schools and colleges are using PCs in record numbers. Children use this new tool for everything from writing papers to solving problems and playing games. For families with school-age children, a PC is practically a must. Hundreds of educational programs help expand the knowledge of the child beyond what was previously imaginable for many adults today.

A sample typing instruction screen that shows the location of fingers on keyboard.

Adults can use their PCs to learn about topics ranging from typing, to cooking, to the stock market, or even a totally new career.

Games and Entertainment

Thousands of games and entertainment programs are available for PCs. Some of them are so vivid and realistic that they are used for training pilots, golfers, doctors, etc. Games vary in price and capabilities, but they provide a tremendous amount of entertainment. PC games are less expensive and offer a greater variety than home video games.

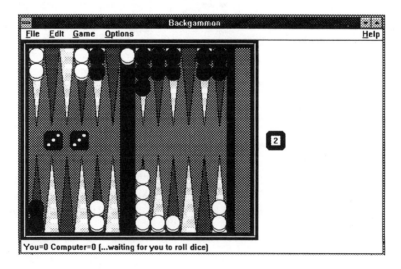

Other

The PC is really a tool with unlimited uses. The categories listed above address only a few of the areas in which we can use our PCs. If you have an idea for an application, you can even develop a program for it yourself. You can also connect your PC to other computers to exchange all sorts of data or send messages to friends, or co-workers.

2.3. PCs are Used Everywhere

With over seventy million PCs in use throughout the country, you can find them virtually everywhere you look. They are in offices, banks, travel agencies, cookie shops, factories, classrooms, homes, and countless other locations. Some people and businesses use PCs because they have to; others use them because it helps them accomplish more. Because the current generation PCs are more affordable and easier to use, they are now available to anyone and can be used anywhere.

Work

Workers in private businesses and in public or government agencies are the primary users of PCs. At work, PCs can help with virtually every aspect of the activities that people are involved with. The most obvious use of the PC is for accounting purposes. Practically all large and medium sized companies are currently using PCs. Small businesses are turning to PCs in large numbers. However, many small business owners and managers have been slow in making a decision to use PCs. Some business owners or managers think that since they have gotten where they are without a PC, they can get along without using one. Unfortunately for them, their competitors have probably computerized their operations and are reaping the benefits.

Home

Using PCs at home is becoming very popular. PCs used to be only for computer hobbyists (the so called Nerds!). Now, businesspeople, students, and others are buying systems for home use. A PC at home can have many uses: Businesspeople can perform some or all of their office work at home and then by using their modem call the computer at work and transfer information back and forth. Entrepreneurs can start a business at home by producing newsletters, brochures, advertising materials, stock market analyses, articles, new programs, etc.

Family members (both adults and children) can connect their computer to on-line computer services to tap into the tremendous resources they provide. Word processing, database management, personal finance, games, and entertainment are among the many uses for a PC at home.

School

Schools and colleges throughout the country are adding PCs to their classrooms by the thousands. Homework is no longer what most adults remember. Although most schools may not currently have enough PCs to give every student a separate unit, they are fast approaching that point. Students can access mountains of information through the school PC. Also, the increased numbers of interactive educational software is helping the learning process. For college students having a PC is becoming a necessity.

Chapter 3. Non-technical Look At PCs And Programs

If you seriously want to learn to use your PC like a pro, you need to have a good understanding of the concepts behind the machine. Various parts in the PC work together to produce the results that you are looking for. This chapter gives you an overview of your PC and the various components and accessories that work with it.

3.1. The Real Meaning of a PC

As you read this book, you'll notice that definitions are somewhat general at first, but as you progress and your level of understanding increases, they become more specific. A personal computer system is defined as the PC unit itself (that's the big box with the drives in the front and cables in the back), plus the monitor, printer, modem, mouse, software, etc. In this book however, we refer to the whole thing as the PC or the system. Ten years ago, personal computers had a standard look and configuration; today, they come in all shapes and sizes.

Hardware (The Stuff that You Can Touch)

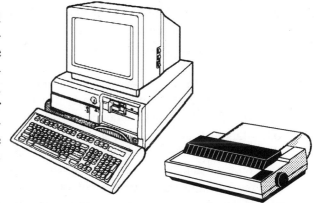

The term hardware refers to all the physical parts and components of the PC, including the main unit, monitor, mouse, modem, printer, and disk drives. Hardware is a term carried over from the early days of mainframe computers. Even the smallest parts of a PC are referred to as hardware.

Software (The Stuff That Works Behind The Scenes)

The programs that tell the computer what to do and how to do it are called software. Software is a classification for various sets of instructions that run a PC. The only physical parts of software are the instruction books and the diskettes that the programs are stored on. Some programs are able to make the computer do some things that could also be done by hardware. The reverse of this is also possible for certain tasks. As we address those areas, we will point out tasks that can be performed by either hardware or software.

3.2. The Binary System (The Way That Nerds Count!)

The most important discovery that led to the development of electronic computers was the binary system. The binary system is based on the two digits, 0 and 1. "Bi" means two (as in bicycle) which refers to a two-wheeled device. The binary system is a method of counting in which a number or a letter of the alphabet is represented by a combination of zeroes (0) and ones (1). In our daily life, we use the decimal system (based on the digits 0 to 9) to express an infinite combination of numbers. We also use the 26 letters of the alphabet (from A to Z) to express ourselves. In the binary system, we only have 0 and 1 to describe the same numbers. Expressing numbers in binary is not as easy as it is in decimal; for example, the decimal number 1994 is expressed as 11111001000 in binary form.

Fortunately, we don't have to know the binary numbers or use them with our computer. Just remember that the "0" and "1" of the binary system can be expressed as the "ON" and "OFF" switches in the PC. By turning switches on and off a certain way, the computer knows exactly what you are talking about. Programs are the medium or the interpreter between you and your PC. They translate the information you express in English into the binary language that is understood by the computer. When the computer responds with the information you have requested, the software translates the binary information back to English. The earlier generation of computers used vacuum tubes and switches to work with the binary system. Today's computers use microprocessor chips containing hundreds of thousands of microscopic switches to accomplish the same thing.

3.3. Key Components of a PC

A PC consists of several small and large components. PCs now come in so many different shapes and sizes, that it's important to understand the function of various components. The key components are described here in general terms:

System Unit (The Main Box)

The system unit, sometimes called the
Central Processing Unit (CPU), houses
the brains of the computer. Other components, like the keyboard, monitor, mouse
and printer are connected to it by cable.
The system unit houses several key components, including the mainboard (affec-
tionately called the motherboard), power
supply, adapter boards, floppy drive, hard
disk drive, CD-ROM, sound board and
possibly, other components.

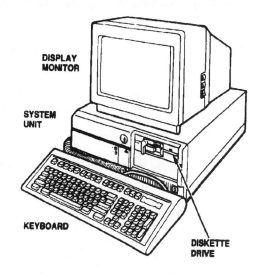

Case

The computer case is a metal or reinforced plastic enclosure that covers the system
unit. The original IBM PC case was designed to sit flat on top of a desk. Millions of
IBM and compatible PCs are still using the same design. These cases are often made

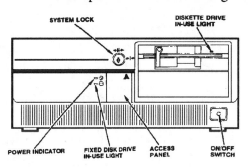

of sheet metal and consist of two parts:
the base unit and the cover. The various
components inside the PC are attached
to the base unit by metal screws. The
cover is then attached to the base unit.
Computer cases are made from materials that prevent electronic frequencies
from interfering with nearby radios,
televisions, and telephone systems. The
Federal Communications Commission
(FCC) has set up specific guidelines for computer emissions. PCs for home use should
have a more strict FCC class B approval, and PCs for office use should have an FCC
class A or B approval.

Power Supply

Personal computers either use AC power from a wall outlet, or operate on batteries.
Battery-operated PCs are usually the small portable units that we will describe later
in this chapter. PCs don't use the AC power that flows directly from the wall outlet
into the computer. Instead, the 110-volt power is fed to a transformer that converts

it to 12-volt DC, much like a car battery. Most power supplies are made of stainless steel and house the transformer and a small fan. The fan cools the various parts of the transformer, as well as circulates air inside the computer.

Motherboard (The Mother of All Boards)

The mainboard of the PC is the real nerve center of the whole system. The processor, memory and other components of the unit are either located on the motherboard or are connected to it. To better understand what a motherboard is and what it does, you should first become familiar with the computer circuit board.

A computer board, often called a printed circuit board, is a green, flat surface, usually about 1/8 inch thick. Its size ranges from about the size of your palm to slightly larger than a sheet of letter-size paper. If you look at the edges of the board, you'll notice that it's made up of several thin layers of hard plastic material. The green surface on top of the board is covered with gold colored veins running in straight lines between small sockets or computer chips. The underside of the board has hundreds of pins with solder spots. The gold colored veins running throughout the board surface perform the role of hundreds of feet of wire.

After engineers design what the board is supposed to do and what components will go on the board, they produce a drawing of the wiring diagram on a large sheet of paper. The drawing is then photographed by a very precise camera that can sharply reduce the size of the page. The image is then transferred to a specially treated flat board, which is dipped into a pool of liquid, conductive metal. The metal attaches itself to the wiring diagram image on the board. The board is then raised out of the pool, cleaned, and covered by another layer of protective surface material. Very small holes are drilled at predetermined locations for attachment of microchips and sockets. This way, thousands or millions of identical boards can be manufactured for various purposes. Computer chips and other components that have short metal legs are automatically placed on top of the board. Their legs are inserted into the holes, and on the underside of the board the

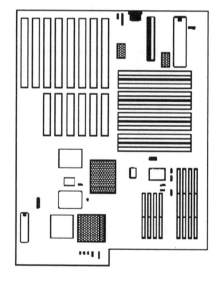

legs are automatically soldered and clipped to a uniform length.

The motherboard often contains the microprocessor, memory chips, the instructional chips (called ROM BIOS), expansion slots, and miscellaneous other components. Although brands and types vary greatly, most motherboards follow the original IBM PC standard for locating drilled holes for screw attachment, expansion slots, keyboard connection, power connection, etc. This standard feature makes it easier to replace defective parts or upgrade a system in the future.

Microprocessor (The Brains!)

The microprocessor (Central Processing Unit) is the brains of the system. It's usually a small matchbook-sized, dark gray item with silver legs. Some microprocessors are rectangular with tiny legs along the two longer sides, while others are square with legs on all four sides. The exterior of the chip is simply a protective shell that encloses the microprocessor itself.

The microprocessor chip is about one inch square. It contains hundreds of thousands (or sometimes millions) of microscopic switches that are etched on silicon wafers in a process somewhat similar to the way boards are made. Tiny, thin gold wires extend from the sides of the processor. Once the chip is placed inside the protective shell, the wires are soldered to the legs and the shell is snapped shut.

Manufacturing microprocessor chips is a very complicated process. It requires extremely clean facilities and a shockproof environment. The latest generation 80486 and Pentium microprocessor chips are manufactured in a Class 1 plant where the employees wear space suits and the air in the room cannot contain more than one 0.2 micron (about 0.2% of the diameter of a human hair) particles per cubic foot. The clean rooms used for manufacturing the chips are isolated from the rest of the building by vibration absorbing seals in the floors to prevent damage to the sensitive silicon chips. Outside vibration and movement in the room cannot exceed 200 micro inches per second. If you thought that threading a needle was tough, you should see this operation!

Math coprocessor (The Little Genius Chip)

A math coprocessor is a microchip specifically designed to work in tandem with a CPU. It takes over the mathematical calculation functions from the CPU, thus freeing up the CPU to perform its other tasks faster. The math coprocessor can be purchased separately as an option. Every motherboard has a built-in socket for adding a math coprocessor. Some new generation microprocessors, like the 80486 and Pentium have the math coprocessor functions built into the CPU chip.

Memory

Your PC needs memory in order to work properly. Think of the combination of microprocessor and memory as a calculator and a sheet of paper. You take information from the paper and feed it into the calculator. Afterwards, you take the results from the calculator and write it on the paper. Microprocessor and memory work the same way.

Computer memory is often called Random Access Memory (RAM). The design of memory chips is somewhat similar to the design of microprocessors. Chips consist of thousands of microscopic switches. When the power to your PC is turned on, the memory chips become active. As you type something on the keyboard, it's first transferred to RAM. The switches in the memory chip turn on or off according to the information you have typed in. The 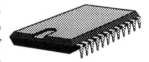 information is then transmitted to the microprocessor for interpretation and further processing. The feedback from the microprocessor is sent to the memory to be stored or displayed on the monitor to indicate the results of the processing and await new input from you.

Memory chips are data storage devices that actively keep information for as long as the power is on. When the power is turned off, all information stored in the chips is wiped clean. The switches go back to their off position. When you turn your PC back on, the chips are blank and ready to accept new information.

ROM BIOS (Chips That Remember)

ROM (Read Only Memory) is a special kind of chip that can be programmed to retain a certain amount of information that can only be read. Once it's programmed, it retains that information and can reproduce it every time your computer is turned on. BIOS (Basic Input/Output System) is an important set of instructions for your PC stored in the ROM chip.

ROM BIOS chips store programs that are used to start your computer, perform diagnostic routines and tests, instruct various components on how to communicate with the microprocessor and with each other, and govern the internal operations of your PC. ROM BIOS chips are usually inserted in sockets on the motherboard, that make it easy to update the chip, if and when necessary.

Expansion Slots

One of the best features of IBM and compatible computers is the expansion slots, which really are the medium for interface between the PC motherboard and other adapter boards. Most importantly, they allow for future expansion and upgrade of your system. Expansion slots, located on the motherboard, are about four inches or longer. An opening about one inch deep runs the length of the slots. Two rows of gold colored teeth run along each side of the slot opening. Adapter boards with plated strips that match the teeth in the slots are inserted into the expansion slots to connect to the motherboard. The origi-

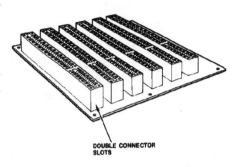

DOUBLE CONNECTOR
SLOTS

nal IBM PC (and its compatibles) had eight expansion slots. However, newer PCs have many of the interface functions built into the motherboard, thus reducing the need for that many expansion slots.

One important advantage of the expansion slots has been the ability to upgrade a PC to higher levels of performance by adding boards that have newer processors or other features.

Adapter Boards

When the IBM PC was introduced in 1981, the motherboard contained the micropro-cessor, memory chips, and ROM BIOS chips. Other functions, such as additional memory, the controller chips for drives and video, interfaces with other devices such as printers and modems, etc. were all placed on adapter boards.

The method of manufacturing adapter boards is very similar to the method described for motherboards. These boards contain the appropriate chips to control specific functions. The bottom of each adapter board has a protrusion the size of the expansion slot, covered with gold colored connections that correspond to the gold colored teeth in the slots. Adapter boards are inserted into the slots and secured to the computer case with a screw.

Memory Board

Various PC motherboards are designed to contain a certain amount of memory capacity. If you need more memory than that capacity, a memory board must be installed in your system unit. Different PCs use different types of memory boards. Memory plugged in directly on the motherboard is always faster than memory accessed on a memory board.

Drive Controller

The drive controller is a printed circuit board that contains the appropriate chips that control the operation of up to two floppy and two hard disk drives. During the 1980's there were several different types and sizes of floppy and hard disk drives. PC manufacturers did not traditionally include the hard disk drive and controller with the system unit. The computer dealer often installed the hard disk drive and controller, based on the buyer's needs and requirements. Today, the majority of the systems are sold with the hard disk drive and the controller installed at the factory.

Video Graphics

The video graphics controller is a printed circuit board that contains the chips that create images and graphics on the screen of your monitor. There used to be several

different types of monitors and video graphics standards. Some PC manufacturers used to leave out the video controller and monitor so that it could be installed by the dealer. Now, there is one popular standard and almost all manufacturers install it at the factory.

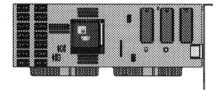

Parallel and Serial

Your PC needs a special set of controller chips to enable it to interact with other devices attached to it. Some peripherals, like printers, modems and mice are attached to the interface board. Many new generation PCs incorporate the so-called parallel and serial interfaces on the motherboard. Parallel interface is usually used for communication between your PC and a parallel printer. It's a special preset standard that permits very fast transfer of data between the PC and the printer. A serial interface is a flexible communication standard that typically runs at less than half the speed of a parallel interface and needs to be specially configured on both ends.

Game

The game controller board contains a set of chips that control the function of one or two joysticks. Joystick is a handheld device similar to the gear shift of a car. It lets you move objects on the screen of your monitor while playing games. The game controller chip is sometimes built into certain brands of motherboards.

Other

Various devices (now and in the future) can be attached to your PC by using an existing or new interface board. The advantage of expansion slots in a PC is that adapter boards can be added as long as there are free expansion slots left in the system. One of the new innovations that's very popular is a multi-media board that turns your PC into a powerful center for computing, live video, high quality sound, and many other yet-to-be-developed uses.

Floppy Drive (Store it and Carry it Around)

Floppy drives were the first devices designed for storing information in PCs. A floppy drive is a magnetic storage device similar to a cassette tape recorder. In fact, the first generation of personal computers in the 1970's used cassette tape recorders for storage. Gradually, floppy disk drives were developed for PCs. Their size and cost have been decreasing while their capacities have been increasing.

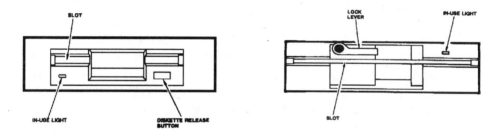

The name "floppy disk" refers to the soft, flexible structure of the disks themselves. Floppy disk is a round piece of thin plastic material coated with a magnetic compound on both sides. It is housed in a square (5.25" x 5.25" or 3.5" x 3.5"), flexible plastic enclosure. When a floppy disk is inserted into the floppy drive, a unit called the drive-head comes in close contact with both sides of the disk. The head has magnetic code reader/writers on each side. As the floppy disk spins inside the drive, the head moves back and forth to read data from or write data to the disk.

Hard Disk Drive (Small Size, Big Capacity)

A hard disk drive is a distant cousin of the floppy drive. As you may have guessed from the name, instead of using a soft, flexible material, the data storage surface is made of rigid material. Hard disk drives are also somewhat different from floppy drives in other respects. They are much faster, store much more data, cost more, and are more sensitive to handling. Unlike a floppy drive, the hard drive is in a sealed enclosure to protect it from dust particles and mishandling.

The storage medium is called a "platter." It's made of thin, rigid metal with magnetic coating on the surface, and concentric circles on both sides, somewhat similar to a music record. The platters range in size from 2 to 5 inches in diameter, depending on the type of drive. Depending on capacity, brand, and storage technique used, the hard drive may contain one or more platters. For every platter, the drive has two read/write magnetic heads which work like the needle on a record player, except that the heads do not touch the platters, but operate microscopically close. They are so close, in fact, that a human hair could not fit in the gap. The platters rotate at approximately 3600 RPM (Revolutions Per Minute), faster than a car driving at 55 miles per hour. Because of the high speed of the platters and the closeness of the heads, the entire assembly is constructed with shock resistant mountings. This is quite incredible for a device about the size of a bar of soap! Newer hard disk drives also include the components that were formerly on the hard drive controller, thus eliminating the need for a separate controller board.

Tape Drive

A tape drive works on a principle similar to a cassette tape recorder. Used for backup purposes, it can record and play back the information stored on special cassettes. The data on the hard disk drive can be copied onto cassette tapes that can be stored for many years. In the early 1980's, hard disk drive technology was not as reliable as it is today. Therefore, hard drives were in danger of malfunctioning and losing all the data they stored. Tape drives were primarily used to copy important data periodically. If the hard drive failed, the data on the tape could be copied to a working hard drive.

Businesses that rely on PCs for important data use tape drives to backup critical pieces of information. Another use for tape drives is the storage of data that's seldom used. Once that data is stored on tape, it can be deleted from the hard disk, thus freeing up more space on the drive for other purposes.

CD Drive (Books, Sound and Video on a Tiny Disk)

The CD (Compact Disk) technology that has revolutionized high-fidelity music is rapidly becoming popular with PC owners. A CD can store the equivalent of thousands of pages of information on a single Compact Disk. The average CD stores about 600 Mega Bytes of data on both sides (equivalent to 300,000 typed pages). CDs use a different principle to store and read information than the magnetic method used by cassette tape players, floppy, and hard disk drives. CD drives are substantially slower than hard disk drives. The CD is coated with a special material that consists of microscopic dots. When data is recorded on the CD, the dots are converted to a series of black and white dots corresponding to the information being stored. The CD player uses a laser head that moves very close to the surface of the spinning disk in order to read the black and white dots. The dots are then interpreted, and the information is fed back to the PC in a series of "ON" or "OFF" signals using the binary system.

Most commercially available CDs can only read from prerecorded CD disks. They are called "Read Only Memory" (CD-ROM) drives. Another, more expensive CD drive can record data only once on a CD, but that disk can be read an indefinite number of times. They are called "Write Once, Read Many" (WORM) drives. Some CD drives are capable of both reading from and writing data to the CD. These CD drives are currently very expensive, and are often used by organizations that need to store thousands of pages of information. The cost of various CD drives is rapidly declining, and has become more affordable for the average PC owner. It's possible that as the cost of read/write CD players decline and their speeds increase, they may; at some point in the future, replace both floppy and hard disk drives.

Input Devices (How You Give Information to Your PC)

Your PC communicates with you by receiving instructions and information (Input) and giving information back (Output). PC output is either displayed on the screen of your monitor, sent through a modem, or printed on a printer. Input, on the other hand, is provided by several different means. Input devices translate instructions or information supplied by you into electronic codes that the computer understands. Some input devices, like a keyboard, input numbers and alphabet characters; others, like a mouse, are used for pointing at items on the screen. Others, like scanners, are used for taking snapshots of printed information and feeding that to the computer.

Keyboard (The Old Fashioned Tool)

Every PC has a keyboard that looks somewhat like a typewriter keyboard. The keys consist of five different groups, as illustrated in the following diagram. The main and largest group looks very similar to the arrangement of keys on a typewriter. The central part consists of letters of the alphabet arranged similar to the standard typewriter called "QWERTY." Named after the arrangement of the top row of the main keys.

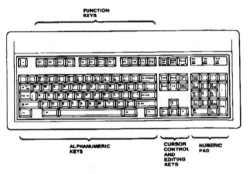

The keys marked F1 through F12 in the top row are called "Function Keys." Most programs use each function key to provide a command shortcut. For example, most programs use the F1 key for Help. Therefore, if you press the F1 key, a set of explanations will appear on the screen describing the topic you are currently working on, just as they would have appeared if you typed the command "help."

The group of keys on the right side of the keyboard look very similar to a calculator. These "Numeric Keys," are usually used in accounting and spreadsheet programs where you need to input large amounts of numbers.

The two groups of keys between the numeric keys on the right and the QWERTY keys on the left are the arrow keys and instruction keys. The arrow keys tell the blinking cursor on the screen which direction to move. The instruction keys (Insert, Delete, Home, Page UP, etc.) tell the PC the commands to execute.

Mouse

Mouse is a pointing device that can speed up using your PC. It works with programs that are designed to accept signals from a mouse. It's a small handheld device the size of a bar of soap. The top of the mouse has two or three buttons, depending on the manufacturer or model.

Under the mouse is a smooth ball about the size of a cherry tomato. Your hand rests on top of the mouse. By moving it on a flat surface near the keyboard, the ball under the mouse turns and sends signals to the PC about the direction and distance the mouse is moving. As the mouse moves, the blinking cursor on the screen also moves in the same direction as the mouse.

Trackball (Upside Down Mouse)

Trackball is a mouse turned upside down. The ball and the keys are on top of the device. The advantage of a trackball over a mouse is that it does not require space to move. Different manufacturers use the same general idea with different designs that create their own unique shape and feel.

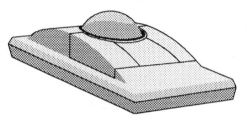

Scanner (From Paper to PC in One Easy Step)

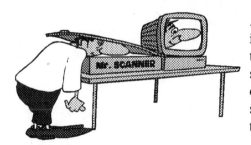

A scanner is a device that can transfer an image of a photograph or written information to the computer. Scanners emit a special light onto the subject. The intensity of the light that is reflected back to the scanner based on the darkness and shape of the image is interpreted and sent to the PC.

Scanners can scan typed or handwritten text, graphs, diagrams, and photographs. The resolution and quality of the scanned subjects vary according to the type and quality of the scanner.

Joystick (The Ultimate Game Handle)

Joystick is a handheld device used for playing PC games that are designed to be used with a joystick. It plugs into the game port of your PC. By moving the handheld stick, the subject on the screen moves in the direction you move the stick. The buttons on the joystick are used to issue specific commands to your PC. Depending on the game you play, some buttons mean firing shots, jumping up, and so on.

Output Devices

PC output is either produced on your monitor screen or on a printer, or sent via modem to another device or computer. Output can also be produced on a combination of all three, if necessary.

Monitor

Monitor is your computer's window to the world. It displays both the instructions and information you give to your computer and the response from the computer. Monitors look much like a TV set and operate on the same basic principle. The size of the screen and the number of colors it can show are the most common ways of differentiating monitors. Desktop PCs use stand-alone monitors. When buying a desktop PC, you can choose among different types of monitors. That choice is governed by your budget, your application, and your needs.

Portable and smaller computers use monitors that are integrated into the system unit. If you purchase one of these units, the model you choose determines the type of monitor that comes with it. The monitors that come with the current generation of portable PCs are flat and usually use the LCD (Liquid Crystal Display) technology that is used in digital watches and calculators. Most portable PCs have the capability to plug into an external color monitor. Most manufacturers also have models with color displays. These PCs cost almost 50% to 100% more than the monochrome versions.

VGA (Video Graphics Array)
The VGA standard was introduced by IBM in 1987. This has quickly become the most popular video standard ever. Currently, almost all PCs are sold with some form of VGA monitor. VGA uses a different method for displaying characters and graphics on the screen. It is capable of showing thousands of colors, making its output close

to what you'd see on a TV. VGA monitors use an analog signal input that will be explained later in this book.

SVGA (Super VGA)

Super VGA is based on the same technology as VGA, but, it has from 50% to 100% better resolution. The small difference in cost between a super VGA monitor and a VGA monitor has made Super VGA the most popular alternative.

Printer (The Power of the Written Word)

Printer is a device that produces written images (numbers, alphabets, graphs, etc.) on paper. Almost everybody has seen a printer of some form: in an office, in supermarket check-out lines, in school, or in other places that provide a written document or receipt. Printers have been available and in use longer than PCs. Printing technology has evolved almost as radically as PCs. The price, performance, and quality of output from the current generation of printers is significantly superior to what was available only five or ten years ago.

Printers come with many different shapes, sizes, and printing technologies. This section gives you an overview of different printer technologies. Although owning a printer with your PC is not an absolute necessity, having a printer is becoming increasingly important.

Daisy Wheel (Modified Typewriter for Your PC)

A daisy wheel printer is basically an electronic typewriter without the keys. The early generation printers were actually modified typewriters that could receive computer signals and print the information. Typewriters gradually became more sophisticated, and in the 1970's, they started using printing elements mounted on a wheel that resembled a daisy. Printers using the same technology became known as "daisy wheel printers."

A daisy wheel printer has over 40 spokes, each containing a numeric or alphabetic character. The wheel is mounted inside the printer. An ink ribbon moves from one spool to the other in front of the wheel. A small hammer-like device is mounted behind the wheel. Paper is positioned in front of the ribbon. When the printer receives an instruction to print a certain character, the wheel rotates until that character is on top. The small hammer-like device quickly hits the character forward against the ribbon, leaving an image on the paper. This action can be performed at more than 10 characters per second.

Because of their relatively slow speed, high mechanical movement, and higher than average noise level, daisy wheel printers are totally extinct. However, their crisp, high quality print has become the standard by which other print technologies are measured.

Dot Matrix (The Popular and Affordable Technology)

Dot matrix printing technology was developed in the 1960's for mainframe computers. Most people may still remember the faint printout on their utility bills, junk mail, and other printed matter that looked as if the characters were formed by small, needle-size dots. In recent years, dot matrix printing technology has advanced to the point where printed matter looks sharp and crisp, similar to that produced by a typewriter.

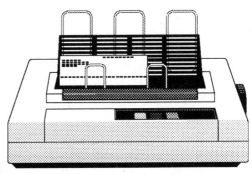

The printing method used by dot matrix printers is somewhat similar to that of daisy wheel printers. A small unit the size of a pencil containing several thin wires is pointed toward the ribbon. The ribbon and paper are mounted similar to those of a daisy wheel printer. When the printer is instructed to print a character, the small pins hit the ribbon against the paper in a way that creates the image of that character with those dots. Obviously, the smaller the dots and the closer they are together, the sharper the character. Dot matrix printers can print at speeds of more than 300 characters per second.

Ink Jet

Ink jet printing technology was developed in the 1980's as a quieter, faster alternative to daisy wheel printers. It uses a technology similar to dot matrix printing. However, instead of pins in the print-head, there are several microscopic holes. Instead of using a ribbon, ink is forced out of the tiny holes directly onto the paper to form the characters.

Ink jet printers are generally higher priced than most dot matrix printers, but their print quality is closer to that of a daisy wheel or laser printer. They make up a small percentage of the printers sold annually. Small, light-weight versions of these printers are very popular with portable PCs.

Thermal Transfer

Thermal transfer printers are somewhat similar to ink jet printers, but instead of squirting dots onto the paper, heat is used to transfer dots from the ribbon to the paper.

Laser (The Ultimate Printing Machine)

Laser printers are the top-of-the-line printing technology for PCs, but their prices are still higher than most other printers. Laser printers use a sophisticated technology for printing, similar to that of a copying machine. When the computer instructs the laser printer to print a page full of characters or graphics, the laser printer waits until it receives an image of the entire page.

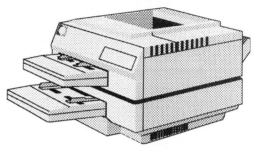

The instructions tell the printer what characters and sizes to use. The printer forms an image of the desired page in its memory. Then, using a laser beam and special mirrors, the image is reflected on a cylindrical device called a drum. The drum is electronically charged to attract fine ink powder particles where the images are. When the ink powder forms an image of the page on the drum, a sheet of paper is electronically charged to attract the ink powder from the drum as it passes under it. After the ink powder is transferred onto the paper, the paper passes under a heating element that melts the ink and bonds it to the paper. Most commercially available laser printers for PCs can print from 4 to 12 pages per minute.

Modem (Your PC's Access to the World)

Modem is a communication device for computers. Using the telephone lines and a modem at each end, two computers can communicate back and forth no matter where they are located. As long as there is a proper phone connection, PCs using their modems can transfer data to each other anywhere in the world. Modem communication is achieved by using special programs developed for this purpose. Recent technological breakthroughs have permitted the addition of Fax capabilities to modems with only a slight increase in price.

Type

Modems come in many different shapes and sizes. There are two types of modems: internal and external. Internal modems look like an adapter board and fit inside your PC in one of the expansion slots. External modems come in a small case and connect

to the serial port of your PC. All PC modems follow a communication standard pioneered by Dennis Hayes founder of Hayes Microcomputer Products, of Atlanta, Georgia. To ensure that they follow that standard, PC modems should be "Hayes compatible."

Speed

Modem speed is based on data transfer rate. That rate is measured by the number of bits per second (BPS). If you recall the description of the binary system ("ON" and "OFF" switches), a bit is a digit (0 or 1) that is part of the combination that represents a number or a letter of the alphabet. PC modems range in speed from 2400, 9600, 14400, to 28800 BPS. The original 300, 1200 and 2400 BPS modems are no longer manufactured. Faster modems can slow down to communicate with an older, slower modem. If you have a slow modem, replace it with a high speed version and enjoy all the pleasure a fast modem gives you.

3.4. Different Types of PCs

In the 1970's and early 1980's, there was only one type of personal computer, and it was designed to sit on top of a desk. The shape and look of desktop PCs was further solidified with the introduction of the IBM PC. In the mid 1980's, creative designers introduced PCs in all shapes and sizes. In spite of the appearance of a PC, the components inside and outside the unit perform a standard operation. For example, a desktop PC has a separate monitor that, like a TV set, may sit on top of the base unit. In a portable PC on the other hand, the monitor is incorporated inside the base unit. Both monitors still perform the same function, but their shape has been modified to accommodate their intended purpose. The same applies to the other PC components we described earlier.

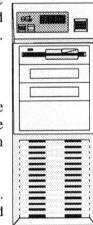

Desktop

Desktop PCs commonly share one major feature: They consist of a base unit, a separate monitor, and a separate keyboard. The shape of the base unit depends entirely on the type of case that is used. As you can see from the following figures, the case may have different shapes and sizes.

Desktop PCs are somewhat heavy and bulky to move around frequently. On the other hand, they generally offer more room for upgrade and expansion. Most desktop PCs use off-the-shelf (standard size and shape) components that make repairs and upgrades easier and less expensive. Desktop PCs are expected to remain popular and their sales are projected to grow at approximately 10% to 15% a year through 1995.

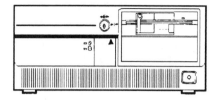

Portable

Portable PCs are getting smaller, more powerful, and more affordable. Currently, portables account for 30% of PC sales. That market share is expected to grow to 50% by 1995.

Transportable (First Generation)

Transportable PCs were introduced in the early 1980's as a portable alternative to the

desktop PC. Essentially, manufacturers took the components of a desktop and squeezed them into a single, portable box that often weighed almost as much as a complete desktop unit. You'd often carry the 25 to 30 pound box around for the first few weeks after its purchase, but then leave it in one place to be used like a desktop unit. Because of their inconvenience, transportable PCs never captured a large share of the market. They are now completely extinct and have been replaced by much lighter units.

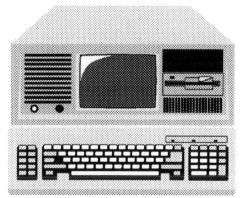

Laptop (Second Generation)

In the mid 1980's, smaller and lighter versions of portable PCs were introduced. Because they could be used on a person's lap, they became known as "laptops." They often weigh between 8 and 15 pounds. Most laptops are battery operated; but those with very powerful CPU's and/or high capacity drives are only AC operated. To accommodate the components inside a much smaller case, manufacturers designed special parts that were often proprietary to each brand.

Although these PCs can operate IBM compatible software, they do not contain standard, off-the-shelf components. This has kept their prices much higher than desktop units, and their shipment volume to a relatively small slice of the total PC market. Laptops have been replaced by notebook PCs that are even smaller and lighter.

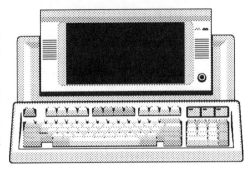

Notebook (A PC in Every Briefcase)

Notebook PCs are the new generation, high performance, lightweight units that are the size of a hard-cover book. They weigh between 4 and 7 pounds, and pack all the

powerful features of desktop PCs. They are all battery operated. The batteries generally last 2 to 5 hours. For people who must have color, most units plug into desktop color monitors. The rapidly declining price of powerful notebook PCs makes it possible for people to use the same computer at work and at home. If you'd like a color monitor, it's possible to connect desktop color monitors at both locations and still save money, compared to having a complete desktop systems at each location.

Physically, different brands of notebook PCs look very similar. The components of notebook PCs, like their laptop predecessors, are often proprietary designs of the manufacturers. Notebook PC sales are projected to grow at approximately 25% a year through 1996. In 1993 they amounted to approximately 30% of total PC sales, a share expected to grow to 50% by 1996.

Palmtop

A new generation of small, lightweight PCs introduced during 1990 are called "Palmtop" because they weigh from 10 ounces to 2 pounds and can be held on the palm of one hand. Some of these units pack more power than the original IBM PC. They currently don't have all the powerful features packed into notebook PCs. Creating a unique market for themselves, they have enough word processing and data storage

capability to serve as a personal time management tool and a note pad for businesspeople who have a larger computer at work or at home. By hooking the two units together, data can be transferred back and forth, thus getting around the smaller capacity limitations of the palmtop.

Pen PC

Keyboardless computers were introduced in 1991. They are constructed somewhat like a notebook PC, with a touch-sensitive screen but without a keyboard. They rely on specially developed operating systems that permit using them without a keyboard. They are primarily targeted for specific applications, such as delivery businesses, food servers, hospitals, inventory checkers, etc. Some models are being offered with handwriting recognition software that lets you write directly on the screen with a special pen.

3.5. Major Software Categories

The greatest advantage of the standard established by IBM PC compatibility has been the availability of thousands of programs that can operate indiscriminately on the millions of IBM and compatible PCs throughout the world. Earlier we discussed the issue of IBM compatibility in relation to the PC hardware. This section gives you an overview of software, and the role software plays in your PC.

Computer hardware, by itself, is not capable of doing very much. The microprocessor, memory, floppy drive, hard drive, keyboard and monitor (among other things), need special instructions to operate as a unit. They also need to have a means of communicating with you, unless you want to spend several years learning programming and computer language. Programs are developed by computer scientists and programmers so that when you work with your PC using their programs, you can communicate with your PC in plain English. The program translates your instructions or questions to computer language and then translates the computer's response from computer language to English. In the 1970's, when PCs were introduced, there were no programs available, so, users had to develop their own.

Current programs are very different from those in the 1970's and 1980's. Programs are written to simplify using the PC. Most programs are designed for specific functions and have simplified the task of using them basically to filling-in the blanks or answering yes or no to questions. Some people who are afraid of using PCs may be thinking of the difficulties involved in the 1970's and early 1980's. In the 1990's, the emphasis is on "user friendliness."

Operating Systems

Operating system is the program that instructs your PC on how to work with its various components. Over the years, operating systems have been upgraded and simplified in order to make using your PC easier. Currently, only four major operating systems are available for IBM and compatible PCs. These programs have distinct differences that make them suitable for different environments. Consequently, choosing an operating system is not very complicated. Frequently, the PC that you purchase is already equipped with an operating system.

Operating systems contain various commands for instructing your PC to perform different functions. Recent versions of operating systems provide so much help that you no longer have to try to remember any of the commands. The commands you use most frequently will eventually become second nature to you.

User Environments

In the past few years the use of IBM and compatibles has become much easier through "Graphical User Interface," or GUI ("gooey") for short. GUI basically converts your PC screen to a pictorial representation of whatever function you are performing. For example, if you are in word processing typing a letter, the screen will have small pictures of single or double spaced lines. To use them, all you have to do is choose the one you want and point at it with your mouse. Small boxes containing pictures of various commands make it easier to use GUI programs. A GUI environment also helps standardize the general look and feel of programs that function under it.

Applications Software (Programs That do it All)

One of the major forces behind the tremendous popularity of PCs at home and office has been the availability of software for specific applications. Called applications software, these programs perform specific tasks. Literally thousands of programs are available for almost everything imaginable: writing letters, manipulating and storing data, number crunching, accounting, tax preparation, recipes, wine lists, publishing, matchmaking, etc. They are available with various capability levels, and range in price from a few dollars to hundreds of dollars.

Word Processing (Writing Made Simple)

Word processing programs help you with writing and composing various written documents like letters, reports, memos, books, newsletters, flyers, etc. These programs contain a tremendous number of essential and conve-  nient features. As far as you are concerned, these programs make the screen resemble a blank sheet of paper with help and other useful commands around the page. You can easily set up the margins on each page or the entire document, decide if you want your text to be single or double spaced, indicate whether you want automatic page numbers, etc. When you type-in your material, if you make a mistake, you can go back on the screen and correct the error; if you want to delete or move a paragraph, you can simply do that. After the shape of the document appears satisfactory, you can have the program check your spelling and point out suspicious words that it cannot find in its dictionary of over 100,000 words. Some programs even have a thesaurus that lets you find words comparable to what you are using.

Some word processing programs have the ability to check your grammar and suggest a more acceptable approach to your writing. Some of the more powerful programs even let you compose your document complete with headlines, graphs, and art work.

Database Management (Keep Track of Everything)

Database management programs help store and sort information in many different ways. In effect a database management program is like a huge sheet of paper with a large number of rows and columns. Each box created by the  intersection of rows and columns is called a "cell." The cells can contain numbers, names, addresses, zip codes, etc. The program can organize the information and sort it by whatever criteria you want. For example, if you enter names and addresses of your friends or customers into the database, the program can sort them by last name, zip code, city, state, etc., in a matter of seconds.

Some organizations customize powerful database management programs for their inventory control and accounting needs. Database programs have a great deal of flexibility and can be programmed to perform customized tasks.

Spreadsheet (Number Crunching and Massaging)

Spreadsheet programs are somewhat similar to database programs, except that various numerical analyses can be performed on the contents of individual cells. For example, your home budget can be set up in the spreadsheet. Based on certain assumptions, you can create a simple formula to have the computer forecast your future expenses.

Data Communication and Information Exchange

Your computer's reach can extend far beyond the doorway of the room in which it's located. Hooked up to a modem and using a communications program, your computer can connect to any computer with a modem anywhere in the world. Communication programs are used together with modems to provide a link between two computers. In order for two modems to connect, a protocol allows the two devices to recognize each other. These programs also provide a systematic method for checking for errors and correcting those errors in data transmission.

Integrated Packages (Jack of all Trades!)

Integrated programs contain the essence of several programs in one package. Typically, an integrated package includes word processing, database, spreadsheet, and communication programs. For some users, especially those with limited needs or little experience with PCs, integrated packages offer an excellent value. They are often less expensive than buying each package separately. Their other advantage is that the commands and operation of each program in the package is consistent with the others, so they are easier to learn and to use.

Personal Finance and Income Taxes

PC programs that help you run your household finances, keep track of your assets and investments, balance your checkbook, and prepare your income taxes are available in many different shapes and forms. These programs are designed to help you manage personal finances as easily as entering check and deposit amounts in a checkbook. They produce an image on the screen of your monitor that may look like your checkbook or a notebook that you would have designed for this purpose yourself. Often the companies that produce these programs seek the opinions of many people regarding their needs and requirements. Then they design the program to meet

those requirements. You benefit from the input of experts as well as ordinary people in the design of these programs.

Business Accounting (Painless Way to Manage Your Business)

Large corporations have been using computers for accounting since the 1950's. Medium sized companies started using them in the 1960's and 1970's. Small businesses (of which there are over 15 million), started using PCs in the 1980's. Today they are the largest buyers of PCs. Still, millions more are waiting for computers to get easier to use and their prices to drop even further. Unfortunately, some of them may wait for a very long time because computers do get easier to use and their prices do keep coming down continuously. The trend doesn't seem to stop.

Businesses that have been using PCs for their accounting have a clear edge over their competitors who do not. PCs help organize vital information and provide timely status reports at the touch of a button. Business accounting programs keep track of income and expenses, keep up-to-date inventory, issue invoices and purchase orders, calculate payroll checks and tax deductions, and perform literally hundreds of other functions for the business owner or manager.

Large or small chains of supermarkets, department stores, and discount stores often use PCs instead of cash registers. As you buy certain food items from your local supermarket, most stores use scanners to read the special code on the items or key in a code from the price ticket into the register. That information not only helps print your receipt, it also helps the store know how many of each item were sold that day. The computer can automatically order more items if they run below a certain level on the shelves, and by keeping track of sales volume at different times of the day, the manager can schedule more people for the peak periods.

Desktop Publishing (Create Your Own Publication)

A few years ago if you wanted to publish a flyer, newsletter, or illustrated manual, you had to go to a special printer to explain what you wanted, go back and forth to proofread the work, and finally have the document produced. PCs have changed all that with special programs called "desktop publishing." These programs are designed to help you create an entire document right on your computer screen. They can create professional looking columns, graphs, illustrations, large and small character sizes in a variety of shapes, etc.

Desktop publishing programs take word processing one step further. They let you move text around on the page, compose the look of the printed page, and create letters and characters of various sizes. A laser printer can print high quality pages that rival professionally prepared material. Most newspapers and magazines are now using PCs to compose their publications. Businesses, schools, churches, individuals, and other groups and organizations are increasingly using PC desktop publishing for their printed materials.

Education (Learning is More Fun With a PC)

The impact of PCs on the education of the younger generation is tremendous. Already, children exposed to PCs are performing unimaginable work with these machines. They can learn almost any topic by using PCs interactively. Educational programs are designed to ask the right questions and lead the students to think and analyze for themselves.

Thousands of educational programs are currently available for PCs. Topics range from mathematics, geography, biology, chemistry, and history, to economics, finance, etc.

Games and Entertainment (Fun! Fun! Fun!)

Some people buy home PCs simply for playing games and helping with their hobbies. However, as you have seen so far, that's just one of the many functions of a PC. Games and entertainment are the largest categories of software available today. The enhancements made to color monitors and powerful PCs make the games more vivid, like those in video arcades.

Parents are discovering that a home computer can help their children do a lot of things in addition to playing games. PCs play games that are more realistic than those played on video game systems. Spending around $200 for a TV video game system and $50 per game cartridge can soon add up to over $1,000. For that amount, you can easily buy a home computer.

Entertainment programs for hobbyists and others are rapidly covering all areas from stamp collecting, and wine lists to gourmet recipes, genealogy, and personal diaries, etc. Every day new programs are developed to address unique areas of interest.

Utilities (Handy Little Programs)

Utility programs are those which help facilitate using a PC or various programs. Some utilities are designed to act like an activity calendar, scheduler, or calculator. Others help you speed up your memory, hard disk, etc. Some others analyze your system's configuration and give you a status report as well as diagnose any problems your PC may have.

Other

Virtually every topic imaginable has been addressed by computer enthusiasts. People continue to develop new programs for activities that were formerly unknown. There are PC programs that help you with your family tree, matchmaking, employee interviews and testing, encyclopedia, world atlas, etc.

3.6. Important PC Terms You Should Know

PCs have spun a whole new vocabulary. You need to become familiar with the following terms before you read any further; others are listed in the glossary.

BAUD
Baud rate is the unit of measure indicating the number of changes in data signal per second. In modems it's used to measure the speed with which they transfer data. The

higher the Baud rate, the faster the modem. Most modems operate at 2400 Baud, 9600 Baud, or 14,400 Baud.

BIT

A BIT is the smallest unit of measure in computer terminology. It represents the "ON" or "OFF" status of a microprocessor switch. Letters of the alphabet, digits 0 to 9, and other special characters are each represented by a combination of 8 bits.

BPS

Bits Per Second is a unit of measure indicating the number of bits a modem is capable of transferring. Newer modems are capable of transmitting more than one bit per data signal; therefore, BPS is a more accurate measure of modem transmission rate than Baud rate.

BYTE

A BYTE is a unit of measure for storage of characters or numbers in the computer. Each BYTE is 8 BITS. Because there are 8 positions of "ON" or "OFF" in a BYTE, there are 256 different values (256 combinations the 0 and 1 can be located in the 8 positions) that can be represented by a single BYTE. The size of the computer memory as well as the sizes of the floppy drive, hard disk drive, tape backup and CD drives are all measured by BYTES.

CACHE

Cache (pronounced cash) memory is very high speed memory that acts as a buffer between your microprocessor and your hard disk drive. There is a significant difference between the speed of the two. Generally, while you are working with a program there are certain instructions and information that you access most fre-quently. The cache controller microchip keeps track of the most frequently needed data and stores it in the cache memory for instant access by the microprocessor. Cache memory can be built into the microprocessor (i.e., 80486 family), the motherboard, hard disk drive, or the hard drive controller.

CPS

Characters Per Second is the unit used to measure printing speed. It's established by the printer manufacturer, and is usually based on somewhat ideal conditions. Printer speed is expressed in draft as well as enhanced or letter-quality modes.

CPI

Characters Per Inch is the unit of measure that determines the number of characters printed per inch by a printer. Most regular correspondence is printed in 10 characters per inch. All printers, except daisywheels, are capable of printing a wide range of characters per inch. Some headings may be as large as 1 CPI, and some fine-prints may be as small as 17 CPI.

DOS

Disk Operating System is the program that tells the various parts of your PC how to work with each other. Since the introduction of the original IBM PC, DOS has been updated and upgraded several times. Two major software companies develop and sell DOS under their own and other computer companies' labels. Microsoft Corporation and Digital Research Corporation market MS-DOS and DR-DOS, respectively. DOS is called a text based operating system because it uses letters and other characters to communicate with you.

DPI

Dots Per Inch measures how many horizontal and vertical dots can be printed per square inch. The higher the two numbers, the smaller the dots, and therefore the better and crisper the printed results. For example, standard laser printers produce 300 DPI in horizontal and vertical. Their output looks sharp and professional. Dot matrix printers are usually capable of 150 to 300 DPI horizontal and 150 to 240 DPI vertical.

Dot Pitch

Computer monitors display information by forming characters that join small dots together. Dot Pitch is the distance between the display dots on a monitor, expressed in millimeters (mm). The smaller the dot pitch, the sharper the characters, and the higher the price. Dot pitch generally ranges from 0.20 to 0.40 mm.

EISA

Extended Industry Standard Architecture was introduced in 1989 (See ISA). It's designed to increase the power and throughput rate of IBM compatible PCs. Motherboards with EISA expansion slots can transfer data 32 bits at a time instead of the 16 bit rate for ISA boards and the 8 bits for XT and PC type boards. An EISA motherboard can work with existing 16 and 8 bit controller boards as well as specially designed EISA controller boards.

Fonts

Various printers create letters of the alphabet, numbers and characters based on a predetermined graphic design called font. Fonts usually come in different sizes and provide different styles such as italic, bold, etc.

GUI

A Graphic User Interface (called "Gooey") is a program that works alongside DOS to convert most commands to graphic images that can be activated by using a pointing device. These interfaces are more intuitive and easier to use than DOS alone. Windows is a GUI program.

IDE

Integrated Drive Electronic refers to a technology used by most hard disk drives sold today. Drives using IDE offer high speed and high data transfer rates at a relatively low cost.

ISA

Industry Standard Architecture refers to the type of expansion slots located on the motherboard of a PC. When the IBM PC was introduced in 1981, it had 8 expansion slots on the motherboard. Those slots were used for adding adapter boards to the computer to operate the monitor, drives, printers, etc. The original slots could only move data 8 bits at a time. When the IBM AT was introduced in 1984, it had a faster 80286 processor and slightly longer expansion slots that could move data 16 bits at a time. That 16 bit bus has become known as the Industry Standard Architecture. ISA is currently the most popular and affordable standard.

Kilo Bytes

A Kilo Byte (KB) is 1000 Bytes of data. The size of computer memory (RAM) and capacity of floppy disks are measured in KB.

Local Bus

Refers to the type of expansion slot that lets your components deal directly with the microprocessor instead of going through several stages on the motherboard.

Mega Bytes

A Mega Byte (MB) is 1,000,000 Bytes of data. The size of computer memory (RAM) or floppy and hard disk capacities are measured in Mega Bytes.

MHZ

Megahertz is a measure of computer processor speed. It's one million beats per second. That's how fast a small clock on the motherboard of your computer regulates electronic signals. The original IBM PC introduced in 1981 ran at 4.77 MHZ. Top speed of some 80486 computers reach 66 MHZ and Pentium systems exceed 100 MHZ. For comparison purposes, MHZ should be used within the same microprocessor family. For example, a 33 MHZ 80386 is faster than a 25 MHZ 80386. However, the same microprocessor is not as fast as the next generation 25 MHZ 80486.

Micro Channel
Micro Channel Architecture (MCA) was introduced in 1987 by IBM, in certain models of PS/2 computers. Micro Channel is a proprietary 32 bit architecture designed to increase the power and throughput rate of the computer. Motherboards with the micro channel expansion slots transfer data 32 bits at a time, and only work with controller boards built with the same microchannel design.

MIPS
Million Instructions Per Second is a measure of data processing rate in a PC. It measures the processing power and speed of a computer.

MNP
Microcom Networking Protocol is an error correction method used in modem communications. If modems at both ends use MNP, the data throughput rate can be as much as two to four times the modems' rated speed. MNP can be on a microchip mounted on the modem, or in the form of software.

PCI Local Bus
PCI is the fastest type of local bus expansion slot available at this time. It moves data 32 bits at a time between your microprocessor and various peripherals connected to your PC. It's designed to work with 80486, Pentium and future generation microprocessors.

Postscript
Postscript is a page description programming language for printers. It offers greater choices for transferring characters and graphics from the computer to the printer. It's primarily used as a hardware or software option with laser printers. Laser printers with postscript can print a wider variety of characters of different shapes, sizes and shades. They are often more expensive than standard laser printers. Windows users may not need Postscript because Windows already comes with a program called "True Type." It creates a wide selection of fonts similar to Postscript.

RAM
Random Access Memory is the main computer memory that becomes active when your PC is powered up. RAM is capable of storing information and passing it back

and forth between the processor and other components of the PC. When the power is turned off, all information in RAM is wiped clean.

ROM

Read Only Memory is a type of memory chip that permanently stores information placed in it at the factory. Unlike RAM, if the power is turned off, ROM retains the data stored in it. ROM-BIOS is one type of ROM which tells your PC what to do at start-up.

SCSI

Small Computer System Interface (called "scuzzy") is a general purpose interface that allows up to seven SCSI compatible devices like hard drives, CD drives, printers, etc., to be connected together and to the PC. If you are buying a PC with the intention of adding a CD-ROM and tape backup, you may consider specifying SCSI for your hard disk drive.

VESA Local Bus

VESA is one of the fastest types of local bus expansion slot available today. It moves data 32 bits at a time. It's designed to work with 80486 systems.

Chapter 4. Get To Know Your PC Intimately

So far, you have been introduced to the history of computers, what they look like, how they work, and what they can do. This chapter goes into greater detail about different hardware products. You'll be intimately introduced to various components. You may skip sections that seem to be too technical for you. We don't want to turn you into a PC Nerd! If you don't currently use a PC or want to upgrade the one you have, you may want to study this chapter carefully. It will give you the knowledge and the tools to use when buying or upgrading your PC.

4.1. Central Processing Unit (CPU)

The CPU, a microprocessor chip that is the brains of your PC, is where all data processing and analysis take place. There are several different families of CPUs. They are called "platforms," because with every generation, they introduce a higher level of performance and capabilities. Only a few companies design and manufacture CPU chips for the IBM and compatible PCs. Since 1981 when the IBM PC was introduced, one of the greatest strengths of IBM and compatible PCs has been the compatibility of various CPU platforms with their predecessors. This has ensured that as newer and more powerful CPUs are introduced, millions of PCs purchased earlier remain compatible and can use the same programs.

Currently Intel Corporation, Advanced Micro Devices Corporation (AMD), Cyrix, Texas Instruments and Chips and Technologies, Inc. are the only manufacturers of CPUs for PCs. However, a few other companies are also preparing to enter that market. As long as these microprocessor chips remain compatible with the established standards, any major brand should work properly.

The speed of CPUs is expressed in Mega Hertz (MHZ). MHZ is one million cycles per second. Special programs, called performance benchmarks, test various CPUs to gauge their speed. Benchmarks test the speed of a CPU by giving it a series of computations that exercise every

aspect of the microprocessor. CPU speeds are a meaningful measure of comparing speeds of microprocessors in the same platform. For example, a 33 MHZ 80386 processor is faster than a 25 MHZ 80386. However, that 33 MHZ 80386 is not necessarily faster than the newer generation 25 MHZ 80486.

Another measure of CPU performance is the number of bits of

data processed and the number of bits moved in and out of the processor (data path). A bit is the smallest unit of binary data, either a 0 or 1. Imagine that a CPU is like an automobile manufacturing plant sitting next to a highway. The plant has a certain number of assembly lines, each of which can produce one car every minute. The highway just outside the plant has a certain number of lanes that the finished cars from the assembly line are driven on to. Currently available CPUs can process either 8, 16, or 32 bits of data at a time. That means the plant has either 8, 16, or 32 assembly lines. The CPUs may have data throughput rates different from their processing speeds. In the factory example, the number of lanes of highway outside the plant may not be the same as the number of assembly lines. As you will see in the following sections, a CPU may process 32 bits of data but move them 16 bits at a time. Like a factory with 32 assembly lines and a 16 lane highway outside.

These units of measuring performance are primarily for comparison and evaluation purposes. Similar to the EPA gas consumption data for cars, they should not be the only criteria for choosing a PC. Your overall criteria will include many other factors in addition to the CPU speed and data throughput rate.

8086

The 8086 microprocessor was introduced in 1978 by Intel in Silicon Valley, California. This chip started the PC industry. It had a 16 bit internal and external data path. Ironically, it never gained the same popularity as its slower 8088 offspring. Faster 8086 chips (referred to as turbo processors) running at 8 or 10 MHZ were developed in the mid 1980's. Hardly any new PCs now use the 8086 chips.

Processor Speed (MHZ)	Performance (MIPS)	Speed vs. 8088/4.77 MHZ
4.77 (Discontinued)	0.3	1.0
8.0 (Discontinued)	0.7	1.7
10.0 (Discontinued)	0.8	2.1

8088

The 8088 microprocessor, introduced by Intel in 1979, had most of the characteristics of its 8086 predecessor. However, it had a 16 bit internal data path with an 8 bit external bus. The initial version of the processor worked at 4.77 MHZ, which was considered fast in those days. The original IBM PC introduced in 1981 made the 8088 a piece of history forever. That processor was used in the IBM PC and XT computers. Faster 8088 chips (referred to as turbo processors) running at 8 or 10 MHZ were developed in the mid 1980's. This chip is now extinct.

Processor Speed (MHZ)	Performance (MIPS)	Speed vs. 8088/4.77 MHZ
4.77 (Discontinued)	0.3	>>> Benchmark 1.0 <<<
8.0 (Discontinued)	0.7	1.7
10.0 (Discontinued)	0.8	2.1

80286

The 80286 microprocessor was introduced by Intel in 1982. It was first introduced by IBM in the AT (Advanced Technology) family of PCs in 1984. The 80286 was a 16 bit processor with a 16 bit data path, making it nearly twice as fast as the comparable 8088 microprocessor. The original IBM AT had a speed of 6 MHZ.

Processor Speed (MHZ)	Performance (MIPS)	Speed vs. 8088/4.77 MHZ
6.0 (Discontinued)	1.0	2.7
8.0 (Discontinued)	1.2	3.6
10.0 (Discontinued)	1.5	4.5
12.0	2.7	5.4
16.0	3.5	7.3
20.0	4.4	9.1

80386-DX

The 80386 microprocessor, introduced by Intel in 1985, helped launch a new power platform for microcomputers. It's a 32 bit processor with a 32 bit data path, which means that the processor works on 32 pieces of data at a time and communicates with memory at the same rate. Additionally, many other improvements were incorporated in the processor that gave it the ability to process several tasks simultaneously, called multitasking.

Processor Speed (MHZ)	Performance (MIPS)	Speed vs. 8088/4.77 MHZ
20.0 (Discontinued)	7.0	10.4
25.0 (Discontinued)	8.5	14.2
33.0	11.4	19.7
40.0	15.2	22.8

80386-SX

The 80386-SX family of microprocessors was introduced by Intel in 1988. It's a scaled down version of the 80386 microprocessor introduced in 1985. The 80386-SX processor is a 32 bit microchip with a 16 bit data path. This processor was introduced by Intel as a lower cost alternative to the powerful 80386 processor. It can run all the programs that are designed to take advantage of the 80386 abilities at a relatively lower cost. Because it took advantage of Windows enhanced mode, it became the entry level system of choice for most users who could afford the slight cost increase over 80286 based systems.

Processor Speed (MHZ)	Performance (MIPS)	Speed vs. 8088/4.77 MHZ
16.0 (Discontinued)	2.5	7.5
20.0 (Discontinued)	4.2	10.1
25.0	5.3	12.7
33.0	7.0	16.8

80386-SL

The 80386-SL family of microprocessors was introduced by Intel in 1990. It's very similar to the SX family in many ways plus it offers some unique features. One of the most important features of the SL family is its low power consumption as well as energy conservation. They were designed primarily for battery operated notebook PCs.

80486-DX

The 80486 processor was introduced by Intel in 1989. It's a 32 bit processor with a 32 bit data path that in addition to enhancements over the 80386, incorporates a math coprocessor and an 8 Kilo Byte internal memory cache. Because of enhancements, the 80486-25 is faster than the 80386-25, even without the built-in math coprocessor and 8 KB cache.

The 80486 based PCs are popular among power users for specific applications which need the high performance abilities of the new processor. They are used as a file server in a computer network environment, as a computer aided design (CAD) workstation, as a high speed number crunching machine, etc.

Processor Speed (MHZ)	Performance (MIPS)	Speed vs. 8088/4.77 MHZ
25.0	20.0	22.4
33.0	27.0	29.9
50.0	40.7	44.8

80486-SX

The 80486-SX, introduced by Intel in 1991, is a scaled-down version of the 80486 microprocessor. The 80486-SX is a 32 bit processor with a 32 bit data path and an 8 Kilo Byte cache memory. The cache memory inside the processor keeps 8000 bytes of the most frequently used information and instructions actively ready for the processor. The processor is identical to the 80486, except that the math coprocessor function is disabled.

Processor Speed (MHZ)	Performance (MIPS)	Speed vs. 8088/4.77 MHZ
20.0	16.5	17.9
25.0	20.0	21.5
33.0	26.5	27.4

80486-DX2

The 80486-DX2 family of microprocessors is also called "DoubleSpeed." The processor runs at twice the speed of everything else on the motherboard. The chip has all the features of the DX family, runs twice as fast and doesn't need an expensive, fast motherboard.

Processor Speed (MHZ)	Performance (MIPS)	Speed vs. 8088/4.77 MHZ
50.0	41.0	43.2
66.0	54.0	49.1

Pentium

The Pentium family of microprocessors was introduced by Intel in 1993. These chips use a 64 K data path, can process multiple tasks, and offer the greatest level of computing power.

Processor Speed (MHZ)	Performance (MIPS)	Speed vs. 8088/4.77 MHZ
66.0	112.0	104.3
100.0	170.0	164.2

RISC

RISC based computers are rapidly becoming popular with business users who demand maximum power and speed from their microcomputers. Reduced Instruction Set Chip (RISC) is a new generation of microprocessors that eliminates unnecessary instructions built into other processors to cover a host of contingencies. As speedy as a regular microprocessor is, it still takes time to sort through all the various instructions and act on them. For most applications, maybe half of those instructions are never used or used very rarely; so reducing them speeds up the processing. RISC chips are a little easier and less expensive to design and manufacture than their 80386 and 80486 counterparts. However, a RISC based system may not run software written for the IBM and compatible machines. As the popularity of RISC based systems increases, special application programs are being adapted to or developed for the environment.

4.2. Math coprocessor

If your application requires a math coprocessor, the selection process is quite simple. The math coprocessor chip number matches the CPU number. For example an 80286-12 MHZ processor needs an 80287-12 math coprocessor. An 80386-33 MHZ processor needs an 80387-33 math coprocessor. Every motherboard has a built-in socket for a math coprocessor. The socket is frequently adjacent to the microprocessor. Adding it to the PC can be done at

any time by simply opening the computer case and
inserting the chip into the socket. Prices of math
coprocessor chips have plummeted over the last couple
of years, as a result of intensive competition between
Intel and other manufacturers.

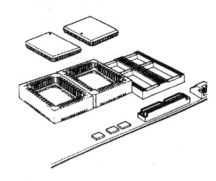

Most applications don't require a math coprocessor.
Specialized applications such as computer aided design (CAD), and number crunching spreadsheets are
the main users of the math coprocessor chip. The
software package you may plan to use will indicate whether it requires a math coprocessor.
Consequently, you don't need to buy a math coprocessor until you have established your needs.

4.3. Memory

Computer memory is divided into four categories. The first 640 K of memory is called
"Conventional Memory." That's the base memory of your PC which DOS and other programs
use as their main playing field. Programs and data use conventional memory to move back and
forth between your hard disk, floppy disk, keyboard and the monitor.

If your PC has more than 640 K of memory, the 384 K that lies between 640 K and 1,024 K
(1 Mega Byte) is called "Reserved Memory." That memory is used to store special ROM
instructions that are used by the BIOS, the video and some other devices in your PC. Using
your RAM memory to store ROM instructions makes them faster to operate and execute. Some
special utility programs are able to move small programs from conventional memory to the
unused portions of reserved memory, thus freeing up your valuable conventional memory.

Memory above 1,024 K is called "Extended Memory." In 80286, 80386, and 80486 systems,
the 64 K of memory between 1,024 and 1,088 is called "High Memory," which can also be used
to store some memory resident drivers and programs for instant access. Systems based on
80286 can handle up to 16 MB of RAM, whereas 80386 and 80486 systems can handle
significantly more memory. Certain programs can use extended memory for a variety of
applications. For example, a part of that memory can act like a drive and store the most
frequently used data for instant access.

Another memory category is called "Expanded Memory." This type of memory is either
installed on specially designed expanded memory boards, or is converted from extended
memory by using special software. In order to use expanded memory, a small portion of the
reserved memory is used as a conduit or channel to fool your computer into thinking that it's

like a bottomless pit. Programs that use expanded memory keep sending part of their data into that channel, thinking that it's an invisible extension of the conventional memory. Some memory management programs convert extended memory to expanded memory.

PC memory come in five different physical categories. Within each category, the memory chips have different speeds to match the requirements of processor speeds. Chip speed is expressed in nanoseconds (ns: one billionth of a second). The 80386, 80486 and Pentium systems require 60 or 70 ns chips for optimum performance. 80386-SX systems can work with 80 ns or faster chips. 80286 systems can work with 100 ns or faster chips. Because there is very little cost difference, slower speeds are no longer manufac- 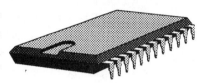 tured. Various PC manufacturers may use different types of memory in their systems for a variety of reasons. When buying a new PC, it's important to ask about the type and speed of memory used in the machine. If you ever intend to upgrade your PC by adding more memory, using the standard type will save you money.

DIP (DRAM)

Dual Inline Package chips are commonly used in older generation PC, XT, and AT compatible systems (8088, 8086, and 80286). These individual chips are inserted into memory sockets on the motherboard or on an add-on memory board. DIP chips have a row of 9 tiny metallic legs on each side. One side of the chip has markings that indicate the manufacturer, size, and speed of the chip. These chips are installed in banks of 9 each. The amount of memory is determined by the number of banks of 9 chips. For example, a bank of 9 chips, 256 KB each, is counted as 256 KB. Two banks of 9 will provide a total of 2 x 256 = 512 KB.

SIMMs

Single Inline Memory Modules are small boards that contain memory chips and fit on the motherboard vertically. The bottom of a SIMMs memory board looks similar to the bottom of an adapter board. The boards are inserted into special memory slots. They have become the most popular memory standard and are used by the majority of motherboard manufacturers.

SIPPs

Single Inline Pin Package memory modules are very similar to the SIMMs modules, but instead of the connector described earlier, there are pins at the bottom of the board. The pins are inserted into similarly laid out pin holes on the motherboard. Don't worry about SIPPs, hardly any motherboard manufacturers use this standard anymore.

SRAM

Static Random Access Memory is a faster type of memory chip than the Dynamic RAM chips used in DIP, SIMMs, and SIPPs. SRAM is much more expensive to manufacture than DRAM. Therefore, SRAM chips are used sparingly and only where they can produce the most benefits. One of the most common places for SRAM is in high speed memory cache for 80386, 80486 and Pentium systems.

ROM

Read Only Memory chips are primarily used for storage of specific instructions for the motherboard or other controller boards. They vary in size and capacity, but their main functions are essentially the same. ROM capacities vary from 8 to 64 KB, depending on the amount of instructions they need to store. ROM chips are placed by the manufacturer and you don't have any control over what is used in your PC.

ROM chips are extremely sensitive to static electricity. The information stored electronically in these chips at the factory can be wiped clean if the chip is zapped by static electricity. If that happens, the only solution is to replace either the chip or the board. This is the main reason for being cautious when you open up your PC to look at or handle any parts.

4.4. Case

A computer case serves as an enclosure for the components of the base unit. Desktop PCs now come in a variety of shapes and sizes. Your computer case often has little or nothing to do with the power and capabilities of your PC. If you are choosing a PC, you should only look for the following characteristics in the case:

● The computer case should have a sticker for FCC Class B approval for home use or Class A for business use. The FCC certification means that your PC will not interfere with TV and radio signals at your location or those near you. The FCC certification is stricter for home use than it is for business use. Therefore, if you plan to use the machine at home, you should have Class B approval.

- The case should have enough room for all the components that you need to have now. You should also anticipate future expansion and upgrade. The case should have room for additional internal drives (drive bays) and adapter boards. Unless your space is very limited, small cases with no room for expansion will limit your ability to upgrade your system in the future.

- Your personal preference for the type, shape, size, and color of the case is important, because you will be looking at it every time you use your PC.

- A solid, high quality case protects your components better.

In the past few years, various PC manufacturers have become quite creative with the type, shape, and size of their PCs. Often, they simply try to differentiate their products from others, but sometimes the case is designed to serve a specific purpose.

4.5. Power Supply

The shape and size of a power supply is often paired with the type of case the manufacturer uses. Pre-assembled PCs already incorporate a power supply deemed to be adequate for the system by the manufacturer. A power supply converts 110 volt AC power into 5 and 12 volt DC power for the components inside the system unit. It also provides a cooling fan. The power capacity, and the cooling capability of the power supply become critical if you plan to add other components to your system in the future.

In transportable, laptop, and notebook size computers, the power supply is already sized for the system and you will not be able to add too much to the system to worry about the power supply. However, in desktop units you can use the following general guideline to select the appropriate power supply for your PC:

PC Type	Minimum Watts	Desired Watts
8088, 8086	100	150
80286, 80386-SX	150	200
80386, 80486, Pentium	200	250

4.6. Adapter Boards

Adapter boards which come in various shapes and sizes are manufactured by hundreds of different companies throughout the world. The most important characteristic they all have in common is the type of "interface bus architecture" they use. The interface is the part of the adapter board that connects to the expansion slot on the motherboard. As you may recall from the previous chapter, currently there are five standard bus architectures: ISA (Industry Standard Architecture), EISA (Extended Industry Standard Architecture), MCA (Micro Channel Architecture), PCI Local Bus (Peripheral Component Interconnect) and VESA Local Bus (Video Electronics Standards Association). Your motherboard and adapter boards all have to conform to one or more of these standards.

Memory Board

First generation PCs were designed with what seemed to be a large capacity for memory, namely 64 K. The original IBM PC was designed to handle up to 640 K, which in 1981 was 10 times the highest capacity of personal computers at that time. But various programs soon started to take advantage of that limit and then demanded more. Memory boards became the only means for adding extra memory to those PCs.

PC motherboards have a certain capacity for the amount of memory they can hold. Additional memory is added by installing memory boards. These boards are basically standard printed circuit boards with sockets for memory chips or memory modules. Depending on their type, they may also contain special chips for specific functions. There are two types of memory boards:

Extended Memory Board: This type of board is very plain and simply adds the chips or modules to the motherboard. The memory is used in its most basic form called extended memory. It was described earlier in this chapter.

Expanded Memory Board: This type of board is similar to the extended memory board plus it has special chips that add the expanded memory capability to the board. It was described earlier in this chapter.

Today's PCs, have a lot of built-in memory capacity right on the motherboard. The majority of 80386 and 80486 motherboards have room for at least 32 MB of memory. Therefore, the need for memory boards is not as great as it was in the older PCs.

Drive Controller

There are five different types and four categories of drive controllers. Almost all drive controllers operate up to two floppy and two hard disk drives. Until recently, drive controllers were actually adapter boards that were inserted into an expansion slot of the motherboard. Now some manufacturers incorporate the drive control chips into the motherboard eliminating the need for a separate board. During most of the 1980's, drive controllers were added by the dealer, depending on the customer's needs and requirements. These controllers were often made by companies other than the PC manufacturer. The six categories of controllers depend on the type of expansion bus used on the motherboard (8 bit ISA, 16 bit ISA, 32 bit EISA, 32 bit Microchannel and 32 bit PCI or VESA Local Bus). These different types of controllers also relate to the technology used for the hard disk drives (MFM, RLL, IDE, SCSI, and ESDI) that will be described a little later.

Floppy Drive Controller

The floppy drive controller is one of the simpler parts of the PC. The floppy drive control chip(s) are often placed on the hard disk drive controller board. Some manufacturers have started incorporating them on the motherboard itself, thus simplifying the controller. Currently, there is only one type of floppy controller. Until a few years ago, the controller that worked in the 8 bit expansion bus of 8088 (PC and XT) type computers was different from the one working in the 16 bit expansion bus of 80286 (AT), 80386, and 80486 type computers. The 8 bit controllers were not capable of operating high density floppy drives (5.25" @ 1.2 MB, and 3.5" @ 1.4 MB), newer controllers have solved that problem.

Hard Disk Drive Controller

Hard disk drive controller technology has advanced rapidly in recent years. Most manufacturers are building hard disk drives that incorporate the controller on the drive itself, allowing them to increase drive performance, as well as reduce overall costs. These drives connect to a special plug on the motherboard (if it has one), or plug into a simple controller board that is inserted

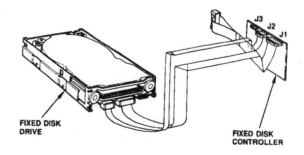

FIXED DISK DRIVE

FIXED DISK CONTROLLER

into one of the expansion slots. The increased popularity of these intelligent drives has phased out the older technology drives (like MFM and RLL).

MFM

Modified Frequency Modulation was the most popular hard disk drive encoding method in the 1980's. Up to two hard disk drives and two floppy disk drives can be connected to an MFM controller. They have been phased out in favor of higher performance intelligent drives.

RLL

Run Length Limited was the second most popular hard disk drive encoding method in the mid to late 1980's. RLL uses a more advanced data encoding method that allows it to record data at a higher density. It stores approximately 50% more data than MFM. Up to two hard disk drives and two floppy drives can be connected to an RLL controller. RLL drives have also been phased out in favor of higher performance intelligent drives. However, an enhanced form of the RLL encoding technique is being used in the newer, more powerful drives.

IDE

Integrated Drive Electronic technology has become the most popular hard disk drive format since 1990. These drives offer high speed and high data transfer rates at a relatively lower cost than their counterparts. They use the Advanced RLL (ARLL) encoding technique. The IDE controller (if needed for a system) is a very basic card. Most of the IDE control functions are built into the hard drive unit itself, and the controller board simply provides the interface between the drive and the motherboard. PC manufacturers in increasing numbers are building the IDE interface right on the motherboard, thus eliminating the need for a separate board and an extra expansion slot. IDE controller/drives are currently capable of transferring 1 Mbps, with future potentials exceeding 10 Mbps.

ESDI

Enhanced Small Disk Interface was developed in the mid 1980's as a high performance alternative to the dominant MFM technology. It led to higher capacity and faster hard drives in a PC. ESDI controller technology has continued to advance, and still offers one of the fastest transfer rates for PCs. Most of the controller functions are incorporated on the drive itself, but the controller board still plays a significant role. High capacity ESDI drives can hold over 1,000 MB (1 Giga Byte) of data at transfer rates faster than 12 milliseconds. They are capable of transferring 1 to 3 Mbps.

SCSI

Small Computer System Interface is a general purpose interface that goes beyond hard disk and floppy control functions. Using the SCSI encoding method, up to seven SCSI compatible components, such as hard disk drives, floppy drives, tape backup drives,

CD drives and other devices, can be connected to the PC. SCSI interface is becoming more popular and its transfer rate is increasing. The current SCSI transfer rate is 1 to 3 Mbps.

Video Graphics

Video graphic standards have been improving dramatically in recent years. The quality of their output is reaching that of high quality TV pictures. The video adapter matched with a corresponding monitor can display a wide range of output, depending on the standard you choose. Currently, the VGA-based standard is the most popular form of computer display, and most programs are designed to take advantage of colorful and crisp VGA images.

When the original IBM PC was introduced in 1981, it did not have a factory-installed video adapter. Dealers installed the video board and the corresponding monitor according to each customer's needs and budget. Most computers sold today still have the flexibility to be equipped with the standard chosen by the customer. Because of the popularity of the VGA standard, most manufacturers install the VGA chips directly on the motherboard, thus eliminating the need for an extra expansion slot.

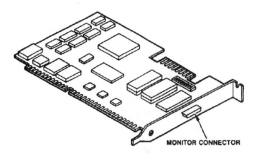

MONITOR CONNECTOR

The video board acts as an interface between your computer and your monitor. It interprets the signals sent by the computer into images displayed on the screen. Video images are formed on the monitor screen by small dots that can have only one color each. In a monochrome monitor, all the dots can have only one color, while in a color monitor, each dot can display one of a variety of colors at a time. The distance between the center of the dots is called dot pitch, and is expressed in millimeters. The smaller the dot pitch, the closer the dots and the sharper the images on the screen. The resolution of the display is measured by the number of horizontal dots followed by the number of vertical dots, such as 640 x 480. The larger the numbers, the more dots you'll see and the resolution will be higher.

MDA (Monochrome Display Adapter)

MDA was the first video standard used by IBM and compatible computers. A carry-over from the standards used for terminals connected to mainframe computers, it was capable of showing only one color on a black background. The color of the display depended on the monitor (either green or amber), not the video board. The resolution was 720 x 350, but the adapter was capable of showing only text characters (no graphics). This standard was quickly replaced by more capable successors, and is no longer manufactured.

CGA (Color Graphic Adapter)

The CGA standard, introduced in 1981, immediately became popular because it could display colors and graphics. Computer enthusiasts who also wanted to play games (although limited at that time) found CGA more appealing than the monochrome standard. However, CGA resolution was not as high as the monochrome standard, and the number of colors displayed was limited to a maximum of 4 at the 320 x 200 level. The highest CGA resolution was 640 x 200 with 2 colors. In 1984 a better color standard was introduced, and by 1988 the CGA standard lost its appeal.

MGA (Monochrome Graphics Adapter)

MGA was introduced in 1982 by Hercules Graphics Corporation as an improvement to the monochrome display standard that was not capable of showing graphics. The adapter had the same resolution of 720 x 350, but it could display drawings, charts, and other business-related images on the screen. The adapters still produced a single-color image. The MGA standard is now obsolete.

EGA (Enhanced Graphics Adapter)

The EGA standard was introduced in 1984, and was an immediate hit with PC users who wanted high resolution text and improved color display. The price of the EGA adapter and monitor was prohibitive, but it gained popularity among businesses. It could display 640 x 350 with up to 16 colors. New high resolution graphics programs and games added to the popularity of the EGA standard. By 1990, the VGA standard (which was introduced in 1987) became the predominant standard, and EGA began to lose ground. The EGA standard is no longer being manufactured.

VGA (Video Graphics Array)

VGA was introduced in 1987 by IBM, and immediately won the hearts of color monitor enthusiasts. However, due to the initial high costs of product introduction, it took a couple of years before VGA became the dominant video standard. VGA has a 640 x 480 resolution with up to 16 colors or 320 x 200 with up to 256 colors. The main enhancement introduced by the VGA standard was using analog signals instead of the digital signals used by all its predecessors. Analog signal is similar to a TV signal, and allows images to have a lifelike appearance. Photographs and similar images appear more realistic on a VGA display.

VGA adapters can work with VGA color or VGA monochrome monitors. For monochrome monitors the adapter sends the signal in shades of gray that allow images to appear similar to black and white TV. Newer and more graphically oriented programs require VGA in order to operate. It's projected that by 1995 even older PCs that were purchased in the 1980's will be upgraded at least to the current VGA standard.

SVGA (Super VGA)

In 1989, enhancements to the VGA standard were introduced by various manufacturers. These improvements affected the resolution, speed, and number of colors displayed by the VGA adapter. The new standard is called Super VGA, and certain adapters produce resolutions from 800 x 600 to as high as 1,024 x 768 with 256 colors. In its highest level, the SVGA image looks better than a TV picture in terms of color and resolution. These enhancements are possible by using special chips and having the required amount of memory on the adapter. SVGA adapters may have 512 K or 1 MB of memory. The higher the amount of memory, the faster the display and the more colors it can display.

High resolution color displays require that the adapter and the monitor work harder than an ordinary display. They have significantly more dots and more lines to display and change every time your screen display changes. In reality, without you noticing, your screen is redrawn several times a second. This is called the "refresh rate" and is expressed in KHZ (Kilo Hertz). Ideally, every line on your screen should refresh simultaneously. However, a price premium is involved with this benefit. Most manufacturers, in order to make high resolution color VGA more affordable, use a technique called "Interlace," which means that the monitor refreshes every other line with each pass. You may notice a slight flicker when you move your eyes on and off the monitor, but, in most cases, the flicker is hardly noticeable. Monitors and adapters that refresh every line with the same pass are called "Non-interlaced". They generally cost 20% to 50% more than their interlaced counterparts, but that price gap is rapidly declining.

SVGA and VGA adapters are supplied with special software called drivers. These programs are supplied by the board manufacturers to help run specially demanding graphics programs like Windows, AutoCAD, Lotus 1-2-3, etc. Drivers play a very important role in the speed with which your computer and monitor work together. Most graphics programs try to include many of the video drivers for the major brands available to them. However, there is always a time lag between when they get the driver and the time their software is released. Because of the importance of having up-to-date drivers, when you buy your system, check the release date on the video driver diskette(s) and make sure that they are fairly recent.

Parallel/Serial Communication

The parallel and serial communication capability in most PCs is handled by an adapter board that contains the necessary chips for that purpose. Some PCs contain the chips right on the motherboard, thus eliminating the need for a separate board.

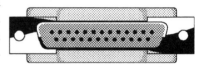

The parallel connector in the back of the PC is a female plug with 25 pin-holes. The serial connector is either a 9 pin or a 25 pin male plug. The end of the cable that you plug into a connector should have the same shape as the parallel or serial connector.

Game

The game adapter board lets one or two joysticks be connected to your PC. In some PCs the game controller chips are installed on the motherboard, but often they are installed on the parallel and serial board. Sometimes the game port is on a separate board by itself. The basic function of most game adapters is the same, but some brands may contain unique features or enhancements. You can check with your supplier if the game board has any special features. Game boards have a 15 pin female connector.

Expansion Bus Architecture

Until 1987, all IBM and compatible PCs had only one standard for their expansion slots. The 8086 and 8088 based systems used an 8 bit bus architecture and the 80286 and higher processors had 8 bit and 16 bit buses. That was known as Industry Standard Architecture (ISA). When IBM introduced the PS/2 line in 1987, some of their higher end models were equipped with a new bus technique called Micro Channel Architecture (MCA). In 1989, a group of major compatible PC manufacturers formed an industry council to develop a new standard that could offer additional features to ISA, yet remain compatible with that popular standard. They developed the Enhanced Industry Standard Architecture (EISA).

ISA

The ISA expansion bus currently used in over 90% of the PCs throughout the world, has become the dominant standard by sheer numbers. The 16 bit ISA bus found in most PCs is more than adequate for most applications. An expansion bus is like a multi-lane highway. If a lot of vehicles are on the road, the higher the number of lanes, the faster you can travel. However, if only one or two vehicles are on the road, you can travel on a two-lane highway just as fast as you can on a multi-lane highway. Word processing, database management and most spreadsheet applications are not really dependent on the bus architecture. Systems based on ISA standard cost less than their comparable counterparts with EISA, MCA or Local Bus designs. For the majority of PC users ISA boards are more than adequate.

ISA based systems don't perform as fast as EISA, MCA or Local Bus, when they are used as a file server in a large network, in a heavy-duty multi-tasking environment or for tasks like CAD (Computer Aided Design) requiring frequent hard disk access. ISA's maximum throughput rate is 4 MB per second.

EISA

The EISA expansion bus transfers data 32 bits at a time. Additionally, it has a feature called "Bus Master" which acts like a traffic cop. The bus master controls and increases the efficiency of data flowing through the bus. The EISA bus looks very similar to the ISA bus, except that the bottom of the bus has two rows of gold colored contacts carefully wedged between the ISA gold colored contacts. This similarity in design means that if you replace your motherboard with one based on EISA, you have the option to use almost all of your existing ISA based adapter boards.

Motherboards based on the EISA standard are manufactured by several companies and often cost approximately $200 to $400 more than their ISA counterparts. EISA's maximum throughput rate using EISA adapter boards is 33 MB per second.

MCA

The Micro Channel expansion bus was originally introduced in 1987 by IBM for some of the IBM PS/2 line of computers. Systems based on the MCA bus work only with adapter boards based on the MCA standard.

Motherboards based on the MCA standard cost approximately $200 to $400 more than their ISA counterparts. Consequently, MCA adapter boards are priced higher as well. MCA's maximum throughput rate is 20 MB per second.

PCI Local Bus

The PCI Local Bus expansion slot was introduced by Intel in 1993. It offers fast throughput rates and the potential to migrate to microprocessor levels beyond 80486 and Pentium.

It has a 64 bit data path and can operate at the speed of the microprocessor. PCI is the expansion bus of the future. Motherboards based on PCI cost approximately $200 to $400 more than their VESA counterparts.

VESA Local Bus

The VESA Local Bus expansion slot was introduced in 1992. It offers fast throughput rates for 80486 based PCs. The local bus allows signals to go directly back and forth to the microprocessor. VESA can transfer data as fast as the microprocessor up to 66 MHZ. It is fast and affordable but long term, it may be replaced by the PCI Local Bus.

Other

The existence of expansion slots lets your PC have various other adapters which help it perform different tasks. Following is a brief list of miscellaneous adapters:

● Network adapters that permit several PCs to be connected to each other in order to share data and peripherals like printers, modems, etc.

● Scanner adapter boards that let a scanner input images to the PC

● Sound boards and voice synthesizers

● Telephone answering systems and automated switchboards

- FAX boards

4.7. Floppy Disk Drives

Floppy disk drives come in two different sizes. Within each size, the drive capacity can be regular or high density. Other than the above mentioned categories, there are no functional differences between different brands of floppy drives.

Size

Floppy drives are either 5.25" or 3.5". Drive sizes are based on the size of the floppy disks. The original IBM and compatible PCs used 5.25" drives, which subsequently became the dominant type in the PC industry. The 5.25" floppy disks became the standard medium for transporting and storing programs and data. In 1986, the 3.5" floppy drives began to appear in portable PCs. Because of their higher capacity and improved construction, they have gradually become popular in desktop systems as well. Since April 1987, with the introduction of the IBM PS/2, all IBM systems are now equipped with 3.5" drives. Currently, more PCs are sold with the 3.5" size drives than the 5.25" drives. It's projected that by 1995, 5.25" drives will be phased out.

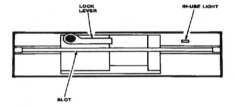 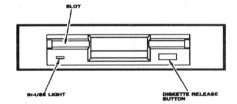

Capacity

Floppy drive capacities are basically grouped as regular (double sided/double density) or high density (double sided/high density). High density drives can read from and write to regular density disks, but regular density drives can work only with regular density disks. The capacity of 5.25" floppy drives is either 360 K or 1.2 MB. The 3.5" drives are either 720 K or 1.4 MB. Regular density drives were primarily designed for the 8088 (8 bit) based family of PCs. All PCs sold since 1992 are equipped with high density drives.

A new generation of 3.5" floppy drives can store up to 20 MB on special floppy disks. In the next few years these drives may replace hard drives in small portable PCs.

4.8. Hard Disk Drive

Having a hard disk drive in a PC has become an absolute necessity these days. Programs are

becoming more powerful, faster, and easier to use, but unfortunately they grow larger with each upgrade and consume more hard disk space than ever before. This trend is expected to continue in the future. Fortunately, the price of hard disk drives has dropped dramatically, and large capacity drives are more affordable than ever. Notebook computers are almost always equipped with a hard drive. The majority of desktop systems are already equipped with a hard drive at the factory. Systems not equipped with a hard drive can easily have one installed. To select a hard disk drive for your new PC or to upgrade your existing drive, you should consider several factors:

Type

The type of hard disk drive used in your PC should match the drive controller (described earlier in this chapter). Most newer PCs are already equipped with a hard drive, so you can only choose the model with the capacity that meets your needs. Otherwise, you can specify the type of drive that is more suitable for you. Drives based on the MFM and RLL technology are now obsolete. Drives based on the IDE technology are now the most popular standard in desktop as well as notebook PCs. Relatively low price, high capacity, and high performance will probably further increase the market share for IDE drives.

Drives based on the ESDI technology are used for very high performance and very high capacity applications such as a server in a network environment, Computer Aided Design (CAD), or demanding number crunching activities, etc.

Drives based on the SCSI technology are also used for very high performance applications. Their main attraction is that up to seven SCSI based devices can be connected to your PC. That makes it possible to have multiple hard drives, CD-ROM drives, etc., in the same PC.

Another feature that differentiates one hard drive from another is the technology used for moving the read/write head back and forth over the hard disk platter(s). Currently that's done by either the "band stepper" or the "voice coil" method. Less expensive drives with band stepper move the head with a combination of a stepper motor and flexible metal bands. This mechanical approach is not as fast or as reliable as the voice coil technology. Voice coil, on the other hand, uses a coil with a cylindrical metal rod in the middle. The rod is connected to the head(s), and when the coil is energized with electricity the rod moves in or out, thus moving the head(s) on the hard disk platter(s). Voice coil is preferred for its accuracy, speed, and reliability.

Size

Hard disk drives are currently manufactured in 3 different sizes. The original hard drive size for PCs in the 1980's was 5.25", but today only a small percentage are still 5.25". Very high capacity drives in excess of 1000 MB (1 Giga Bytes) are also made in that size.

In the past few years 3.5" drives have become increasingly popular because of their newer technology, higher performance, fewer moving parts and lower costs. Notebook computers use 2.5" drives that are specifically designed for that purpose. They weigh less, consume less power, and cost more than their 3.5" counterparts.

Capacity

Shortly after the original IBM PC was introduced with 64 K of memory and one floppy drive, several manufacturers began designing and manufacturing hard disk drives patterned after the technology used in mainframe and mini computers. In 1982, the IBM XT was introduced with a 10 MB hard disk drive. At that time 10 MB seemed to be a tremendous amount of storage capacity. By contrast, today most applications software take up at least 5 MB by themselves. Data generated by a program often need as much capacity as the program itself. Therefore, today's capacity requirements far exceed the imagination of PC pioneers. Hard drives are available in capacities ranging from 80 MB to over 1,000 MB (1 Giga Byte). The price of a hard disk drive is directly related to its capacity, as well as its type, speed, and manufacturer.

Read/Write Speed

The speed of a hard disk drive is determined by how fast it can read and write specific information located at various parts of the hard disk. Special tests are designed to calculate the average time it takes the drive to perform numerous read and write commands. The average seek time is expressed in "ms" (milliseconds: thousandths of a second). Currently, most drives have an average seek time less than 18 ms. High performance drives have an average seek time in the 10 to 12 ms range. Obviously, the faster the drive, the higher the cost.

Data Transfer Rate

Another very important factor in determining the performance of a hard drive is the data transfer rate expressed in Kbps (Kilo bits per second: 1,000 bps) or Mbps (Mega bits per second: 1,000,000 bps). When comparing various hard drives, you should use both the average seek time and data transfer rates to select the best drive for your needs and budget. The average seek time obviously has a direct bearing on the data transfer rate. Other factors also influence the data transfer rate. One of those is the existence of 8 to 256 K of cache memory on the drive. This memory acts as a buffer between the drive and the CPU, because the CPU is significantly faster than the drive. Information that's used most frequently is held in the buffer memory for immediate access. Therefore, when comparing hard drives, use the data transfer rate together with the average seek time and the size of cache memory.

4.9. Tape Backup Drive

Tape drives have become very affordable lately, and PC owners buy them for a number of reasons. The most important is obviously to have a backup copy of important data on the hard disk. Copying on tape drives is considerably faster and more convenient than copying on floppy disks. You can also use them to store less frequently used data on tape and off the hard drive. Adding a tape drive to your PC is very similar to adding a floppy drive. However, you need to make sure that the drive is compatible with your PC and your controller. Like floppy drives, tape drives can be either internal or external.

Type

There are three different tape drive standards. All three work with PCs, but their tapes are not interchangeable.

   ● QIC-40 (Quarter Inch Cartridge) generally stores from 20 to 60 MB, depending on tape size. With data compression, their capacity can almost double. QIC-40 drives can use the existing floppy drive controller in your system, if you don't already have two floppy drives.

   ● QIC-80 tape drives use higher density tapes and store from 40 to 120 MB, depending on tape size. With data compression they can store up to 240 MB. QIC-80 drives, like the QIC-40, can use the existing floppy drive controller in your system.

● DC-6000 tape drives use 5.25" tape cartridges for very high capacity data storage. These drives use their own proprietary controller and can store up to 700 MB, using data compression.

Size

PC tape drives, similar to floppy drives, are either 3.5" or 5.25". The size of the internal tape drive is similar to the size of the internal floppy drive. They can fit into the same size drive bays in your base unit.

Capacity

The capacity of tape drives depends on the type of drive, the type of tape cartridge, and the use of data compression software. Data compression software can more than double the capacity of a drive; but it may slow it down a little.

Read/Write Speed

Tape drives are intended for storing and later retrieving large amounts of data each time they are used. This makes their usage different from hard and floppy disk drives. Therefore, read and write speed is not a meaningful measure of performance for tape drives.

Data Transfer Rate

Data transfer rate is measured in Kilo bits per second (Kbps). The type of expansion bus on your PC, as well as the type of controller, largely determine the transfer rate. The average rate for 8 bit PCs based on the 8088 family of processors is about 250 Kbps. PCs with 16 bit expansion buses can transfer about 500 Kbps. Some special controllers can transfer data in excess of 1,000 Kbps (1 Mbps). A QIC-40 or QIC-80 based tape drive can store 40 MB of data in slightly over 10 minutes. A DC-6000 based drive may store as much as 100 MB in the same length of time.

Backup Software

Tape drives are often supplied with their own proprietary software. These programs are generally written to work with the manufacturer's own units, and all contain similar, basic features. Some contain additional features that may make them more attractive to users with special needs. Standard features include easy-to-use menus, tape formatting, automated unattended backup, selective backup and restore. Advanced features include tape diagnostics, data compression, security erase, and sophisticated unattended backup.

4.10. CD-ROM Drive

CD-ROM (Compact Disk - Read Only Memory) drives are rapidly gaining in popularity, and, as their prices continue to decline, they may soon become an integral part of every PC. They offer a huge amount of storage capacity on Compact Disks. If the cost and speed of CD drives capable of reading and writing to the disk approach that of hard disk drives, they may someday replace hard disk and floppy disk drives altogether. CD drives used with computers include sophisticated error correction circuitry to ensure that the data which is stored or retrieved meets your computer's strict requirements. CD drives can be easily added to a PC. Most of them work with SCSI controllers, but a few use their own proprietary controller. If your PC already has an SCSI controller for the hard and floppy drives, you may not need to buy another controller. If  possible, when buying a CD drive, choose an SCSI specification because it has greater flexibility for future expansion. Most CD-ROM drives are sold as a complete kit that includes the drive, the drive adapter, cable, software driver, and external terminator (if necessary).

Working with a CD drive is as easy as working with a floppy drive. You simply insert the CD disk into the drive and read from it as if it were another drive with its own drive letter. Most CD drives come with their own searching software that's often installed automatically when you follow their setup instructions.

Type

There are two basic types of CD drives: the ROM (Read Only Memory) type that can only read data from pre-recorded CDs, or the WORM (Write Once, Read Many) which, as the name implies, can record your data once and then can be read an indefinite number of times. The current price of WORM drives keeps them out of the reach of the range most of us can afford. CD-ROM drives, on the other hand, are becoming more popular and more affordable.

CD drives, like their floppy and hard drive cousins, come in two different configurations: internal or external. The internal drive is mounted inside the base unit, and is attached to your existing SCSI controller or to its own controller. The only drawback to the internal drive is that it occupies an accessible drive bay in your PC case. If you have the extra drive bay to spare, an internal drive is often less expensive than its corresponding external version. The external drive is basically the same as the internal unit, except that it has its own case and power supply and can be placed somewhere near the base unit. A cable connection to the back of the case transfers data and supplies power to the unit.

The predominant standard for CD drives is the "High Sierra" format, or the more recent upgrade called the "ISO 9660". When you are buying a CD drive, besides making sure that it's the PC version, you should make sure that it complies with at least one, preferably the latest, version of the above standards. Also make sure that the software driver supplied with the drive is the latest Microsoft CD-ROM extension version.

Capacity

Compact Disks have a capacity of over 300 MB per side. CD-ROM drives can read both sides of the disk, thus giving them a capacity over 600 MB. CD-WORM drives, on the other hand, can only write to one side and thus have a 300 MB capacity. By using data compression hardware and software, the CD capacity continues to increase even further.

Read/Write Speed

The data transfer rate for CD drives is measured in Kilo bits per second (Kbps). Another unit of measure is the average access time expressed in milliseconds, similar to a hard disk drive (except that they often range from 200 to 600 ms). However, where available, use Kbps to compare CD drives with one another. Also make sure the drive has at least a 300 Kbps data transfer rate, so that it will be able to take advantage of the upcoming multimedia features.

4.11. Input Devices

Input devices have become so standard that there are literally hundreds of manufacturers producing various products according to those standards. Often the differences between these products are in small features, appearance, feel, quality of construction, and price. You use the input device as often as you use your PC; therefore, choose it carefully and, if possible, look at it and try it out before you buy it.

Keyboard

The basic functions of different keyboards are essentially the same. The main difference is in the number of keys and their arrangement. Early generation PC keyboards had 84 keys. The function (F) keys were on the left side and some of the other keys performed more than one function. For example, the numeric keys on the right hand side also contained the arrow key functions. The enhanced keyboard design which is now the standard, increases the number of keys to 101 and separates some of the multiple function keys, like the arrow keys from the number keys. The function (F) keys are at the top row of the keyboard.

Another important feature of keyboards is the feel of the keys. Some keyboards have the click feature. When a key is depressed it presents a little resistance and makes a little clicking sound. Other keyboards feel soft and mushy. Before choosing a system, try out the keyboard to decide which type is more appealing to you. On the other hand, if you buy a computer and later decide that you are not

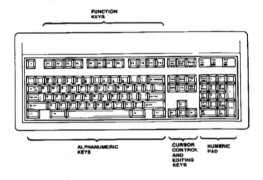

happy with the keyboard, you can buy another keyboard from most computer stores. Their prices range from as low as $30 to about $75.

Mouse

There are two different types of mice: opto-mechanical and optical. The opto-mechanical mice use a roller ball under the unit. The mechanical movement of the ball establishes the optical location of the cursor on the screen. Optical mice, on the other hand, don't have any moving parts. Under the mouse is a light source which emits a narrow beam of light onto a special plate. When the mouse is moved around on the surface of that plate, the light that is reflected back to the mouse points to the location of the cursor on the screen. Although optical mice tend to be more precise than their opto-mechanical counterparts, they are not as popular, because of their higher price and the inconvenience of the reflective plate.

A mouse can have 2 or 3 buttons. Two buttons are all you need for most applications since the 3rd button on some mice basically performs the same role as depressing the 2 buttons simultaneously. The third button is not necessary, but a convenience feature. Some applications like CAD and desktop publishing programs will let you program the third button to perform specific tasks.

Another important feature of mice is the resolution. That determines the level of detail you can manipulate with the mouse. A 200 DPI (Dots Per Inch) resolution is the minimum necessary. Some mice go as high as 800 DPI, which is nice, but not essential.

Every mouse should be supplied with special software called drivers. Most mouse manufacturers try to follow the dominant standard established by Microsoft Mouse. If you plan to use Windows, it will be very helpful if your mouse is definitely Microsoft Mouse compatible. That will make it easier for you to use the driver supplied with Windows, and save some valuable memory.

A mouse needs to be connected to your PC in order to communicate with it. Most mice connect to the serial (RS 232, COM 1, or COM 2) port of your system. If you have a port available, then you can purchase a "Serial Mouse" that connects to that port. If you don't have an available port and have an empty expansion slot inside your PC, then you can use a "Bus Mouse" that comes with its own interface board. Before buying a mouse, carefully evaluate your needs, because a bus mouse and a serial mouse are not interchangeable.

Because your hand is supposed to rest on the mouse while you are using it, you should test the shape and feel of various brands of mice before buying the one that feels most comfortable to you.

Trackball

Trackballs are identical to mice in every respect, except that they are only opto-mechanical. Rapidly gaining in popularity because of their convenience and compactness, they also use the same drivers as mice. You should test the shape and feel of various trackballs before buying one.

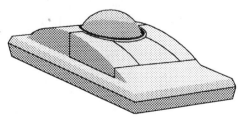

Pen

Pen style pointing devices are divided into two categories. The most common type looks like a fat pen. At the bottom of the pen is a small roller ball similar to a mouse. By holding the pen and moving it around on a flat surface, the cursor moves on the PC screen. These pen style mice cost slightly more than a typical mouse or trackball. They are not as popular as mice and trackballs.

One very specialized type uses a light pen which looks like a fat pen with light coming from the end. By pointing the pen and touching a special monitor, the computer executes your commands. These are mainly seen in some hospitals, and have been in use since the 1970's.

Digitizer

Digitizers are very specialized input devices from the mouse family. A digitizer consists of a tablet and a pointing device. The tablet can be as small as a sheet of paper or as large as a poster. The pointing device looks like a mouse with four or more buttons and a cross hair.

Digitizers are special purpose devices. They are primarily used with CAD (Computer Aided Design) programs. In most cases your applications software dictates the minimum requirements. Some of the components and variables in a digitizer are the size of the tablet, the number of buttons, and the resolution. If you need to buy a digitizer, make sure that it's compatible with most major CAD software.

Scanner

Scanners are becoming increasingly powerful and popular as their prices go down to more affordable levels. They are, however, somewhat specialized tools that most PC users may not need. If you have desktop publishing applications or a Fax board, you may consider adding a scanner to your system. Scanners require their own interface board inside your PC, so having an available expansion slot is a necessity. Several important characteristics can dramatically affect the type of results you get from a scanner:

Type

There are two types of scanners: handheld and flatbed. Within each type there may be some variations in size and features. Handheld scanners are primarily 4" wide. Previous generation hand scanners were about 2" wide. A few manufacturers make full-page, handheld scanners that fill a need somewhere between a handheld and a flatbed scanner. With handheld scanners, the image you want to transfer to your PC is placed on a flat surface and the scanner is slowly moved across that image. A steady hand is a major requirement!

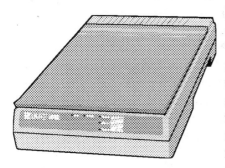

Flatbed scanners are more expensive and more convenient if you plan to scan a lot of images. They are somewhat similar to a small copying machine. You place the image that you want to transfer to your PC on top of the scanner, and a moving beam of light scans the surface and transmits the image to your system. Some flatbed scanners may have a sheet feeder that makes high volume scanning easier and more convenient.

Features

Several important features are provided in different brands and models of scanners. It's very important to match these features with your specific application and budget. Internal components and the software supplied with each scanner play an important role in the quality of output generated by that scanner. Two scanners with the same resolution and gray scale level may still produce dramatically different quality results. Therefore, it's very important that you see the actual output before choosing a brand and model.

Resolution

The resolution of a scanner determines the sharpness and clarity of an image when it's scanned and transferred to the PC. Almost all scanners have a 100 DPI (Dots Per Inch) resolution, which is basically the minimum level. Most scanners go up to 400 DPI, which is sharper than the output of a regular laser printer. For really professional applications that will be produced on commercial high-resolution printers like those of magazines and books, the resolution can be up to 1,500 DPI. When you scan an image for insertion into a document, and store it on your hard disk drive, you should know that the higher the resolution, the more disk space will be required. Some images, like photographs, can use over 1 MB of hard disk space.

Gray Scale

Gray scale is the number of shades of gray that can represent an image. A black and white photograph is based on numerous shades of gray. If you look at a color photograph next to a black and white you'll see that shades of gray are used to represent various colors and their degree of intensity. Photos in newspapers are also composed of shades of gray. Early versions of gray scale scanners could produce only 32 shades of gray. Some high performance scanners can now show as many as 256 shades of gray, which is considered magazine quality.

Optical Character Recognition (OCR)

In recent years, powerful programs have been developed that can analyze a scanned image of printed or typed text and interpret the written document with a high degree of accuracy. The software matches the image of every character with its database to determine the letter or digit closest to it. Some recent versions of these programs claim as much as 99.9% accuracy. This means that while reading a full, typed page, the software may only miss two characters.

Optical Character Recognition (OCR) offers great savings to businesses and organizations that have massive amounts of paperwork to input into their computer systems. Flatbed scanners are more appropriate than handheld units for OCR applications. There are several OCR programs on the market. If you need to have OCR software for your application, make sure it's one of the top-ranked programs. Otherwise, a program full of errors wastes more time than it can save. Unfortunately, manufacturers' claims of accuracy may not be fully representative of the actual performance of the OCR program. Looking up comparative reviews in various computer publications will help you make a better decision.

Joystick

The principle behind joysticks is pretty basic; there are not many significant differences between various brands and models. Some joysticks may have different features that make them more versatile or provide quicker response. Some joysticks may have more buttons, or have the buttons in more convenient places. The main features to look for when buying a joystick are a solid quality, the feel of the unit, and the extent and type of warranty.

4.12. Monitors

Computer monitors are manufactured by several major companies in the U.S. and the Far East. These companies market their monitors under their own names, as well as under the labels of dozens of other companies. When choosing a monitor, you need to choose a video standard. The video adapter and the monitor need to match one another. Note that in desktop computers, the monitor and its video adapter are independent of the PC. Therefore, if sometime after buying your system, you decide to upgrade your monitor, you can do so without replacing your computer.

Several features differentiate one monitor from another. These features are important considerations when you are comparing monitors within the same group.

Resolution: is determined by the number of horizontal and vertical dots that make up the images on the screen. It's expressed as 640 x 480; 800 x 600; or 1,024 x 768. Obviously, the higher the numbers, the higher the resolution.

Dot Pitch: is measured in millimeters (mm). It's the distance between the dots of red, green, and blue that form a grid on the surface of the monitor. The monitor sweeps an electron beam across the grid several times per second. The closer those dots are together, the sharper the image. It generally ranges from 0.20 mm to 0.40 mm.

Frequency: is measured in KHZ (Kilo Hertz). Video graphics adapters generate frequencies that are dependent on how many dots they can address on the monitor. The higher the resolution of the monitor, the higher the frequency rate has to be. Additionally, the monitor has to be able to match or exceed the frequencies sent by the video adapter.

Size: is measured diagonally and expressed in inches, like a TV set. The most common size is 14", which is less expensive than larger screens because of its popularity in the PC marketplace. The next available sizes are 15" or 16", which are often 25% to 50% more expensive than their 14" counterpart. There are also 19" and 25" monitors, which are primarily used for special applications.

Monochrome

Monochrome monitors can have only one of the three colors of green, amber, or white on a black background. The choice of color depends on your personal preference. The only other factor to consider is the size of the screen. Most monochrome monitors have a 12" screen. Some manufacturers offer a 14" model at slightly higher cost. The 12" monochrome monitor remains the least expensive type available today. However, due to the increasing popularity of the VGA standard, regular monochrome monitors are now obsolete.

CGA (Color Graphics)

The color graphics monitor standard was introduced in the early 1980's as an improved alternative to the monochrome monitor. It was capable of showing as many as four colors on the screen. The monitors were also called RGB, which stood for Red-Green-Blue. Those were the colors of the dots that made up the images on the screen. The resolution of CGA monitors was not as sharp and crisp as monochrome. But at least games and graphics oriented programs could be used with them. CGA monitors are now obsolete.

EGA (Enhanced Graphics)

EGA monitors were introduced in 1985 as an enhanced version of earlier CGA color monitors. EGA offered a much sharper and crisper picture. The text output of EGA monitors was similar to the quality of text on monochrome monitors. They were capable of showing up to 16 colors. EGA monitors are now obsolete.

VGA

VGA monitors have become the most popular standard in the PC industry. Almost all programs are designed to take full advantage of the features offered by that standard. VGA monitors can be either color or monochrome. Monochrome VGA monitors cost about half as much as color VGA monitors, and about 50% more than regular monochrome monitors. For people whose applications don't require a color monitor, and who have a limited budget, monochrome VGA may be adequate.

VGA monitors come in standard screen sizes ranging from 14" to 16", 19", and 25". The 14" monitors are the most common. Larger sizes cost significantly more and are only used for specific applications like CAD or desktop publishing.

Other important factors to consider are the resolution, dot pitch, and scan frequency (expressed in KHZ). VGA monitors should have a minimum resolution of 640 x 480. This should match the capabilities of the VGA video board. Their dot pitch (distance between dots) ranges from 0.20 to 0.40 mm (millimeter). The smaller the dot pitch, the sharper the images, and the more expensive the monitor. Scan frequency (expressed in KHZ) is the number of times per second that the CRT (Cathode Ray Tube) beams move vertically across the screen to update the images. Most VGA monitors have a standard frequency of 60 HZ vertical and 32 KHZ horizontal.

SVGA

Super VGA monitors are very similar to VGA monitors in most respects. They are capable of higher resolutions of 800 x 600, 1,024 x 768 (technically called 8514/A) or 1,280 x 1,024. SVGA monitors usually have a smaller dot pitch of 0.28 to 0.31 mm to match their higher resolution. They also operate at higher scan frequencies. At higher resolutions, another factor becomes important. Very high resolution monitors need to scan the screen more frequently in order to produce the sharper details required. Higher scan frequency means higher cost. Therefore, some manufacturers scan every other line in the first pass and then scan the remaining lines in the second pass, a process called interlaced scanning. Interlaced images have a slight flicker that's usually not noticeable. However, if your computer is going to be used under fluorescent lighting, the flicker will be more noticeable, because the flicker of fluorescent light magnifies the flicker of the monitor.

SVGA monitors that can scan every single line on the screen in one pass are called non-interlaced. They cost more than interlaced, but produce a flicker-free screen. Non-interlaced monitors generally have a 72 HZ vertical frequency and a 48 KHZ horizontal frequency. If you can't afford a non-interlaced monitor, sometimes a high quality SVGA board with either 512 K, or preferably 1 MB of memory on the board can help minimize the perceived effects of the flicker.

Multi-Frequency

Multi-frequency monitors are more versatile than VGA or SVGA monitors. They have the ability to be hooked-up to different types of graphics adapters such as monochrome graphic, color graphic, EGA, VGA, and SVGA. For most of us who plan to have a VGA or SVGA video board in our PC, the multi-frequency monitor doesn't offer any advantage. It does cost more than a standard VGA or SVGA monitor.

4.13. Printers

Printer technology has advanced dramatically in recent years. As the quality of printer output has improved, prices have declined, making printers more affordable than ever before. These days it's almost impossible to have a PC without a printer. Therefore, the printer you have or plan to buy must meet your needs and fit within your budget. Knowing which features are essential and which ones are nice to have will guide you through the selection process among the hundreds of brands and models of printers. It's always helpful to see a few printers, hear them operate, and look at their output before buying one.

Dot Matrix

Dot matrix printers were the dominant type of printer in the 1980's and will continue to lead in the 1990's. Every year, over 5 million of these printers are sold in the United States alone. Their print quality has continuously improved, and various convenience features, coupled with low prices, make them especially attractive to home PC users. Today, even the least expensive dot matrix printer 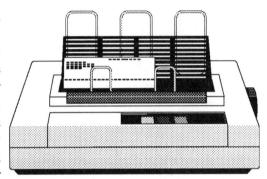 produces very acceptable letter quality output. When evaluating dot matrix printers, check the following points carefully:

Manufacturers' reputation & types of printers they make: Since dozens of companies manufacture hundreds of printer models, it's prudent to make sure that the printer you choose is made by a reputable company.

Type of warranty and location of service: Printers come with at least a one year parts and labor warranty. Nothing less is acceptable, and more than that is even better. Also, having a local service center is more favorable than having to ship the printer out for service.

Printer speed: Printer speed, expressed in characters per second (CPS) for both draft and letter quality mode, is a good measure for comparison. In the draft mode, the print-head makes just one pass over each line; so this is the fastest mode. In letter quality mode, the print-head makes two passes over the line, which enhances the resolution but reduces the speed.

Emulations: There are dozens of printer manufacturers and literally hundreds of models. To make sure that various software programs work with the variety of printers available, printer manufacturers try to give their printers the ability to emulate (act like) certain printer models that have become accepted industry standards. Therefore, if a software does not specifically recognize a particular printer, you can make the printer act like a model that the software recognizes.

Paper width: Printers come in two sizes: regular width printers that can print on 8.5" wide paper, and wide-carriage printers that can print on 14" wide paper. Wide-carriage printers often cost 20% to 50% more than their regular width counterparts. The regular width printer does everything most of us need.

Buffer memory: The amount of buffer memory in a printer is measured in Kilo Bytes. It usually ranges from 2 KB to 64 KB. Because the computer works much faster than the printer can print, the print buffer memory stores several pages worth of data, and frees the computer to perform other tasks sooner. Divide the number of buffer "KB's" by 2 to get an estimate of the number of pages your printer can hold in its memory. For example, a printer with a 16 KB buffer can hold close to 8 pages of information while printing. The amount of buffer memory is definitely an added convenience, but it should not be the deciding factor.

Maximum number of multi-part pages: Almost all dot matrix printers can print on 3 part forms. Some can print on 4, 5, or even 6 part forms. If you plan to use your printer for business, and you intend to print multi-part forms, you need to look into this feature.

Push versus pull feed: Push feed brings up the top of each page to the point where printing starts. It's used by most manufacturers on many models. Pull feed, as the name implies, pulls the paper through, so every time you print, the first page of that printout will be wasted. This can be particularly expensive if you use pre-printed forms or stock. Make sure your printer has push feed.

Top feed, rear feed, and bottom feed: Most printers are capable of feeding the paper from all 3 positions. The first two are particularly important. The bottom feed is only useful if you plan to use relatively thick paper in your printer.

Paper parking capability: This feature makes the printer automatically pull the continuous paper back and lets you feed single sheets like letterheads through. After you are finished, pressing the paper parking button makes the printer automatically pull the continuous sheets back to the ready position. This is a handy little feature that you'll appreciate.

Number of built-in fonts: Most printers have at least two or three built-in fonts that lets them quickly print the documents specifying those fonts. All printers have the courier and elite fonts that are a carry-over from typewriters. Having more built-in fonts is a nice feature but most programs bypass them all together.

Ability to accept font cards: If you plan to use your printer to produce a lot of documents with different types of fonts, having the ability to add font cards is a plus. For most home PC users, however, the built-in fonts are more than adequate.

Color printing capability: Some printers can produce multi-color documents by using a special print-head and multi-color ribbon. This is a nice feature to have, but most home PC users rarely need it. Plus, the multi-color ribbon costs three to four times more than the black ribbon.

Life of the print-head: For comparison purposes, the life of the print-head is useful to know. It's often expressed in millions of characters. By simply dividing that number by 2,000 (the average number of characters per page), you can approximate the life of the head in terms of the pages it can print. Most print-heads last several years.

Number of characters printed per ribbon: Different printers use their ribbons differently. Some printers are designed with a very small ribbon cartridge, which forces you to buy ribbons more frequently. Some are poorly designed and consume more ribbon. By comparing the number of pages printed per ribbon, you can determine your operating cost.

Ease of use: As more features are added to printers, they usually become more complex, but some manufacturers have found innovative ways to keep their printers easy to use. Remember that if something is easy to use, it will be used frequently and to its full potential. If something is difficult to use, only the most necessary features will be used regularly.

Noise level: Dot matrix printers generate a certain amount of noise, which is measured in decibels. The smaller the number, the quieter the printer.

9-Pin

9-pin printers are the most popular type of dot matrix printer on the market. Some of these printers sell for as low as $150 and often have all or most of the features listed above. As the name implies, they have 9 pins that do the printing. The pins form the characters and graphics. In recent years, the quality and sharpness of their printouts have improved significantly. Their printout looks almost comparable to that of a typewriter.

24-Pin

24-pin printers are more advanced cousins of the 9-pin printer. They have smaller pins that form smaller dots. These dots are printed closer to each other than on a 9-pin printer. Because of the smaller dots, their characters and graphics are sharper and crisper. These printers generally cost from 20% to 50% more than their 9-pin counterparts.

Ink Jet

Ink jet printers are gaining in popularity, because their output looks almost as sharp as that of a laser printer, but they cost about half as much. Most ink jet printers produce 300 DPI resolution. They fit somewhere between a 24-pin dot matrix printer and a laser printer. Most home PC users don't need the higher quality printing capability of ink jet printers, so the added cost may not be justifiable. However, for people who wish to produce newsletters, advertising, and other desktop publishing output on a limited budget, an ink jet printer may be the answer. Some models can print in color.

Like dot matrix printers these printers, are made either for regular or for wide size paper. The wide versions cost from 30% to 60% more than their regular models. Because these printers use individual sheets of paper, an automatic paper feeder is almost a necessity. Most newer models have a built-in sheet feeder. Otherwise, you must stand by the printer and feed it one page at a time. Another point to consider is that ink jet printers cannot print on multi-part forms.

These printers work on the same principle as dot matrix printers. The computer sends signals to print certain characters and graphics to the printer. The printer executes the command one character and one line at a time. Characters are formed by dots, much like dot matrix printers.

Thermal Transfer

Thermal transfer printers are becoming popular, because of their small size and high quality output. They print by using heat to transfer dots from the ribbon to the paper. Similar to ink jet printers in many respects, some of these printers are designed to be very small and lightweight so they can be used as companions to notebook computers. These printers generally have a regular width. If you are interested in buying a thermal transfer printer, look at different models and check the projected life of the print-head and ribbon cartridge. These printers, like ink jet printers, work on the same principle as dot matrix printers.

Laser

Laser printers are becoming increasingly popular among home PC users and businesses. In the past two years, the prices of laser printers have plummeted. Today several brands are available for $600 or less. Laser print-ers, as described earlier, work on a principle very different from dot matrix printers. The only thing they have in common is that both form characters from dots. Other than that, laser printers need a large amount of memory to form an exact copy of the entire page before printing it. The following are some key features to look for in a laser printer:

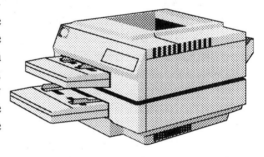

HP LaserJet compatibility: Hewlett Packard LaserJet printers became a standard of compatibility for laser printers in the 1980's. The HP LaserJet II was the predominant printer in that period. In 1990, the HP LaserJet III was introduced with several enhancements to its predecessors. In 1992 HP introduced the HP LaserJet IV. Several manufacturers make compatible printers. If you plan to buy a laser printer, it should be at least HP IV compatible to ensure proper operation with various software.

Number of pages per minute: The performance of laser printers is determined by the number of pages per minute. For most laser printers, that number ranges from 4 to 12 pages per minute. Slower printers are usually more affordable for home buyers.

Amount of memory: Almost all laser printers come with at least 512 K of memory. Some come with 1 MB standard. The 512 K memory is adequate for forming a page full of standard text; but for pages containing graphics or large letters, 1 or 2 MB maybe necessary.

Capacity for additional memory: The more memory inside a laser printer, the faster it can form and print the page. Having the ability to upgrade memory to 2 or 4 MB is very advantageous for increasing the printer speed.

Number of built-in fonts: As described above, laser printers need to have fonts of various characters available to form them in their memory and then to print them. Most laser printers come with several built-in fonts. Printers with more built-in fonts are advantageous for desktop publishing.

Ability to accept additional fonts: Most laser printers come with one or two special slots that will accept font cartridges. Some users may never need to add those cartridges. Some may opt to use software that create the fonts in the computer instead. Using software instead of font cartridges is slower but less expensive.

Postscript compatibility: Postscript is a high resolution laser-printing technique of font creation that uses a special method to create fonts of different shapes and sizes. Some laser printers have the postscript program installed on chips inside the printer.

Resolution: Almost all commercially available laser printers have a 300 x 300 dot per inch resolution. Some printers use resolution enhancement techniques to further improve their output. Others produce 600 x 600 resolution, similar to those used by commercial printing businesses. Some companies make laser printers and special boards that can produce 800 x 800 or 1200 x 1200 resolution.

Laser Printer Types

There are two types of laser printers.

Standard
Most laser printers are standard printers (as opposed to Postscript printers). Standard laser printers have most or all of the features listed above, and they work only with their built-in fonts and specific font sizes. These printers regularly cost less than corresponding postscript printers. Programs that work under Windows use the fonts supplied by Windows and therefore don't need Postscript.

Postscript

Postscript is a high resolution laser-printing technique that uses a special algorithm to create fonts of different shapes and sizes. Postscript lets the printer form different shapes and sizes and shades of the fonts that it has built in. Postscript printers have the postscript software installed on one or more chips inside the printer. They also have a fast, specialized processor chip which speeds up the forming of each page. Postscript printers generally cost from 50% to 100% more than similar standard models.

4.14. Modems and Fax/Modem Devices

Once the favorite toy of computer hobbyists and long distance computer users, the modem has become almost as necessary as a printer. In recent years, modem prices have dropped while their performance and features have increased. Millions of PC users have modems with their systems, and through their modems and telephone lines they have access to a world of information. Businesspeople use their modems to communicate with computers at work. Virtually any PC equipped with a standard modem can communicate with another computer over a telephone line.

Recent technological advances and mass production have made modems very affordable. Newer ones also contain more features that help increase their speed and accuracy. In the last couple of years modem manufacturers have been able to incorporate faxing capabilities into their modems with only a 10% to 25% increase in the modem price. By 1995, all modems are expected to have fax capability. New and powerful software now let you fax whatever document you can create on your computer. You can also incorporate a fax received by your computer into your documents. If you are interested in buying a Fax/Modem device, you should make sure that the fax can operate in the background to avoid tying up your PC while it's sending, receiving, or printing faxes.

Several important new features have been added to most modems in recent years, including data compression and error correction that are built into the hardware. These features, in effect, increase the actual speed of the modem. Most of these features, however, do require that the modem at the other end have a corresponding capability. MNP is an error correction or data compression protocol that comes in several different levels. The most popular levels are MNP 5, 6, or 7. These versions primarily offer powerful data compression features. Each level is compatible with its predecessors, making it easier to communicate with modems manufactured at different times. Modems are capable of automatically detecting the MNP levels of their counterparts, then adjusting their transmissions to the same levels. Other powerful features, expressed as v.29, v.32, v.42, v.32 bis, or v.42 bis let the computers at both ends of a phone line send and receive data simultaneously on the same frequency. These two features are added features that help current and future generation modems transfer data faster.

A few other features that may be bundled with a modem include remote operation, background file transfer, unattended file transfer, direct PC-to-PC file transfer, and virus detection. Some of these features may also be found in utility programs.

- Remote operation lets your computer (called the terminal) call another computer (called the host), and take over the operation of that system as if you were sitting in front of it. This is particularly useful for computer consultants and technical support people, who can solve most problems without actually traveling to the site of another PC.

- Background file transfer lets you work on other applications while the PC communicates with another computer sending or receiving files.

- Unattended file transfer lets you set up special instructions so that your computer can communicate with another system at a predetermined time without your presence.

- Direct PC-to-PC transfer lets you connect two systems together (e.g., a portable to a desktop to transfer files).

- Virus detection lets your system detect the existence of computer viruses that may be downloaded to your PC.

Type

There are basically two physical types of modems: internal and external.

Internal

Internal modems resemble a regular adapter board that fits inside the computer. These modems have various microchips plus a small speaker and 2 phone jacks built onto the board. The board fits into an expansion slot, requiring the use of one of the COM ports (serial port designation). Some modems are capable of operating as COM 3 or COM 4, leaving your COM 1 and COM 2 available for other uses. If you plan to use both COM ports, then finding an internal modem that can operate at COM 3 or 4 may be very important.

The advantages of internal modems are that they don't clutter the work area, they don't need one of your serial ports, and they are less expensive. Their disadvantages are that they don't have all the visual indicator lights that the external type have, and they occupy an expansion slot inside your computer.

External

External modems are small boxes that contain a board similar to an internal modem. Most of them also include a small power supply. The modem is connected to the computer by a special serial cable that hooks up to an available serial port. The front

of the modem usually displays several small indicator lights that show whether the modem is connected, if data is being transferred, what the transmission speed is, etc. Some external modems are as small as a bar of soap. Their power needs are often supplied by the serial port they are connected to.

The advantages of external modems are that they can be easily moved from one computer to another, and they have indicator lights that show the status of the modem at all times. Their disadvantages are that they cost more than internal modems, occupy desk space, and use up one serial port.

Speed

Modem speeds for PCs range from 300 to over 115,200 BPS (Bits Per Second). The actual data transmission speed of some modems can be even higher if data compression and error correction features are used at both ends. The 300, 1200 and 2400 BPS modems have been completely phased out.

1200-BPS

In the 1980's, 1200 BPS modems were the most popular series. However, they have been phased out in favor of faster and more powerful modems.

2400-BPS

2400 BPS modems were very popular until 1993. Using data compression and error correction features, some of these modems were capable of 9600 BPS performance. These modems are being phased out and can be found for well under $50.

9600-BPS

9600 BPS modems are 4 times faster than the 2400 BPS series, and cost under $200. Because of their slight cost difference with 14,400 BPS modems, they are being phased out.

14,400-BPS

14.4 KBPS modems are currently very popular and their prices are often under $200. They offer very high speed modem and fax capabilities at reasonably low prices.

4.15. Accessories and Consumables

When you buy your new PC, monitor, printer, mouse and modem, you don't have everything yet! Buying a PC is like buying a car; you still need to buy gas, oil, coolant, tires, etc. For your computer system, you need some small accessories that help you get better use out of your PC. You'll also need consumable supplies that will satisfy your needs. The quality of some accessories plays an important role in the performance you may get from your entire system. You should treat the accessories like you treat the tires on your car and consider the quality of your consumable supplies like you do for the gasoline you put into your car.

Diskettes

There are two distinct sizes of diskettes. The 5.25" diskettes which have been around since at least 1980, are still found in millions of older PCs. The double sided/double density diskettes have a capacity of 360 K. Although 360 K drives are no longer used in new PCs, millions of them still exist in older models. It's projected that by 1995, 360 K diskettes will be eliminated. The double sided/high density diskettes have a capacity of 1.2 MB. They were introduced in 1984 with the IBM AT based on the 80286 microprocessor. The 1.2 MB floppy drives have gained a larger market share than their 360 K cousins. Almost all new desktop PCs that may be supplied with a 5.25" drive offer the 1.2 MB capacity. The major advantage of 5.25" diskettes is their  low cost. Their major disadvantages are that they are bulkier than 3.5" diskettes, and are more vulnerable to abuse.

3.5" diskettes have slowly moved into the dominant position for the 1990's. Initially they were started with the 720 K, double sided/double density version. The double sided/high density 1.4 MB version followed shortly thereafter, and quickly took over the 3.5" market. Today more 3.5" high density drives are sold than any other type of floppy drive. Notebook computers use 3.5" drives exclusively, and most desktop units are supplied with that drive. This has made 1.4 MB floppy disks the most popular version for the 1990's. The major advantage of 3.5" diskettes is that they have slightly more capacity, are smaller, and are better protected. Their disadvantages are that they cost almost twice as much as their 5.25" counterpart and are slightly slower.

With almost all new PCs equipped with hard disk drives, floppy disks are not used as heavily as they were in the early 1980's when PCs had no hard disk drives. They are now used primarily for installing software and backing up important data. Each diskette is now used only a few times during its almost unlimited lifetime. Because all diskettes have to meet certain accuracy standards, and because formatting eliminates most defective or weak areas, the differences between the various brands and qualities of diskettes are very small. You can save a great deal of money by buying the most economical diskettes available. However, if you'll be using certain diskettes more frequently than others, you should buy high quality disks for that purpose.

Cables

Almost all external devices that need to be connected to a PC's base unit are connected via cables. There are various types of cables for each type of device. Most standard devices come with their cables attached and ready to be plugged into the appropriate connection on the back of your PC.

● The PC power cord is supplied with the PC. It connects the power supply on the base unit to a wall outlet on the other end.

● The keyboard cable is attached to the keyboard. The other end of the cable has a unique shape and connects to a corresponding plug on the front or back of the PC.

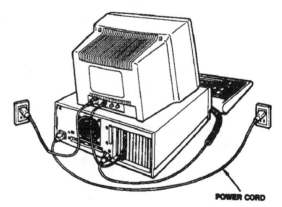

POWER CORD

● Monitor cables consist of a power cord that needs to be connected to the wall outlet and a video cable that has a unique shape resembling an elongated "D" surrounding several pins. This cable needs to be connected to the video plug that has a similar shape on the back of the base unit.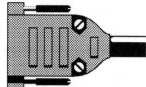

● The mouse or trackball cable is attached to the unit. The other end of the cable has a unique shape. If the device is a bus version, the shape of the plug could be proprietary and similar to the corresponding shape on the adapter board installed inside your PC. If the device is serial, then the end of the cable is shaped like an elongated "D" with several pin holes. The cable attaches to the serial port with a similar shape on the back of the base unit.

● Printer cables consist of a power cord and a data cable. The power cord is attached to the printer and plugs into the wall outlet. The data cable depends on whether the printer is parallel or serial. Parallel cables are the most common type of printer interface. Both ends of the parallel cable resemble an elongated "D." The end that has a series of gold colored teeth attaches to the printer; the other end that has 25 pins attaches to the parallel port on the back of the base unit. If the printer is serial, it needs a serial cable specially modified for that printer. Both ends of the cable resemble an elongated "D" with a certain number of pins. One end attaches to the printer and the other end attaches to a serial port on the back of the base unit. The standard printer cable is 6' long; however, if you need to locate your printer a little farther away from the PC, you should buy a 10' or longer cable.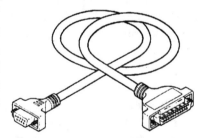

● Other cables may be needed, depending on the device. An external modem uses a serial cable specially modified for that modem. A scanner, digitizer, plotter, or other device may come with its own proprietary cable or use a serial cable specially modified for that device.

Printer Ribbons

Printer ribbons are consumable items whose usage depend on the type of printer and the number of pages you print. Most printers use ribbon cartridges that are clean and easy to replace. For every printer brand and model, ribbons are often available from several different sources. If a name-brand printer has been on the market for more than a few

months, companies other than the printer manufacturer usually offer compatible ribbons that
cost less than the name-brand version. Although compatible ribbons are supposed to
meet or exceed the original manufacturer's
performance and quality specifications, always
test a compatible brand by initially buying a
single ribbon to compare with your printer's original ribbon. Some compatible ribbons
lack the lubricant necessary for smooth operation of your print-head.

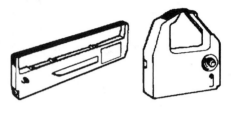

Businesses and organizations that are heavy users of printer ribbons can buy re-inking kits
that lets them reuse a ribbon a few more times before disposing of it. If you choose to re-
ink your ribbons, mark the ribbon cartridge each time you re-ink it and dispose of each
cartridge after two or three uses.

Laser Printer Cartridges

Laser printers use special, disposable ink cartridges (called toner cartridges) that are very
similar to those used by small copiers. These cartridges often contain most of the moving
parts of the laser printer engine as well as a certain amount of ink powder. Each cartridge
lasts from 1,000 to 3,000 pages, depending on your type of printer. With the increasing
popularity of certain brands and models of laser printers, a few companies are starting to
manufacture compatible ink cartridges.

In recent years, hundreds of small companies have started offering ink cartridge refills.
They recycle used cartridges by opening the cartridge, cleaning and lubricating it, and
refilling it with ink powder. These recycled cartridges often cost half as much as a brand
new unit. If these cartridges are refilled by a reputable company, their performance should
match that of a new cartridge. Because the moving parts in the cartridge are designed with
a certain life expectancy, dispose of a cartridge after two or three refills.

Paper

The type of paper you need depends on the type of printer you have. Daisy wheel, ink jet,
thermal, and laser printers use single sheets of paper. Daisy wheel printers can use both
letter (8.5 x 11") and legal (8.5 x 14") size paper, fed manually or by an automatic sheet
feeder. Laser printers, ink jet, and thermal printers need separate paper trays for these two
sizes.

Dot matrix printers can use single as well as continuous
sheets of paper. Wide-carriage printers can handle sheets as
large as 14 x 17". Continuous sheets are also called tractor-
fed paper because of the series of equally spaced holes on
both sides. Both sides of the paper have a perforated strip
with the holes punched. When looking for a certain type of
paper, check to make sure that the perforated edges can be
torn off easily without leaving any trace on the sides of the
paper.

Depending on your application, the types of paper you choose and the prices you pay may
vary. The most popular type of paper for general use is 20 lb. bond. For business purposes,
you may use higher quality stationary paper. However, if you plan to use that paper in a
laser printer, check with your supplier or the printer manufacturer first. Some laser
printers can safely use paper only up to a certain weight, thickness, and texture. For that
same reason, if you plan to use labels in your laser printer, only use labels specifically
marked for laser printing.

Surge Protector

Surge protection is very critical to preserving your investment in your computer system.
A surge is an unusually high electric voltage that can be caused by several factors. The
most common cause of an electric surge is the cycling (turning on and off) of large
appliances or other large electrical machinery working on the same circuit as the computer
system. Another common cause of surges is electric "blackouts" or "brownouts". The
most devastating damage is caused by lightning, which fortunately does not happen very
often. Some areas of the country are more susceptible to lightning strikes than others.
Parts of Florida have the potential for more than 100 strike days per year. The potential

number of strike days per year gradually decreases as you move toward
the West Coast. Southeastern states
have between 60 to 80, midwestern
states have 40 to 60, northern and
southern states have 20 to 40, and the
West Coast has less than 20 potential
strike days per year.

A surge protector is a small device that stands between the AC wall outlet and your
computer system. Instead of plugging your PC, monitor, and printer directly into the wall

outlet, you plug them into the surge protector, and then plug the surge protector into the wall. Certain models of surge protectors also have two outlets for connecting your modem or fax board to the phone line.

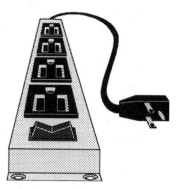

The inside components of a surge protector are the most important parts of the unit. A surge protector is supposed to have one or more fast action fuse(s) and a circuitry that prevents the power surge from going beyond the unit itself. Any surge protector you buy should definitely have the UL (Underwriters Laboratory) approval. When comparing surge protectors, the two most important factors to consider are the clamp time, expressed in nanoseconds (typically 5 ns or less), and the highest spike voltage absorbed, expressed in volts (typically 6,000 volts or more). The smaller the clamp time and the higher the spike voltage, the better the surge protector.

Some of the other features you should look for when comparing surge protectors are as follows:

- The number of outlets on the unit

- Modem and fax phone line protection

- The number of circuit breakers (at least one 15 Amp breaker)

- An EMI/RFI (Electro Magnetic Interference/Radio Frequency Interference) noise filter

- UL 1449 listing (establishes the pass-through voltage at less than 400 volts)

- The number of switches (some units have one switch per outlet)

Battery Backup

A battery backup consists of a battery and special circuitry that lets it connect to and work with a computer. The size of the unit varies from that of a book to that of a two drawer file cabinet. Size is based on the amount of power supplied and the length of time that power is available. Some small backup units can fit inside a PC and can support the unit for only a few minutes. Larger units may support several PCs, monitors, and printers for several minutes or close to an hour. The battery power is intended only to help you quickly wrap up whatever you are working on and save your work to the hard disk drive before shutting down. It's not intended to sustain a long operation.

The main function of a battery backup is to support the continued operation of the computer in case of a brief or long power outage. The computer is very sensitive to instantaneous power fluctuations. When power to the PC is interrupted, all information on the RAM memory is wiped clean, including everything you have changed or added since the last time you saved data to your hard disk. The function of the backup unit is to be on standby and provide instantaneous power, when necessary.

Backup units primarily supply the power for a few minutes while you shut down properly and save your work. Other more sophisticated units, which are frequently hooked up to computer networks, can automatically shut down the main unit unattended. These units need a special connection to the main PC and special circuitry to work properly with the network software.

For organizations that have a computer network, battery backup is an absolute necessity. Other organizations may have to evaluate their needs based on the frequency of power problems in their area and the value of the backup. Some small battery backups sell for under $100.

There are three different technologies for power backup: off-line (standby), on-line (UPS: Uninterruptible Power Supply), and internal.

● Off-line systems are the most common and the least expensive of the three (some vendors incorrectly call them UPS). They simply wait on standby for a power interruption, then they switch on within milliseconds, and supply battery power to the system. Generally, the very brief time lapse does not wipe data off the system.

● On-line systems (UPS), on the other hand, are continuously supplying power through the battery while the battery is also being charged. In case of power interruption, the computer doesn't detect any difference. These units often cost 50% to 100% more than their standby counterparts.

● Internal power backup systems are a cross between the two previous technologies. They don't have enough power to operate the monitor; but, they have special software that automatically records on the hard disk the state the system was in at the time of the interruption. After power is restored, the software automatically returns the system to its last state. These units cost about the same as their standby counterparts.

Furniture

In recent years, computer furniture has become a specialized product. As millions of people spend more hours in front of their computers, comfort, convenience, and health safeguards gain more importance. Most computer furniture are designed to address the special needs of a PC user. The most commonly used pieces of furniture are the PC table and the printer stand. The PC table supports the PC and the monitor at a comfortable height while making efficient use of the space. Printer stands usually have one or more shelves for holding the paper, either in a stack or in a box. They also have cut-out sections for the paper to be fed directly to the back or the bottom of the printer.

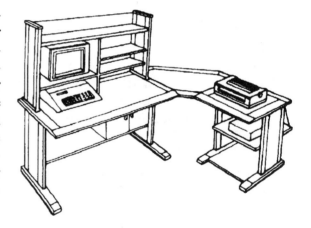

When looking for computer furniture, you should first pay particular attention to the ergonomics that determine your comfort and convenience. Then you can look for other features that you would like to have in any piece of furniture. Keep in mind that most computer furniture is sold unassembled, and is somewhat heavy. If you plan to buy your furniture from an out of town supplier, check the shipping costs.

Chapter 5. Software You Can Use

There are literally thousands of computer programs for every imaginable purpose. Every category of activity has at least a handful of programs from small or large companies. Each program has certain characteristics and works a certain way. One of the most important points to remember is that when you buy a software and learn to use it, you have already invested a certain amount of time and money into that particular program. The longer you use that program and the more data you generate with it, the more you'll be committed to it. After a while it becomes more difficult and, sometimes, more costly to switch to a completely different program. Therefore, whenever possible it's important that you choose the most suitable software to begin with.

If you are just starting to use a PC, you are facing a major dilemma. You may not know anything about software, or what little you know may be based on feedback from friends and co-workers. The danger of feedback from others is that most people have a tendency to recommend the programs they have become familiar with. Without having tried other programs, they often think that theirs is the best. Magazines and other periodicals dealing with PCs are an excellent source of comparison information; but a magazine can only review a few programs in each issue. Therefore, if you are in the market to buy software now, you should find a collection of these magazines to research your needs. Programs are updated and revised so frequently that a book comparing them may often be outdated by the time it reaches store shelves.

If you have had some experience with or exposure to PCs, you probably know a few programs and have already spent some time learning to use them. Now that you have to choose programs for your own use, your tendency might be to choose those you have grown accustomed to. Sometimes having a starting point like this is helpful, but that may force you to spend more on software than your budget allows. You will still benefit from researching the available programs to find the most suitable ones for your needs.

Most programs are designed to become active when you call upon them to do so. Other programs are called "memory resident" because all or part of them reside in memory (RAM) at all times. These programs are also called TSR (Terminate and Stay Resident). They come in two categories: pop-up or interrupt-driven. A pop-up program is activated when you press one or more designated keys. This type includes certain utility programs that offer a calculator on screen, an appointment scheduler or a phone dialer, etc. An interrupt-driven program stays dormant in the background until a certain event occurs or a certain date or time arrives. This type includes programs that blank your screen after a few minutes of no activity, hard disk cache or appointment reminder, etc.

5.1. Operating Systems

An operating system is like gas for your car: your PC cannot operate without it. Today, most PCs are sold with an operating system, so in most cases, you don't have to choose. If, on the other hand, your PC is not bundled with an operating system, you must select one that meets your needs and budget. Fortunately, there is only a small amount of difference between the two types of DOS (Disk Operating System) programs currently available.

Feed Me

Some organizations may require a more powerful operating system with the ability to perform multiple tasks simultaneously, or the ability to work in an environment where multiple users can access a central computer. In that case OS/2 or UNIX/ XENIX may be appropriate. Following is a description of the major PC operating systems on the market:

MS-DOS

DOS, the Disk Operating System, is a character-based operating system that runs one program at a time. It was initially developed by Tim Patterson of Seattle Computer Products under the name 86-DOS. It was developed before IBM introduced the original PC in August 1981. In July 1981, Microsoft purchased the rights to 86-DOS, adapted it for the IBM PC (which was secret then), and renamed it MS-DOS. Since then, MS-DOS has gone through several major updates and upgrades.

MS-DOS 6.2 was introduced in October 1993. It has many features that were lacking from previous versions of MS-DOS and were often provided by other companies as utility software. If your new PC is not supplied with DOS, we recommend that you buy the latest version. You'll not only benefit from the latest features, but you'll also find it easier to learn and to use.

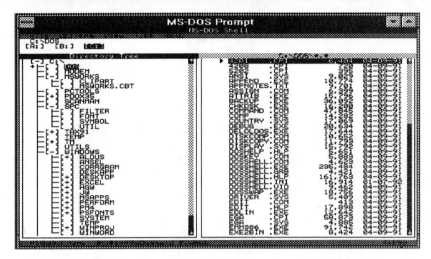

A sample screen that shows an MS-DOS directory shell and tree structure.

DR-DOS

DR-DOS is a product of Digital Research Corporation, one of the pioneers of operating systems. Like MS-DOS, it's a character-based operating system that runs one program at a time. In fact, one of the most popular operating systems before the introduction of the original IBM PC was called CP/M which belonged to Digital Research. According to PC folklore, in 1980, when IBM was putting together the team of suppliers for its secret PC project, Digital Research was considered the primary source of the operating system. However, IBM executives had a difficult time getting in touch with the young president of Digital Research. On the day they went to California to meet with him, he was out flying his airplane. Rebuffed by the young entrepreneur, IBM turned to the even younger Bill Gates and Paul Allen of Microsoft for the operating system. Today, Bill Gates is the richest man in America, Paul Allen is also a Billionaire and Microsoft is a major powerhouse in the PC industry, the rest is history.

Digital Research continued marketing CP/M for a short time later, until it was totally overwhelmed by MS-DOS. A few years ago Digital Research began developing an MS-DOS compatible operating system that offered more features than MS-DOS. It first introduced DR-DOS 5.0 in May 1990, which offered many advanced features that a year later appeared in MS-DOS 5.0.

The latest version by Digital Research is DR-DOS 7.0. It is state of the art and contains several enhancements to both DR-DOS 6.0 and MS-DOS 6.2. Digital Research is now a division of Novell Corporation (a major computer networking software maker). DR-DOS is compatible with MS-DOS and works well with Novell networking software.

OS/2

OS/2 stands for Operating System 2, and was introduced in April 1987 by IBM (version 1.0) along with their new PS/2 line of computers. It was a joint development venture between IBM and Microsoft. The intent was to develop a new and powerful operating system from scratch for the new generation of PCs. OS/2, unlike DOS, was designed with the ability to run multiple tasks or programs simultaneously. Instead of being character based like DOS, it incorporates a graphical user interface called Presentation Manager, similar to Windows.

The graphical user interface lets you communicate with your computer by using small graphic pictures called icons. You simply point with your mouse pointer at the icon or the text for the action that you want performed, and click a button. So, instead of typing commands, you simply use your mouse. There are some strong similarities between OS/2 and Windows interface.

The multi-tasking capability of OS/2 lets the computer break a program into different processes. It then allocates CPU time to each process as needed. By efficiently allocating time between processes, OS/2 can perform several tasks or programs simultaneously. It also has the ability to pass the results of one program to another while performing various tasks.

Since its introduction in 1987, OS/2 has been primarily used by corporations purchasing high-end IBM PS/2 computers. Although it offered many features and benefits over the DOS and Windows combination, it required about 4 MB of RAM, at least 10 MB of hard disk space, and a powerful processor. OS/2 can step down to the level of DOS to run DOS programs, but then it's not able to benefit from most of OS/2's features.

OS/2 version 2.1, released in 1993 by IBM, is a major enhancement over the previous versions. OS/2 provides significant advancements over the features offered by a combination of the latest versions of DOS and Windows. However, it does require at least an 80386-SX microprocessor, 4 MB or more of RAM, and about 25 MB of hard disk space.

UNIX/XENIX

UNIX is a multi-user operating system that was developed by AT&T Bell Labs in the 1970's. XENIX is a version of UNIX developed by Santa Cruz Operations to work in the PC environment. Both have gone through several versions and upgrades in the past few years.

Unix is a much more comprehensive operating system than DOS or OS/2. Like OS/2, it offers the ability to perform multiple tasks simultaneously, and it allows simultaneous multiple users. Because UNIX was developed as a multi-tasking and multi-user operating system, it offers a more solid environment than both DOS and OS/2. DOS was originally developed as a single-task and single-user operating system. Other features have been added on top of DOS while trying to maintain compatibility with previous versions. OS/2 was developed from scratch with multi-tasking capabilities but it still maintained a close relationship with DOS. Although UNIX offers a more solid operating environment, it's not as prevalent as the millions of DOS based systems throughout the world.

5.2. User Environments

As described earlier in this chapter, DOS is a character based operating system. Therefore, you must type a command for it to be understood and executed by your computer. User environments have been developed to make it easier for you to use your PC. They fill the screen with a pleasing view of small graphical pictures called icons. Commands that are not graphically represented are shown in text form. By moving the mouse pointer to the icon or text and clicking a button, you execute that command. The graphical user interface was initially developed by researchers at a Xerox research center in California. First introduced by Apple Computer Corporation on the Macintosh systems, it soon became very popular. In November 1985, Microsoft introduced Windows 1.0 which was based on a somewhat similar idea. It was later upgraded in November 1987 to Windows 2.0. In June 1988 Microsoft introduced Windows 286 and Windows 386. However, all these Windows programs were very slow and inefficient compared to the Macintosh interface. In the past couple of years, newer and more powerful versions have been introduced.

Windows

Microsoft introduced Windows 3.0 in May 1990. During the first two years it sold more than 10 million copies and became a major factor in the added popularity of PCs. The program required at least 2 MB of memory, occupied about 5 MB of hard disk space, looked best when used with a VGA color monitor, and worked best with at least an 80386-SX or faster processor.

Windows 3.1, was introduced in April 1992 with significant enhancements over version 3.0. It offered many new features such as sound and multi-media. Windows NT, Windows for Workgroups and Windows 4.0 resulted from the success and popularity of Windows 3.1.

Every day more software designed to operate under Windows is introduced. The advantage of these programs is that if you install Windows on your system and then add these programs, they have a consistent look and feel that makes them easier to learn and to use. For example, a word processing program will be started the same way as a spreadsheet program. The basic windows containing pre-defined commands on the top of your screen will look basically the same. This uniformity in mode of operation also makes it possible for data to be transferred from one program to another relatively easily.

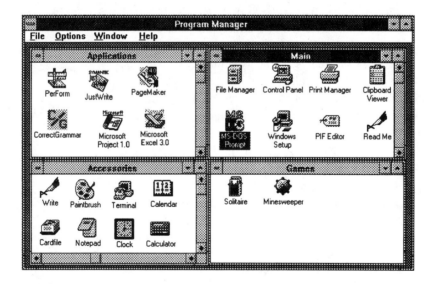

A sample Windows screen that shows the contents of Program Manager.

For example, you can transfer a list of your household goods from a database program and use it in your word processing program in order to write a letter to your insurance company.

PC/GEOS

PC/GEOS, a product of GeoWorks International, is an alternative graphical user environment to Windows. There are many similarities between the two. PC/GEOS is very popular with the owners of 8086, 8088, and 80286 based PCs who are not capable of running Windows. It uses graphical icons, **works** with multiple applications at once, produces WYSIWYG - pronounced wee-zee-wig (What You See Is What You Get), on the screen, and offers many other features.

PC/GEOS is often included as part of a software bundle, called GeoWorks, which includes word processing, database manager, spreadsheet, planning calendar, phone directory, dialer, drawing tools, communication, scrapbook, notepad, calculator, and many other necessary and convenient modules.

Pen-based

The recent introduction of pen-based, notebook-sized PCs **has given** rise to pen-based user environments. It's an environment somewhat like **Windows and** has various graphic shapes (icons) and commands on the screen. By touching these icons on the screen, you can access a document or instruct the computer to execute a command. Some computers have a touch sensitive screen which you can activate with the touch of your finger. Others use a special electronic pen that's attached to the PC.

Several companies such as Microsoft and Go Software Corporation, have introduced their own versions of user environments for pen-based PCs.

5.3. Applications Software

Applications software is designed to perform specific functions within the framework of an operating system and possibly a graphical user interface. When buying software, it's very important to check the disk size the program comes in, as well as the DOS version(s) it operates with. One of the features of applications software is that it gets updated or upgraded periodically, usually about once a year. Before choosing a software, it's wise to check the frequency of upgrades and the date of the last upgrade. If a program is upgraded frequently, you should be a little more cautious. If it's almost time for a new update, you might want to wait a little longer for the new version to be released.

Since the introduction of Windows, software has been divided into two groups: those that work only with DOS and those that work only under Windows. Before you buy any programs, you should decide whether you want to operate Windows. Whichever option you choose, you can then buy software that's appropriate for that environment.

Word Processing

Word processing programs are the driving force behind the growth of personal computers. PCs are used for word processing more than 80% of the time. Word processing programs have almost reached the top of their evolution. The high-end packages contain so many features that software developers are running out of things to add.

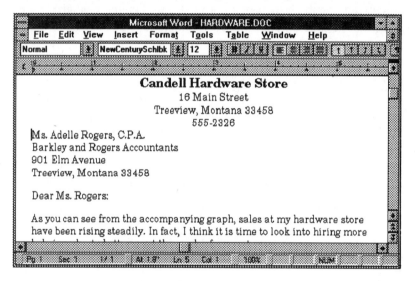

A sample screen that shows a windows-based word processing page.

Word processing programs are divided into three levels: high-end, mid-range, and low-level. The high-end programs are powerful, sophisticated, and full of features such as page layout, spell checking, and thesaurus. The mid-range programs have most of the features listed above, while low-level programs are fully functional but somewhat simplistic packages that are adequate for generating simple documents.

Word processing programs are not very demanding of processor and hard drive speed, but if you use the Windows version you'll need a fast processor.

When you begin a word processing program, the screen looks like a blank sheet of paper. Depending on the program, you may see one or two rows of summary commands on the top or bottom of the screen. Programs often start with a set of guidelines called "default values." These default values include information about the size of the page; the margins on the sides, top, and bottom of the page; the size of the characters, etc. Default values apply to most standard documents. You can change the style of your page or the entire document. As you type characters on the screen, you can go back to correct an error or replace a word. With most programs, you can move sentences or entire paragraphs from one place to another. You can even divide the page into several columns or bring a graph, drawing, or photograph from another program into your page. If your program has a built-in spell checker, you can have the computer check your spelling and suggest correct alternatives for suspected words.

Database Management

Database programs have advanced to high levels of power and performance. In the more than ten years that database programs have been in use, they have gone through an evolution similar to that of word processing programs. Unlike word processors, these programs rely more heavily on the processor and hard drive speed. These programs basically present a very large accounting (ledger) sheet with many rows and columns. You can change the width of each column to match the information you store there.

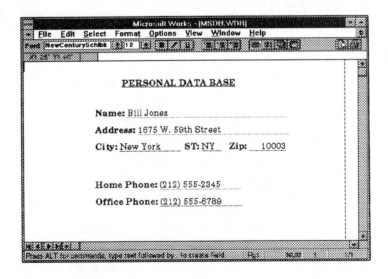

A sample screen that shows a Windows-based database management page.

A database program is like a huge filing cabinet that can store thousands of pieces of information. The great advantage of these programs over manual storage is that you can manipulate the data in many different ways. For example, you can sort names alphabetically or by city, state, or zip code

Spreadsheet

Spreadsheets played a very important role in introducing PCs to the work place. About the same time that the IBM PC was brought to the market, a program called Visicalc caught the attention of corporate America. Armed with a PC and Visicalc, employees and accountants were suddenly able to develop budgets, financial forecasts, performance reports, and hundreds of other number-related reports. With the introduction of the powerful Lotus 1-2-3 program in 1983, corporate America was permanently hooked on PCs.

Parallel to the evolution of the PC and the increasing power of the microprocessors, spreadsheets have grown to become powerful tools for just about any activity dealing with numbers. They are used by organizations large and small for budgeting, forecasting, what-if analysis, and so on.

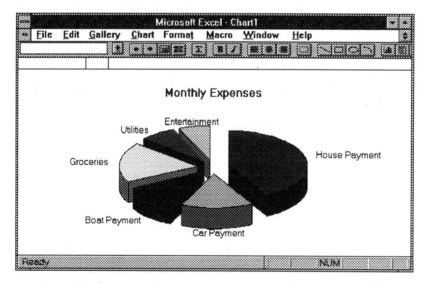

A sample pie chart of monthly expenses created with a spreadsheet program.

Spreadsheets resemble an accountant's ledger sheet with rows and columns. At first the number of rows and columns handled by these programs was 40 rows and 26 columns. Now it has grown to thousands of rows and hundreds of columns. Each individual box created by the intersection of a row and column is called a cell. Spreadsheets can take the contents of one or more cells and perform various mathematical computations based on whatever formula you specify. For example, if you enter all your monthly household expenses into one column and want to see what would happen if your expenses grew by 5% across the board, all you have to do is tell the spreadsheet to create a new column by increasing all the numbers in the cells of the original column by 5%.

The performance of spreadsheets is very dependent on the speed of your processor and hard drive. When choosing such a program, you should make sure that the package can work well with your system. For example, if you have an old 8088 based XT computer, but the software you choose is primarily designed for an 80386 or faster processor, you'll notice tremendous performance degradation in the spreadsheet program's response time.

Data Communication

Data communication programs tend to be somewhat complex, with protocol settings and other functional requirements. A wide variety of communication programs with different features and capabilities are on the market. An increasing number of programs feature a graphical user interface. This type of interface makes them easier to use, but it also makes them a little slower than text-based programs. Another important feature is the type of menu the program uses to interface with you. Each program has its own unique approach to this. Sometimes, if you have access to these programs, you can make a better decision by experimenting with various types before choosing one.

Most basic data communication programs lets you connect to other computers via your phone line to send data back and forth or to carry on an on-line conversation on your computer screen. You can actually talk to a person on the other end of the line by typing your statements into your computer and receiving the other person's reply on your screen. Almost all these programs let you send data from your computer to the other system. For example, you can send a letter or a database directly to the other person.

Another group of communication programs let you call up a computer from your PC and make it act as if you are sitting in front of the other system. After the phone connection is made, these programs take over the operation of the other computer and give you total control over it. These programs are particularly popular with computer consultants and technical support staff who can help customers out of a jam without having to travel to the customer's location. Businesspeople also find these programs helpful, because they can call up their work computer from their homes or on the road, and operate it as if they were sitting in their office.

An increasingly popular type of program used by computer hobbyists and some businesses and computer companies is called a Bulletin Board System (BBS). These programs make a designated BBS computer available to other callers' computers. Those providing the BBS often place various information, programs, and other notices on their system for access by others. Most cities have one or more computer user groups. These groups use a central BBS to post information for their members, exchange electronic mail, and work on other activities on-line. Manufacturers of computer products often use a BBS to provide updates, notices, or corrections to their software problems for their customers.

Integrated Packages

Integrated programs combine the features of word processing, database management, spreadsheet, and communications into one convenient package. Unlike the full-featured stand-alone programs they represent, each part of an integrated package contains most of their basic functions, without some of the frills. Since their introduction in the mid 1980's, integrated programs have kept pace with the improvements made to their full-featured cousins. The programs available today contain many features that make them more than adequate for most PC users. Although they may not contain most of the "bells and whistles" available in their full-featured counterparts, their absence is not noticeable to most people who don't use those features anyway.

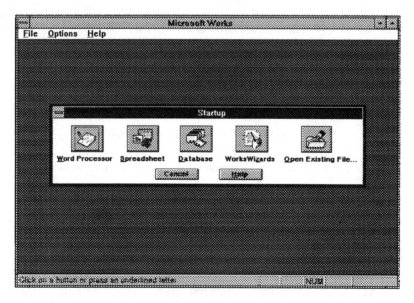

A sample screen that shows a Windows-based integrated program.

PC users are beginning to rely on integrated programs for all their needs at home, as well as at work. These programs use less disk space than individual programs. Increased use of portable computers has further added to the popularity of these programs. Ease of use and economy are also very important factors. Overall, with the backing of some of the major software manufacturers, these programs continue to be very popular.

Personal Finance and Income Taxes

In the early 1980's, individuals who could afford to own a PC at home were quick to take advantage of the power of spreadsheets to keep track of their personal finances. They customized their spreadsheets to create programs that suited their needs. Soon people started to share or sell their modified programs to others who were interested in them.

In the mid 1980's, some software companies started to develop programs specifically designed for home finance. Over the years, these programs have become quite powerful, with many features that go beyond a simple checkbook recorder. Most of these programs now let you print checks with your PC, keep track of your investments, sort your expenses by category to facilitate your work at tax time. They also advise you on ways to improve your tax position, keep a record of your household goods, and so on.

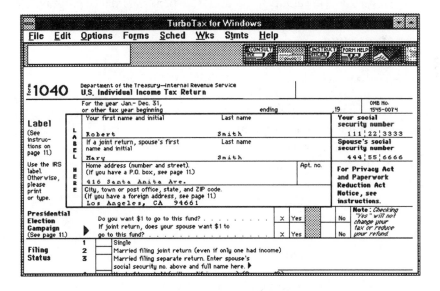

A sample federal income tax 1040 form displayed by a tax preparation program.

Some programs give you the ability to pay your bills electronically. Using your modem and special software, you can instruct the service to take a certain amount of money from your bank account on a certain date and send it electronically to the account of the receiver. You can pay your utility bills, mortgage, insurance, etc., right from your PC.

Since the late 1980's, another group of programs has also become increasingly popular with home PC users. These programs help you prepare and file your federal and state income taxes. You still have to keep track of all your income and expenses, but the programs are designed to ask you a variety of questions to get all the necessary numbers. Then they simply put the numbers where they belong. These programs are capable of printing all the relevant tax forms on your home printer. The IRS has approved the printout from most of these programs, so you no longer need to fill out any forms by hand. Another feature that some of these programs offer is the ability to use your modem to send your tax forms electronically to a special service which forwards them to the IRS. This procedure expedites your refund and saves the IRS from manually entering all your numbers into their computers.

When evaluating income tax preparation programs, you should look for several factors: the availability of your state's income tax package as well as the Federal package, the number of tax forms and schedules handled, the cost of annual updates, ease of use, electronic transmission, the ability to get data from personal finance programs, and so on.

Business Accounting

The current prices of computers and accounting programs make it almost mandatory for every business to have a computerized accounting system. The increasing volume of information and competitive pressures make this a matter of survival, rather than a luxury. Accounting programs come in many different shapes, sizes, and prices. If you operate a business, large or small, you can choose from a wide assortment of programs regardless of the nature of your business. There are two types of accounting programs: general and specialized (called vertical).

General accounting programs are designed to address most the of the needs of a business. Often divided into modules, each module addresses a different part of the accounting requirements. The most common modules are the following:

>**General Ledger (GL)** is like the glue that holds all the other modules together. It also contains the information that will create financial statements and reports.

>**Accounts Receivable (AR)** can issue invoices and keep track of income.

Accounts Payable (AP) keeps track of purchases and expenses as well as purchase orders.

Inventory (IN) keeps track of items in your inventory.

Payroll (PR) keeps track of employee payroll, issues paychecks, and determines payroll tax deductions and FICA.

Some programs further divide these functions into other modules. Some accounting programs sell each module separately, while others sell a complete package that includes several modules. Generally, complete packages are less expensive, but have fewer frills and less flexibility than those sold as separate modules. In recent years, most accounting packages have reached such levels of refinement and power that a low price does not necessarily make them any less desirable. They often meet all established accounting standards and perform accurately. Most smaller businesses find complete accounting packages to be more suitable for their needs. These programs are usually available from various retail sources. Some packages also support multi-user operations, which makes them more attractive for organizations that use several computers on a network.

More expensive programs that are sold as individual modules are often sold and installed by authorized dealers. They are usually more sophisticated than the complete packages sold at stores. Most of them offer greater flexibility to be modified to suit the special needs of a specific business.

One of the factors to consider when buying accounting programs is the frequency and cost of updates and upgrades. Most software companies have a tendency to upgrade their programs every year, then stop supporting the older versions from six months to a year after releasing the newer versions. Although upgrading to a newer version does not cost nearly as much as the initial purchase, it can still be a sizable amount. To avoid any future surprises, when you are evaluating programs, always check and verify the frequency of upgrades, their cost, the need for the upgrades, and the length of support time for each version.

Some of the other points you need to check before buying an accounting package are questions like:

● Is an easy-to-understand accounting primer included?

● Is a network version available or included?

● Is the Chart of Accounts editable?

● Are tutorials and sample company data included?

● Does it offer on-line, context-sensitive help?

● Does it have a report generator?

● What is the number of standard reports? Customizable reports?

● Does it have account number look-up feature?

● Does it provide tax tables? How frequently are they updated?

● Is error correction after closing a period possible?

● Does it have check writing?

● What is the total number of open periods?

● Ability to reverse an entry in Accounts Payable and Accounts Receivable?

● Can it print forms (Invoice, PO, etc.) on blank paper?

Specialized accounting programs (called vertical market programs by the computer industry) are specifically developed for their respective industries. For example, there are programs for dentists' offices, shoe stores, construction companies, personnel offices, video stores and so on. These programs are developed for a relatively smaller market because of their specific focus on one industry. They are often available only through authorized dealers, and usually cost more than a general purpose accounting program. If you are looking for business software and feel that generalized programs don't meet all your needs, you can probably find a handful of vertical programs for your situation. These programs are often advertised in trade publications for your industry. When you find a list of software providers, you can call them to get the number for their local authorized dealer(s). The dealer should show you a demo and explain the program to you at no cost. If there are no local dealers in your area, ask the software provider for a free or inexpensive demo kit. Don't hesitate to evaluate several packages and several dealers before making a decision. Before buying a program, get at least five references each from the software company and the dealer in order to check and verify their claims. Then make sure that you get a detailed written proposal that shows exactly what you will receive. Verbal promises that the software will do everything you want can lead to major disappointments after you pay for it and discover that certain things don't meet your expectations.

Desktop Publishing

Desktop publishing programs have become quite sophisticated in recent years. Powerful programs, currently used by magazines and newspapers, are also available to PC users for several hundred dollars. These programs not only let you compose the appearance of your page(s), determine the shape and size of your text, and allow you to place photographs and drawings on the page, but also let you prepare sections for multicolored printing. One of the features of desktop publishing programs is called WYSIWYG (What You See Is What You Get). This feature lets you see on the screen exactly what your document will look like when it's printed.

Other less sophisticated programs are easier to learn and to use than the ones used by professionals. These programs are used mostly by individuals and organizations that need to print simple newsletters, flyers, advertisements, etc.

Some of the more powerful word processing programs have in recent years incorporated many of the features that were previously found only in desktop publishing software. If you plan to produce some flyers or newsletters with your computer, you should first explore the capabilities of your word processor. Word processing programs based on the Windows environment offer features that satisfy most desktop publishing needs. If you need more power, then you should find a way to evaluate some of the high end packages before making a purchasing decision.

Education

Educational programs are proliferating continuously. Literally thousands of programs aimed at educating people of all ages are directed at various topics with different degrees of difficulty. Because of their diversity, there are no specific guidelines for selecting these programs. The best sources for information are other users, educational institutions and related publications.

Games and Entertainment

One of the most popular uses of home computers is playing games and working with entertainment software. Since the introduction of "Pong," the first black and white home video game in the 1970's, computer games have duplicated the sophistication and dazzling colors found in video arcade games.

Games use various forms of animation on the screen to represent different scenes. These games have advanced to the point of producing very high quality visual effects. Obviously, to get the most visual enjoyment from these games you have to use a high resolution VGA monitor. Some of these games use very high quality animations. Others are card games like poker and solitaire, or board games such as chess and checkers. Other games let you participate in fighter airplane dogfights, sea battles, football, baseball, golf, etc. Most PC games cost under $50. Before you buy a game you have to make sure that it works with your system. Most games specify their requirements in terms of the DOS or Windows version, microprocessor, amount of memory, hard disk space, video board, and monitor type. If your system does not meet one of these requirements, you may not be able to use it.

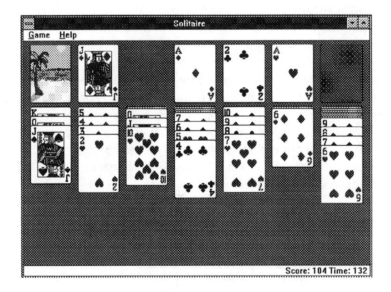

A sample screen that shows a Windows-based solitaire card game.

Utilities

Utility programs perform hundreds of functions to make using your PC easier. Until recent versions of MS-DOS and DR-DOS, the main function of most utilities was to complement the shortcomings of DOS.

Some utility programs show you the DOS screen in an easier and more informative way, find files faster, and make disk backups faster and more efficient. Some utilities turn your computer into a calculator, schedule appointments, keep a mailing list and a phone directory so that you can simply find a name and have your modem dial the number, clean unnecessary files from your hard disk drive, bring back a file that was accidentally erased and so on.

Utility programs can also complement applications software packages. For example, a utility program that works together with a word processing package can check your grammar and style for possible improvements. Another type of utility program may help you print a variety of letter and character sizes with a plain word processor and printer. Yet another type may help you create an instant graph of your data. All these programs are helpful to have, but are not the type that a novice computer buyer has to purchase at the same time as the system. After becoming familiar with your computer and applications software, you'll be in a much better position to determine exactly what you may or may not need.

```
┌──────────────────────────────────────────────────────────────┐
│                     Calendar - [Untitled]                      │
├──────────────────────────────────────────────────────────────┤
│ File   Edit   View   Show   Alarm   Options   Help             │
├──────────────────────────────────────────────────────────────┤
│         12:17 PM    ▓▓▓       Saturday, July 11,               │
│          7:00 AM                                               │
│          8:00                                                  │
│          9:00       bring car in for oil change                │
│         10:00                                                  │
│         11:00       take Jennifer to Lisa's birthday party     │
│         12:00 PM                                               │
│          1:00       mow the lawn                               │
│          2:00       clean out the garage                       │
│          3:00       pick up Jennifer                           │
│          4:00                                                  │
│          5:00       take Uncle Bob to the airport              │
│          6:00                                                  │
│          7:00       pick up the baby-sitter                    │
│          8:00       attend "Marriage of Figaro"                │
└──────────────────────────────────────────────────────────────┘
```

A sample daily calendar and activity scheduler with alarm.

Other Applications

Besides the application programs listed above, thousands of other programs perform a variety of functions. These programs usually address areas of special interest like cooking, genealogy, stamp collecting and so on. The field is so broad that it's almost impossible to describe all the different topics available. When you are buying your PC, you can delay buying any miscellaneous programs until you become a little more knowledgeable.

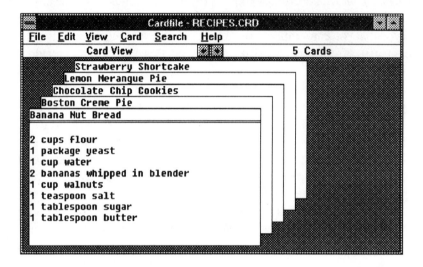

A sample screen showing recipe card file maintained and sorted by computer.

Chapter 6. Best Way To Choose Or Upgrade Your PC

If you don't have a PC or want to upgrade your existing computer, the next two chapters will help you do just that. So far, you have developed a good understanding of what a PC is, how it works, and what it can do. This knowledge and the following chapter will give you the tools necessary to choose and buy the system that best meets your needs and fits within your budget.

6.1. Selection Criteria

Making a choice is an activity that we all do several times a day: We decide what clothes to wear in the morning, what to have for breakfast, what route to take to work, and what to buy at the grocery store. We compare options and make decisions all the time. In making a selection, we follow certain criteria. Some selections happen so frequently that they become second nature to us. Others happen only once or a few times in a lifetime. Buying a home, a car, or a personal computer is in that category. In these cases, you can't make a selection just on a hunch. The more knowledgeable and prepared you are, the better your system will be and the more pleased you will be with your selection.

In this chapter, we will review various criteria that you can use in choosing the system that is most appropriate for you. All the factors mentioned here may not necessarily apply to your situation, but you should choose as many of them as possible. Remember that the more prepared you are, the better your choice will be.

Available Resources

One of the most important selection criteria is the resources that you have available to you. These resources are unique to you and your situation. Most of them are readily available to you in some measure. You have a great deal of control over how you utilize these resources.

Budget

Money is the most important criterion in selecting your system. How much money you can budget for your purchase will determine what type and brand of system you can afford to buy. How do you go about reaching a dollar amount for your budget? Budgeting for a computer is very different from budgeting for a car. When you decide to buy a two-door car, you know that a year later you are not going to want to add two more doors to that car.

When you buy a computer, you are entering a wonderful world of challenging and interesting experiences. The more you use your computer, the more features you will wish for. You'll want it to be faster, have more storage capacity, have a better color display, and do more things. You'll be anxious to try the new products that are introduced frequently. If you buy the wrong system, you will be limiting your options for growth and expansion.

Establishing a budget for your computer purchase is a little more involved than merely looking at your bank balance or your credit limit. When you sit down to establish a budget for yourself, you should consider several points. Write your answer to each of the following questions on this page.

● How much money all together are you willing to spend for your entire system, including the PC, monitor, printer, mouse, software, etc.? $_____

● How do you plan to pay for the purchase? Cash, credit card, finance, or lease?

● If you and your family or your business really enjoy using the computer, how much more are you willing to spend to upgrade your system during the first year, second year, and third year? $_____, $_____, $_____

● If necessary, are you willing to spend a combination of cash and credit for your purchase?

● What is the absolute maximum that you are willing and prepared to spend for the system now? $_____

Later in this chapter you can record the numbers you have established for your budget. Remember that at this point, to you this is just a purchase. Based on our accumulated years of experience buying PCs as well as selling them, we know that if you limit yourself improperly at this time, you'll spend more money later upgrading your system to where it should have been to begin with.

Time

Another important resource is time. Buying the right system takes time: time to become a knowledgeable computer shopper, time to select the appropriate type of system, time to shop around, and time to set up your system properly. To determine how much of this valuable resource you have available, answer the following questions:

● After reviewing this program, how many hours are you willing to spend shopping around for a system? _____

● After buying your system, how many hours are you willing to spend to set it up properly? _____

● After setting up your system, how many hours are you willing to spend to learn to use your software? _____

Advice and Feedback

An equally important resource that almost everyone has available is advice and feedback from friends and co-workers. People love to talk about their experiences and give advice. This valuable resource is there for the asking. If you know several PC users, choose a few who are close to your age and educational background, and who use their PCs for activities similar to those you plan to do. The following are some of the questions you should ask them about their systems and experiences:

● Kind of computer (processor type, speed, brand name, model, etc.)

● Total amount of RAM memory.

● Hard disk drive (type, size, capacity, speed, etc.)

● Floppy drive (type, size, capacity, etc.)

● Monitor (Mono or color VGA, brand name, model, screen size, resolution, dot pitch, etc.)

● Printer (dot matrix, laser, brand name, model, size, etc.)

● Pointing device (mouse, trackball, brand name, model, etc.)

● Modem (type, speed, features, etc.)

● Operating system (type, version)

- User environment (type, version)

- Applications software (type, name, version, etc.)

- Name and address of supplier (local retail supplier, mail order, etc.)

- Warranty (type, coverage, length, etc.)

- Experience with sales and support staff

- Any equipment failures or malfunctions

- Any recommendations (computer, software, supplier, etc.)

Find out as much as possible about their experiences with their systems and their suppliers. Record the positive as well as the negative feedback.

Performance

Ever since the original IBM PC was introduced in 1981, computers have become more powerful and offer a lot more features. As of this writing, the most powerful system on the market, the Pentium, is more than 100 times faster than the original PC. Based on the

performance tables in Chapter 4, you can see that there are several systems for every performance level. When you are selecting a system, performance is just one of the many factors you should consider. If you have ever bought a car, home, or color TV, you have experienced the type of balancing act that goes into looking at all the factors, including performance.

Almost every two years a new microprocessor generation is introduced. The higher performance level and features introduced by each new generation can be very tempting to most PC users. The important thing is to choose a performance level that meets all of your criteria, including your budget.

The types of programs you plan to use have a direct bearing on the type of performance you need. Your operating system does not depend on your processor speed. However, if you plan to use a graphical user interface like Windows, you should consider an 80386-

SX as a minimum. Actually, an 80486-SX is recommended as a starting point. If you don't plan to use Windows or anything beyond word processing, then an 80386-Sx based system should perform adequately.

The speed of a microprocessor determines the amount of time it will take the computer to process your commands. With word processing programs, you spend most of your time typing characters into the computer, and very little processing is involved. Other programs, however, rely on the processor quite extensively. Database, spreadsheet, and accounting programs, in particular, put great demands on the processor. If your system is too slow, it will take the program longer to go from one step to another. For some people, speed may not be very important, but our experience has shown that PC users, in general, grow more sensitive to their processor speed after a while. So, you should not settle for minimum speed. If you become dissatisfied a few months later, it will cost you a lot more to upgrade your system than if you had spent that money at the beginning. Don't feel pressured to spend over your budget to get the very highest speed. In most cases, after one or two years you can upgrade your processor.

Brand Name

IBM established a standard for the PC industry in 1981, and that inadvertently gave birth to hundreds of large and small companies. During the early 1980's, the entire industry was in a learning process. In recent years the industry has matured and quality control has reached very high levels.

Among the hundreds of PC manufacturers in the United States are several nationally recognized brand names. Some of these companies are multi-billion dollar organizations. Although the size of an organization is not an indicator of the quality of its products or its commitment to the PC industry, some people feel more comfortable with a nationally recognized brand name.

Fortunately, most PCs use standard off-the-shelf components. These components are generally manufactured by multi-billion dollar companies that specialize in making those components. For example, Intel, IBM, AMD, Cyrix and Texas Instruments are major manufacturers of microprocessors. Seagate, Conner, and Maxtor are major manufacturers of hard disk drives. NEC, Mitsubishi, Sony, Samsung, Gold Star, and Panasonic are major manufacturers of monitors. Literally hundreds of companies manufacture various components for the whole PC industry. As long as the components used inside your PC meet certain quality standards, the name on the outside of the box is no longer a critical factor.

Ease of Use

IBM and compatible computers share many standards, so they are quite similar in the way they interact with you. Therefore, ease of use is limited to a number of issues that individually are not very critical, but collectively become an important consideration. Among the factors that contribute to ease of use are the following:

- Location of on/off switches and cable connections

- Shape, size, and weight of the base unit

- Shape and feel of the keyboard

- Tilt and swivel of the monitor

- Accessibility of floppy and tape drive(s)

Quality

Quality is a term that has been overused and abused by many manufacturers. It's not a very visible, objective or measurable criterion. Advertisements tout the quality of various products to the point that some people may feel that nothing ever breaks down.

Most parts used in computers are solid state electronics, which means that there are very few moving parts in PCs. The low voltage operation inside the PC makes it less vulnerable to electric shorts or overheating. Most systems, regardless of brand name, have proven to be quite reliable. Most manufacturers, even the nationally known brands, use components in their systems that are mostly supplied by reputable vendors. The result is that PCs are becoming increasingly standardized. The quality of a system is now dependent on the quality of the components that go into it.

Very few objective quality comparison programs are available. One of your best sources can be friends and co-workers. With the variety of brands available, it's increasingly difficult to get good feedback based on more than one or two units of the same brand. Another option is to research various computer magazines to find PC quality polls. Although they may not always be very current, they give you a good indication of the quality of several well known brands.

When you are shopping locally for computers, you can inspect some of the external quality features such as the sturdiness of the base unit, the feel of the keyboard, the switches, and the floppy drives. Make notes so that you can compare your impressions from one brand to another.

Service and Repair

When you go out to buy a brand new computer system, the last thing on your mind is the prospect of having to service it. If you do your homework beforehand, you'll minimize your chances of having problems and reduce your aggravation if a problem ever arises. Any piece of equipment will eventually have a malfunction at some time in its active life. Computers, with so many parts and components, are no exception. To put your mind at ease, you should know that the solid state electronics in your PC have a very long life expectancy. It's not unusual for most systems to work for five or more years without any maintenance.

When you are evaluating computers, you should ask the suppliers about periodic maintenance requirements, repair frequency statistics (if available), and the average type and cost of repair. Another question you should ask, is where service is performed during and after the warranty period. Also ask about extended maintenance contracts and loaner systems, in case your repair takes too long. Again, remember that the frequency of breakdowns is very low. PC repairs often require nothing more than the quick replacement of a component.

Support

If you are a computer novice, you probably don't know much about technical support. On the other hand, if you are a PC user, you are already familiar with the term. Technical support for PCs is quite important, especially during the first few months of operation.

When you unpack your PC and find a missing or incorrect part, it helps to have someone to call right away to correct the problem. Or, when you start setting up your system and accidentally erase something important, you need to call for help. The technical support staff at your supplier is your first line of help.

Thank You For Holding...
Hello! Are You There?...

Technical support can be handled in one of two ways. Most of your questions can be answered by phone. However, there are times that all your explaining and all the technician's prodding will not solve the problem. In these situations you'll need to get the system or the component to the supplier for service.

During your evaluation process, it's important that you find out about technical support. If the supplier is local, ask about their technical support staff and their level of expertise. Check to see whether service is performed at your location or theirs, both during and after the warranty. Also ask about the service hours, and the response time after you call for service.

If the supplier is not local, check to see whether they have a toll free number, and ask about their hours. If they offer on-site service during the warranty period, ask the name of the company providing the service in your area. If possible, get that phone number and verify their service level in terms of hours and response time. If the supplier does not offer on-site service, ask about the level of phone support you will get. Also check to see if support calls use toll free phone numbers. If a part or the whole system needs to be shipped back, ask what part of the shipping cost you will be responsible for and what part they'll pay for. Get a service policy in writing that states the turnaround time if your system, or part of it, is sent back for service.

Upgradeability and Expandability

Once you become an expert at using your PC, you'll be more aware of the developments in the computer hardware and software field. At some point, you'll develop a need to upgrade or add to your system. Some systems are specifically designed to be easily upgraded. Find out about expansion potentials. How much more room does the PC have for adding another floppy or hard disk drive? How do you add more memory? How do you upgrade the processor?

During the selection process, keep an eye out for upgrade and expansion potentials. It's important to know not only that the system can be upgraded, but also how complicated or involved the process is. Another question to ask is whether your supplier will upgrade during the warranty period free of labor charges.

Portability

One of the important factors that you have to consider is how and where you plan to use your computer. In particular, you have to decide what degree of portability, if any, you need to have. A desktop computer consists of a base unit, monitor, and keyboard. Together they generally weigh over 30 pounds and are bulky to move around. They cost significantly less than comparably equipped portable units and are easier to upgrade or service. However, if you need to move your computer frequently, a desktop is not appropriate for you. Therefore, portability is a factor you have to decide before you start to shop around.

With the increasing power and capacity of notebook computers and significant price reductions in recent months, there is one possibility you might consider. If you are buying a PC for work and considering one for home, you might save some money by buying a notebook computer to satisfy both needs. If you prefer, you can buy a color monitor to hook up to the notebook at either or both locations. With most notebook PCs you can even hook up a regular sized enhanced keyboard, if you prefer.

If you need portability, and can afford the extra premium in price, obviously we recommend that you buy a notebook PC. Other types of portable computers have been discontinued. Following are some important features you should look for in a notebook PC:

- At least an 80386-SX microprocessor

- Battery powered and capable of running at least 3 hours on one charge

- Battery rechargeable in less than 5 hours

- VGA display with at least 16 shades of gray and 640x480 resolution

- At least 1 MB of RAM memory, expandable to 4 MB or more

- 1.4 MB floppy drive and at least an 80 MB hard disk drive

- Weight less than 7 lbs. (with battery) and no larger than 8.5"x11"x2"

- LCD display with backlighting

- Ability to work and charge the battery while hooked up to AC power

- Auto power saving capability to extend the length of battery usage

- Battery power level indicator

- Internal slot for adding a Fax/Modem device

- External plugs for VGA monitor, keyboard, mouse, parallel, and serial

- FCC class B certification

- Parts and labor warranty with a specified service turn-around commitment

- Extended warranty with annual cost not exceeding 10% to 15% of value

Warranty

The length and type of warranty offered can be an important determining factor in your choice of PC. Almost all PCs are offered with at least a one year parts and labor warranty performed at the seller's location. Any additional extensions or features above and beyond those mentioned above should be considered a plus. Some variations to the basic warranty are described below:

- Service performed at your location

- Warranty longer than one year. Be wary of warranties longer than 2 years for unknown brands.

- Replacement of defective parts with overnight shipment

- Availability of reasonably priced extended service contracts

Certifications

Electronic systems are required by the laws of the United States to be approved by two separate organizations. The Underwriters Laboratory (UL) tests equipment for safety. The Federal Communications Commission (FCC) tests equipment for compliance with radio frequency interference. It's very important that both your base unit and monitor display valid UL and FCC approval stickers.

6.2. Selection Guides

Before you go out and start shopping for a system, you should have a clear idea about what type of system you need and about how much you plan to spend. The following section guides you through the selection process. It'll be helpful for you to have a good understanding of the criteria described earlier in this chapter. If you need to review a topic again, feel free to do so. Armed with your newly acquired knowledge and the selection guide provided here, you should be able to arrive at the approximate type of PC that will satisfy your needs and fit within your budget. Be prepared to encounter as many variations as you would if you were shopping for an automobile. After determining that you need a four-door sedan, your wallet will tell you if you can afford a Chevrolet, Cadillac, or Mercedes.

PC Selection Guide

The "PC Selection Guide" in the back of the book has two parts: Short Form and Long Form. If your budget is under $2,500 and you don't need the PC to do any high power or unique work, then use the Short Form to see what type of system fits your needs. The majority of people fit in this category. If you have special needs or a higher budget, then use the Long Form to determine which system is most suitable for you.

PC SELECTION GUIDE

Short Form

Locate the desktop or notebook box with the cost that is within your budget for PC, software & peripherals.

DESKTOPS

$1000

80486-SX 25 MHZ
4 MB RAM
3.5" floppy drive
120 MB hard drive
parallel/serial/game ports
Super VGA board
VGA monochrome monitor
9-pin standard dot matrix printer
DOS
integrated software package

$1500

80486-SX 33 MHZ
4 MB RAM
3.5" floppy drive
170 MB hard drive
parallel/serial/game ports
Super VGA board
Super VGA color monitor
24-pin standard dot matrix printer
DOS + Windows or OS/2
integrated software package
mouse or trackball

$2000

80486-DX 50 MHZ - Multimedia
4 MB RAM
3.5" & 5.25" floppy drives
250 MB hard drive & CD-ROM 2X
parallel/serial/game ports
Super VGA board & Sound board
Super VGA color monitor
24-pin standard dot matrix printer
DOS + Windows or OS/2
integrated software package
mouse or trackball

$2500

80486-DX2 66 MHZ - Multimedia
8 MB RAM
3.5" & 5.25" floppy drives
340 MB hard drive & CD-ROM 2X
parallel/serial/game ports
Super VGA board & Sound board
Super VGA color monitor
24-pin standard dot matrix printer
DOS + Windows or OS/2
integrated software package
mouse or trackball

NOTEBOOK

$2000

80486-SL 25 MHZ
4 MB RAM
3.5" floppy drive
120 MB hard drive
parallel/serial/game ports
VGA plug for external monitor
VGA monochrome LCD monitor
9-pin standard dot matrix printer
DOS + Windows or OS/2
integrated software package
mouse or trackball

$3000

80486-SL 25 MHZ - Color
4 MB RAM
3.5" floppy drive
200 MB hard drive
parallel/serial/game ports
VGA plug for external monitor
VGA color LCD monitor
24-pin standard dot matrix printer
DOS + Windows or OS/2
integrated software package
mouse or trackball

PC Guide ™   © **Inter Trade Corporation, Norcross, Georgia**

Using the Short Form is very simple. Write down the total amount you have budgeted for your purchase on the top line of the form. Then simply find the box that has the amount closest to your budget. More than likely, that's the type of system that will fit within your budget.

If your needs are a little more complex or your budget lets you get a more powerful system, then you should use the Long Form. With the Long Form you can choose from various types of software, printers, and peripherals. Then with your remaining funds you can put together the PC that's right for your needs. The procedure for using the Long Form is to determine the approximate cost of software, printer, and peripherals, then subtract that amount from your budget to arrive at the amount you'll have available for the PC.

Page 1 of the Long Form will ask you for your total budget for the PC, software, printer, and peripherals. Then you are presented with various choices of software categories and their approximate costs. Circle around or write-in the cost of various software that you need.

Page 2 of the Long Form will help you find out how much a printer and other peripherals will cost. Circle the costs of those items that you are interested in, and enter the total in the appropriate boxes on the page.

Page 3 will help you determine how much you'll have left after subtracting the cost of software, printer, and peripherals that you selected in pages 1 and 2. The "Cost Matrix" will help you put together the system that's suitable for your needs. In each microprocessor family (each column on the form) select the features and components that you would like to have and then circle the cost. At the bottom of the form, total the costs circled for each column. You'll have an approximate figure for the type of system that you can buy for the amount of money you have available. If it turns out that after subtracting the cost of software, printer, and peripherals, you don't have enough left for an appropriate PC, you can adjust the items you have selected to arrive at a combination that's more suitable for your needs and within your budget.

PC SELECTION GUIDE

Long Form - Page 1

Write the maximum amount you are willing to spend for the PC, software and peripherals:$_____
Select or write-in the cost of the software packages that you need, then circle each item.

Word Processing

Basic features: margins, line spacings, bold, italic, underline, multi-column, spell checker, thesaurus
Advanced features: all of the above plus hyphenation, grammar checker, outlining, cutting/pasting
Average advertised prices: Basic $50 Advanced $200 Other$_____

Spreadsheet

Basic Features: over 256 rows and 256 columns, formulas, templates
Advanced features: all of the above plus macros, charting, 3-D
Average advertised prices: Basic $50 Advanced $200 Other $_____

Database

Basic features: multiple fields, descriptions, formatting, sorting, reports
Advanced features: all of the above plus import/export filters, query functions, templates
Average advertised prices: Basic $50 Advanced $200 Other $_____

Integrated Packages

Basic features: word processing, spreadsheet, database, spell checking
Advanced features: all of the above plus charting, telecommunications, page layout
Average advertised prices: Basic $50 Advanced $150 Other $_____

Business Accounting

Basic features: chart of accounts, credits, debits, general ledger, A/R, A/P, financial reports
Advanced features: all of the above plus inventory, payroll, billing, order entry, forms design
Average advertised prices: Basic $100 Advanced $200 Other $_____

Other Types of Software

	Basic	Advanced	Other
Personal Finance	$35	$100	$
Desktop Publishing	$85	$400	$
Utilities	$30	$150	$
CAD	$75	$1500	$
Games	$10	$50	$
Entertainment	$10	$50	$

PC Guide ™   © **Inter Trade Corporation, Norcross, Georgia**

Long Form - Page 2

Circle the amounts for the printer (s) and other peripherals that you need.

Printers

Printers with advanced features have the following advantages over the basic models:

higher speed	more emulations	better resolution	more fonts
more memory	better paper handling	color upgrade	low noise

Dot Matrix	Basic	Advanced	Other
9-Pin, standard	$150	$250	$
9-Pin, wide	$220	$320	$
24-Pin, standard	$225	$350	$
24-Pin, wide	$350	$500	$
Ink Jet	$300	$600	$
Thermal Transfer	$300	$500	$
Laser			
Standard	$600	$1500	$
Postscript and/or 600x600	$1500	$3000	$

Other Peripherals

	Basic	Advanced	Other
Mouse/Trackball	$15	$100	$
Joystick	$15	$50	$
Fax/Modem			
14,400 internal	$150	$250	$
14,400 external	$200	$300	$
Scanner			
handheld	$150	$300	$
flatbed	$500	$1500	$
CD-ROM drive			
internal dbl speed w/controller	$250	$400	$
external dbl speed w/controller	$300	$500	$
Sound Card/ 2 Speakers			
16 bit, stereo, digital	$100	$250	$
Tape Backup	$250	$400	$

PC Guide TM   © **Inter Trade Corporation, Norcross, Georgia**

Tally up the total amounts you have allocated for Software, Printer and Peripherals from Pages 1 and 2, and write it in this box: $

Subtract the amount in the box from the total budget you have allocated for the entire system on page 1 and write it in this box: $

Cost Matrix

In each microprocessor family listed in the table below, circle the cost of the items you need to have in your system. Total the numbers circled in each column and enter the amount at the bottom of the table. Compare the amount you have left for the PC with the totals below to see which PC family you can afford within your budget.

Bare bones system consists of the following components:				
case	motherboard	power supply	floppy drive	1 MB RAM
keyboard	drive controller	parallel/serial		

Components	386DX	486SX	486DX	486DX2
Bare bones system	(300)	(400)	(500)	(700)
4 MB RAM (total memory)	120	120	120	120
120 MB hard drive	220	220	220	220
170 MB hard drive	260	260	260	260
250 MB hard drive	300	300	300	300
340 MB hard drive	350	350	350	350
additional floppy drive	60	60	60	60
VGA card + mono monitor	160	160	160	160
VGA card + color monitor	250	250	250	250
SVGA card + color monitor	350	350	350	350
SVGA card + non-int monit.	400	400	400	400
Totals				

Recommended PC Types

If you have completed the selection form at this point, you have developed a keener appreciation for the tremendous choices that you are going to face. When you start approaching various suppliers you'll notice that the number of choices will increase again. Selecting a PC recommended by someone else is a very subjective process. The friend or co-worker who recommends a PC may be speaking from very limited exposure to one type of system. The salesperson may be inclined to favor the brands he sells. If you are a novice, you don't have easy access to or understanding of the highly technical comparisons performed by various organizations.

Based on our years of combined experience in using, manufacturing, selling, and supporting PCs, we have developed some generic recommendations. As discussed earlier, this process is very subjective. Use our recommendations as a guideline that you can and should modify according to your specific needs and circumstances. For example, if you live in Ames, Iowa, where a few computer stores sell a limited selection mostly at list price, you face a different set of circumstances than if you live in Atlanta, Georgia, and have hundreds of suppliers competing for your business with cut-throat prices.

We don't recommend buying an 8088, or 80286 based system (XT or AT compatible) anymore. Even if your budget is very limited, you can cut out some of the frills but at least get an 80386-SX system. Newer programs offer so much more power and so many more features that they really need at least an 80386-SX based system.

In our opinion, the most suitable entry level system is based on the 80486-SX processor. It offers you the 32 bit processing power that's fast being incorporated into software, yet it's the least expensive of the 80486 family. Therefore, if you don't have a specific performance requirement for home or even business use, we recommend that you start out by considering the 80486-SX systems. If you find out that your budget lets you buy a more powerful system, by all means do so.

We don't have any opinions on various brand names. This area is somewhat subjective and depends on many different variables. Suffice it to say that the majority of systems on the market today are very high quality and very reliable. Our only word of caution is to avoid purchasing from fly-by-night operations. From what we described earlier in this book, you should know by now that the brand name on the box does not mean that all the components inside are from that manufacturer.

The amount of memory you should buy depends on your needs and your budget. We recommend that you get at least 2 MB of RAM. If you plan to use Windows, then you should have 4 MB of RAM. Just make sure that your system has built-in sockets for at least 16 MB of RAM on the motherboard. Avoid systems that require proprietary memory modules. They'll usually cost more when you are ready to upgrade.

The size of your hard disk drive depends on your needs and your budget. Newer programs offer a wealth of features, but also gobble up a lot of hard disk space. Chances are that, over a period of time, you'll add more software and more data to your hard disk, an easier task if you start with a reasonable amount of storage capacity. Just as you can live in a one bedroom apartment or a five bedroom house, your comfort level is the determining factor in choosing the hard disk capacity. We recommend an 80 MB hard disk drive as a bare minimum. Ideally, you may opt for 120 or 200 MB.

As far as floppy drives are concerned, you can choose either high density 5.25" or 3.5", or both. 3.5" disks are easier to handle and to store. They also have a slightly higher capacity than their 5.25" counterparts. We definitely recommend that you have a 3.5" drive. However, if you don't have access to another PC with both drives in it, you may at times receive software or data on 5.25" disks, and have no way of using it. In that case, having both drives in your system might be useful.

The monitor plays a very important role in how you feel about your system. When you use your computer, you'll be staring at your monitor all the time. If you buy a monitor that you are really not happy with, you'll be unhappy with the entire system. Therefore, choose your monitor carefully and don't skimp. Fortunately for most of us, the available video standards have become more straightforward than other components. As indicated in earlier chapters, the CGA and EGA standards have been completely phased out. At the very low end you can buy a VGA monochrome monitor and a VGA board. If your budget permits, we strongly recommend that you buy a VGA color monitor. The pleasing, multi-color VGA display will definitely help you enjoy your computer a lot more. Within the color VGA range of performance, you can choose one that satisfies your needs and meets your budget. It's important for you to make special note of the brand of monitor you buy. Unlike a computer that has several independently replaceable components, if your monitor breaks down, the cost of the repair is often close to the cost of a new unit. Therefore, make sure that the monitor has at least a one year parts and labor warranty, and the brand is serviced locally.

As far as pointing devices are concerned, you definitely need to have one. Most programs, with or without Windows, are easier to use with a pointing device. You can choose a mouse or a trackball for that purpose. The selection is purely subjective, and is also tied to your budget. Some people feel more comfortable resting their palms on top of the mouse and move it. Others prefer to rest their palms on the trackball and move the ball with their thumb or fingers. In either case, make sure the device you choose is Microsoft Mouse compatible, and has at least a one year parts and labor warranty.

You have a wide selection of printers to choose from. Literally hundreds of models and brands are on the market today. Most of them are high quality products, and should give you several years of trouble free service. If you have a specific application that requires something like a laser, ink jet, or thermal printer, then you should look at several brands and compare their features, prices, and operating costs. Otherwise, we recommend that you buy a name brand dot matrix printer. If your budget is somewhat limited, look at a 9-pin standard size printer. If you can spend a little more, then we suggest a standard size 24-pin printer. Unless you will definitely need to print on paper wider than 11 inches, we recommend that you stay with a standard size printer.

As far as modems are concerned, you have a lot to choose from. Unless you have a specific application that requires otherwise, we recommend that you buy an internal 14400 BPS modem with send and receive fax capability. As long as the modem comes with at least a one year (preferably 5 years) parts and labor warranty, you can choose just about any Hayes or Hayes compatible brand that meets your budget.

Chapter 7. How And Where To Buy PC Products

This chapter will help you find the PC or the components that are right for you. You now have the knowledge and the tools to evaluate various PCs, you are ready to buy the best possible system that meets your criteria and gives you the greatest value. Of course, the easy way out is to walk into the nearest store and buy whatever the salesperson recommends. Or, pick up the phone and call a mail order company and order from an ad that sounds good. An astute buyer, on the other hand, takes a little more time to get the best, and the most bang for the buck. Since you have taken the time and the effort to come this far, you already are an astute buyer. This chapter will give you the tools to find the most appropriate system.

Before you start your shopping "adventure" make sure that you collect and review several pages containing computer advertisements in your local paper as well as at least one or two computer magazines. Mark the advertised prices for the systems that are of interest to you and within your price range so that you can compare them with the quotations you'll receive. Some computer suppliers may try to match prices with valid and similarly equipped systems, if you provide the necessary documentation.

7.1. Where to Buy a PC

When PCs were first introduced in the 1970's, they were initially sold in kit form to hobbyists through magazine ads. As PCs grew more sophisticated and more expensive, it became apparent that a specialized retail channel was necessary, and computer dealerships were born. In the early 1980's, computer dealers mushroomed all across the United States. Manufacturers preferred selling to computer dealers because, with proper training, they could better sell and support the manufacturer's computers. Customers preferred buying from computer dealers, because they needed the local support and availability of after-the-sale service.

In the mid 1980's, PC mail order companies were appearing out of no-where. Initially, they simply sold their systems based on lower prices. However, over the years they started to offer on-site warranty service by national service organizations, setup and preparation before shipping, and telephone support. The late 1980's gave birth to the computer super stores, which move high volumes of products at lower margins. At about the same time, warehouse clubs and office supply chains began carrying pre-configured PCs. So did department stores, discount stores, and other chain stores. The widespread availability of PCs through thousands of suppliers has helped drive down prices and bring them within easy reach of most people. The following is a description of the various suppliers.

Computer Dealers

A handful of computer stores opened for business during the latter part of the 1970's. They mostly sold the first generation personal computers that were offered as individual components by their manufacturers. The dealers themselves were computer hobbyists turned businesspeople. They assembled various components in the backroom to create a system. When the original IBM PC was introduced in 1981, IBM and other PC manufacturers found it necessary to sell their products through computer dealers. Since then, thousands of computer dealers have opened stores and offices in practically every community in the United States.

The first generation PCs were quite basic. The IBM PC, for example, included the case, power supply, motherboard with 64 K of memory, a floppy drive, and a floppy drive controller. The dealer added the monitor, the video board, memory board, parallel and serial board, hard disk drive, hard drive controller, and other peripherals. The dealer's role was crucial in putting the whole system together to fill the customer's order. Some major computer manufacturers went so far as to sell only to dealers that they had authorized according to certain criteria. In the mid 1980's, as the number of IBM compatible PC manufacturers increased, so did the number of dealers who carried brands other than IBM, Compaq, and Apple. Computer dealers are divided into two primary groups: independents and national chains. Most national dealers, and some independents, are authorized dealers for the major computer brands.

Independent dealers are often privately held. They may operate out of a store or an office and purchase most of their products from distributors who, in turn, buy from hundreds of manufacturers. They may also purchase some products directly from manufacturers or be authorized dealers for certain product lines. Most of them have a few products on display. In most small communities, the only computer dealer is usually an independent dealer. The advantage of buying from an independent dealer is that the owner often runs the business with a personal touch. If you are not familiar with computers, they may take the time to explain things to you, and often you deal with and get to know the same person over the years. The disadvantages of buying from small dealers are that they may not have the strong financial backing to survive very weak economic periods, they may not have a wide selection on display, and, for more sophisticated applications, some may not have the necessary in-house expertise. You can find the name and address of your local dealers in the Yellow Pages under "computer dealers."

Dealers with national chain affiliation are divided into two groups: company owned and franchises. As far as you, the customer is concerned, they are both the same. Most of these dealers are very similar to an independent dealer. Their operations do follow a chainwide pattern, however. Some chains have better training programs for their sales staff and technicians than smaller independents. However, the fact that a dealer is part of a chain is not a guarantee of quality. For most home PC buyers, the fact that a supplier is affiliated with a dealer chain will not make any difference. Large organizations with facilities throughout the United States often establish national contracts with the national dealer chains for the sake of uniformity. These dealers can also be found in the Yellow Pages.

There are no hard and fast rules about which supplier to choose. Some dealers charge the full manufacturer's suggested retail price plus the added cost of consulting and service, while others may charge as low as 5% to 10% over their own costs. The quality of product knowledge and technical support may range from poor to excellent. If you like person-to-person interaction during and after the purchase, the right dealer offers an excellent alternative.

When buying from a local dealer, you may be able to negotiate the price. Often, you get a few miscellaneous items thrown-in for free. The following is a brief list of suggestions:

- Take along pages of recent computer advertisements in the local paper.

- Be prepared to negotiate the price.

- Ask about a 30 day money-back guarantee.

- Ask about their service and repair policy and capabilities.

- Ask for free cables, disks, and shareware programs.

- Try to get free on-site service, at least during the first few weeks.

Computer Super Stores

During the past few years mega size (20,000 to 40,000 square foot) computer super stores have sprung up in most major cities. These stores often carry between 3,000 to 5,000 different computer-related items and have average annual sales of $20 to $60 million per store. They are often divided into departments, with one or more assigned salespeople who are often knowledgeable about the products in their respective departments. Their large space and huge variety of products may awe some people.

Their large sales volume per store enables them to buy most products directly from the manufacturers at distributor discount levels. They usually operate with margins ranging from 10% to 20% over their cost. This puts their prices at about what dealers often pay to their distributors. Individuals who are knowledgeable about computers and some organizations who have internal computer experts find the prices and availability offered by super stores irresistible.

Office Supply Stores

In the past few years, a large number of office supply stores have begun carrying computers and related products. Office supply super stores often have a separate department for PC hardware, software and supplies. They cater primarily to businesspeople. In some ways, they offer an environment similar to a computer super store. Unlike computer stores, they may not have as large a number of computer-related items or a service department. You may find that buying from an office supply store that offers wide selection and competitive prices is just as convenient.

Department Stores

In the early 1980's, a number of department stores got into the computer business, but got out of it a couple of years later. At that time computers and software were more complex to package and sell than they are today. In recent years, with the pre-packaging and preparation work performed by most PC manufacturers, department stores are again finding it profitable to sell computers.

PCs are often sold in the audio/visual departments, and the salesperson(s) working in that area may or may not be familiar with the product. The lines of computers they sell are often specifically prepared so that they can be purchased and hooked up almost like a TV or VCR. People who are traditional department store shoppers may find it more convenient to buy a home computer from their favorite store. Obviously, these stores don't carry nearly the number of PC related products that are carried by specialized computer stores.

Discount Stores

As the cost of PCs decline, more people can afford to own a home computer. A number of discount store chains have begun to carry low-end, competitively priced systems. They offer an environment similar to department stores. Their low prices and heavy promotions attract a large number of customers. Depending on where you are located and the bargains offered by your local discount stores, they may be able to satisfy your needs.

Wholesale Clubs

Wholesale membership clubs, which offer large warehouses full of products, have become a major supplier of PCs for small businesses. They operate on the basis of very large volumes, very low margins, and a few product lines. They often carry one or two models of computers and printers at deeply discounted levels. These stores usually don't have in-store sales and service experts. They usually suggest that you call the manufacturer's toll-free phone number for questions and service.

Mail Order Companies

In recent years, the mail order computer business has mushroomed into a multi-billion dollar industry. Mail order companies have grown quite sophisticated in their products, operation, sales, and service. Some of these companies, although less than ten years old, have annual sales exceeding a billion dollars. There are two groups of mail order companies in this industry: The first group manufactures or assembles computers for sale under their own label. The second group sells computers, peripherals, and software produced by other companies. Currently about 20% of all PCs are sold through the mail, a number projected to increase to 25% by 1995.

Mail order suppliers used to be the least expensive and, sometimes, the riskiest type of supplier. Now some of them have grown to be more reliable than traditional channels. Some mail order computer companies now invest a noticeable amount of their revenue in research and development. They design and build their own systems. The majority, however, buy components from various manufacturers and assemble them according to customers' orders. The quality and the reliability of the components they use determine the quality of the systems they produce.

Almost all mail order companies have a toll-free 800 phone number to place orders. Some also have toll-free technical support lines. Most systems come with a warranty on parts and labor. Some offer on-site warranty service performed by national service organizations. When ordering systems from mail order suppliers, it's very helpful to know about the size of the company, the length of time they have been in business, and their return policy.

The second group of mail order companies sells computers plus various peripherals and software. They often sell national brand names at deep discounted prices. Well-established and solid organizations often provide a very viable and convenient service.

Following is a list of things you should check when choosing a mail order supplier for your system:

- Look for companies that advertise regularly.

- Avoid companies with no street address in their ads.

- Look for a thirty-day money-back guarantee with no restocking charges.

- Insist that if parts fail shortly after your purchase, they should be replaced with new parts immediately.

- If your purchase is based on an ad or a catalog, keep a copy for your records.

- The printed document is legal; the verbal promise of a salesperson is not.

- Make sure that they offer (800) toll-free numbers for sales and service.

- Ask by whom and where the warranty service is performed.

- Before ordering the system, get the exact amount of shipping and handling charges.

7.2. How to Pay For Your System

Whether you are buying your computer system from a local supplier or through mail order, we strongly recommend that you pay by credit card, if possible. You are buying a complex system made up of many diverse components. Your supplier could be an outfit that sells a complete system from a major manufacturer, or it could be purchasing components from various manufacturers and assembling them to your needs and requirements. In either case, the first few weeks of operation are critical to the long-term health of your system. If there are major defects in your system, they'll show-up during the first few weeks of rigorous use. Having paid by credit card, you have much stronger leverage to return the unit to your supplier for repair, replacement, or refund.

Most purchases from local suppliers are not as critical as those from out-of-town companies. With a local supplier, you have more access to the seller, as well as law enforcement and legal support. However, with our ever-fluctuating economy and occasional failure of small and large businesses, it's still a good idea to charge your PC purchases.

Buying your system by mail often saves you more money, but it does pose some risks. When you buy from an out-of-town supplier, you have no clue as to the size and stability of the supplier. On top of that, you are buying a system without having seen it. Mail order computer sales are measured in the billions of dollars a year. For the most part, the process works successfully, but there are rare occasions when a customer does not receive the product or service ordered. Paying by credit card lowers your risk and gives you the peace of mind that you are protected in case anything goes wrong during the first few weeks. There are several guidelines and laws that you should be aware of:

> ● The Federal Trade Commission (FTC) has a law called the Mail-order Rule, which requires the mail order merchant to ship the ordered merchandise within thirty days from receipt of the order and payment, or offer the buyer a chance to cancel the order with a full refund. Under this law, the merchant can charge your credit card at the time of your order, but not ship the order to you for thirty days.

> ● The financial organizations that process credit card sales for the merchants have a different rule that dictates that sellers specifically cannot submit a credit sales slip unless the merchandise has been shipped or the services for that transaction have been performed. Therefore, although the FTC rule may not protect you during the first thirty days, the financial organization that pays the merchant can reduce your risk.

> ● Reputable merchants want to keep your business and keep you happy for their own continued growth and success. The financial institution that accepts the credit sales receipts from a merchant knows that if a seller keeps charging bogus sales or has unfulfilled sales, it will be challenged by the card holder, and eventually the financial institution will have to foot the bill if the seller fails. Therefore, you have two forces besides the federal government to protect you in most situations when you charge your PC purchase.

7.3. PC Buying Guide

The "PC Buying Guide" supplied with the book will help you establish some basic prices for the type of system you have selected from the previous chapter. After you complete the form, you can start shopping around. The form has five columns. The first column lists the various components and peripherals. The second column is for you to enter the specific items you have selected for your system. The remaining three columns are for entering specific information or costs from three different suppliers.

PC BUYING GUIDE

Item	Desired PC System	Supplier A _____	Supplier B _____	Supplier C _____
Bare bones System				
RAM				
Hard disk drive				
Extra floppy				
Video + Monitor				
DOS				
Windows				
Mouse				
Modem				
Printer				
CD-ROM				
Sound card				

Total $_____ $_____ $_____

Cache memory on motherboard	☐	☐	☐
On-site warranty	☐	☐	☐
Extended warranty beyond 1 year	☐	☐	☐
Non-interlaced SVGA monitor	☐	☐	☐
Utilities or integrated software included	☐	☐	☐

PC Guide ™   © **Inter Trade Corporation, Norcross, Georgia**

For best results, follow these steps:

● Make extra copies of the Buying Guide and use a pencil to complete the form.

● At a local book store, library, computer store or supermarket, look at several computer magazines. Choose one that has quite a number of PC advertisements complete with prices and descriptions. Buy it or check it out.

● Carefully review the magazine and choose two PC advertisements from companies that sound familiar to you or have prominent ads, have fully detailed information, and have prices that are in-line with most of the rest.

● In each of the two advertisements, choose a PC that closely matches the system you selected from the previous chapter.

● Enter the cost of each system separately in the first and second columns. Note any differences they may have from your list of selected system components.

● At the bottom of the "Buying Guide" is a box that contains a list of several unique items that may be included with some systems. They are listed separately because there are so many variations that it will be confusing to attach a value to them. Simply check off the items offered by each supplier, and at the end, assign your personal value to those items.

● Use this form and a blank copy of the "Buying Guide" to shop for your system. You can start by visiting or calling suppliers that you are familiar with or that have been recommended to you by friends and co-workers.

● Write down the prices and features offered by these suppliers in the available columns. Also note any special differences that you may have observed between the products, the salespeople, and other important factors.

● After you have checked prices with at least three suppliers, you can start comparing total prices. If some items are not similar to those you have selected, use the costs in the cost matrix on page 3 of the "PC Selection Guide" to equalize the differences. For example, if you are looking for a 200 MB hard disk drive and one of the suppliers offers a 120 MB drive instead, you can find the price difference between the two drives from the cost matrix and then add that amount to the cost of the system.

● While you are shopping around, remember some of the points discussed earlier in this chapter. Make sure that the supplier appears to be a financially stable company. Observe the helpfulness of the salespeople. Ask about their technical support and service staff. Above all, make sure you feel comfortable buying from them.

● One of the important documents that you should read carefully (before making the purchase) is the equipment warranty. They are usually no more than one or two pages, but what they say and what they cover may save you hundreds of dollars, if anything goes wrong with your system.

● After you have completed your shopping, carefully review the "Buying Guide." As much as possible, using the cost matrix if necessary, try to equalize the offerings from various suppliers.

● You should be able to arrive at one or two top candidates. At this point if you have developed a personal preference, take the Buying Guide to that supplier (or call them if it's a mail order firm), and review it with a salesperson. If their price is higher than others, don't hesitate to let them know that you would like to buy from them except for the price difference. You'll be surprised to find that in most cases that supplier will try to meet or come close to your price. This is a very competitive industry, and if suppliers discover that you are a smart shopper they'll try to meet your price. You may save hundreds of dollars and buy your system from a supplier that you will enjoy dealing with.

● Before ordering the system, ask the salesperson if he will throw in free diskettes, some paper, the printer cable, and even a surge protector. It never hurts to ask. More than half the time, to your surprise, they may agree to do so!

Following is a sample of a completed "Buying Guide" based on systems offered by three different suppliers. This is just a sample and not an indication of the type of prices you may find.

PC BUYING GUIDE

Item	Desired PC System	Supplier A Dealer	Supplier B Super Store	Supplier C Mail Order
Bare bones System	486-SX 33 MHZ	1,150	1,250	1,099
RAM	4 MB	incl.	incl.	incl.
Hard disk drive	170 MB	incl.	incl.	+40 120 MB incl.
Extra floppy	Don't need	—	—	—
Video + Monitor	VGA Color	incl.	incl.	incl.
DOS	MS-DOS	incl.	incl.	incl.
Windows	Yes	+55	incl.	+50
Mouse	2 Button Serial	+22	incl.	+15
Modem	14,400 BPS/Fax	+155	+130	+145
Printer	9-Pin Standard	+170	+160	+165
CD-ROM				
Sound card				
Total		$1,552	$1,540	$1,514

	Supplier A	Supplier B	Supplier C
Cache memory on motherboard	☒	☒	☒
On-site warranty	☐	☐	☒
Extended warranty beyond 1 year	☐	☐	☐
Non-interlaced SVGA monitor	☐	☐	☐
Utilities or integrated software included	☐	☒	☐

PC Guide ™   © **Inter Trade Corporation, Norcross, Georgia**

7.4. Buying a Used PC

Almost everyone has bought a used car, pre-owned home, or at least some kind of used electrical equipment like a TV, stereo, or calculator at sometime in his or her life. After the first few days, the sensation of ownership is basically the same whether the item was bought new or used. On the other hand, the cost of ownership may be very different. Other than real estate, which normally appreciates in value, all other personal property has a tendency to depreciate over time. Sometimes the value drops immediately after a product is purchased and taken out of the box. PCs depreciate somewhat faster than other equipment, because of time and usage. Technological obsolescence is a major factor in the low price of used PCs. As mentioned earlier, new advances are made almost daily and, unless a PC is at a reasonably advanced technological and performance platform, it may not be able to take advantage of the speed, power, and conveniences offered by new programs.

Pros

If you are a real bargain hunter, you might be able to find a used PC that meets your needs at a fraction of the cost of a new system. Often the PC has worked for several months or a few years, it has the operating system already installed, and as a bonus, you may be able to get some useful applications software. Other than technological obsolescence, PCs usually don't deteriorate significantly with age. Therefore, an old PC doesn't necessarily mean higher maintenance and repair costs.

Cons

Used PCs usually don't carry any type of warranty, and unlike an automobile, you can't check the mileage. Therefore, along with the savings, you do accept a higher degree of risk. The majority of PCs operate flawlessly for many years. As with any product, there is the occasional lemon to watch out for. When fixing a problem with a used PC, you have fewer resources to call on for help. It's also important to check that the system is not stolen.

Sources

The best sources for used PCs are often large businesses which upgrade their systems frequently. Their systems are usually better cared for and may have better quality components inside. However, those businesses don't advertise to the general public. Their PCs are usually sold through dealers and used computer sources. Most larger cities and metropolitan areas have computer exchange companies that act as brokers between buyers and sellers. They charge the seller a fee of around 10% for listing the equipment and advertising. The equipment usually stays with the seller until the sale is completed. This may sometimes make it difficult or impossible to test the PC. To locate a computer exchange near you, check the local phone directory under "Used Computer Dealers." Also check with other computer dealers to see if they have any used computers for sale. Sometimes they may be able to offer some sort of warranty protection against defects.

Pricing

Prices of used PCs don't follow a precise formula. With hundreds of manufacturers and rapidly declining prices, it's difficult to establish a reliable benchmark like the used car price book. If you intend to buy a used PC, your first step should be to find the price of a new, comparable system. Based on what you have learned so far, you know that comparable means same brand and similarly equipped. Some of the nationally known sources for current pricing of used PCs are the National Computer Exchange in New York City (800-359-2468); the Boston Computer Exchange in Boston, Massachusetts (617-542-4414); and the American Computer Exchange in Atlanta, Georgia (800-786-0717).

As a rule of thumb, you can use the following guideline for determining the approximate value of a used PC.

● Keep the cost of the PC system (system unit including memory, floppy drive(s), hard disk drive, graphics card and monitor) separate from the printer, modem, scanner, tape backup drive, CD drive, mouse, software, etc. They depreciate differently.

● Find the current cost of similarly equipped PCs and peripherals from magazine ads.

● Subtract 15% of the cost of the PC if the used system does not come with a one year parts and labor warranty.

● Subtract 15% of the cost of the PC for every year of age of the used system.

● Used printers, modems, and other peripherals are usually worth between 40% to 60% of their current new pricing.

● Software that is installed on the hard disk of a system often has no resale value because it is upgraded by the manufacturers so frequently. However, having good, current versions of software and accompanying documentation with a used PC may just be the icing on the cake for some buyers.

Test Before You Buy

When buying a used PC it's very important to test the system very carefully. After you have agreed on a satisfactory price for the used PC, ask if you can test the system. There are several tools you may need to take with you:

- A pair of flat blade and Phillips screwdrivers.

- A bootable DOS disk and several blank floppy disks.

- A diagnostic program like Checkit, AMI Diag, ASQ, PC Tools, or Norton Utilities.

Testing the system and peripherals may take up to an hour. Make sure the seller does not mind your poking into and playing with the computer for that long.

- Carefully inspect the exterior of the system. Existence of dirt and dents may indicate carelessness or abuse.

- Listen for unusual noises. There are only three moving components in a PC; the fan, the floppy drive, and the hard disk drive. The fan and the hard disk drive always run when the computer is turned on and should make a consistent whirring sound. The floppy drive should make a faint whirring sound only when it's reading from or writing to a floppy disk. Unusually loud noises or rattling may be a sign of trouble. A faulty fan or floppy drive may cost between $60 and $90 to replace. A problem with the hard drive may cost more than $200 to fix or replace, depending on the type and capacity of the drive.

- Try out the keyboard by just typing random characters. Make sure you are comfortable with the feel of the keyboard. Some keyboards click when you press a key, some are mushy, and some have a strong springy feel. Check each individual key to make sure it works and does not stick. As you press each key, verify that it appears on the monitor correctly. The "Cap Lock," "Num Lock," and "Scroll Lock" keys should light up when you press them. Lift up the keyboard and gently shake it while you turn it upside down. There should be no loose parts inside the keyboard, and the keys should not fall out. If there is a problem with the keyboard, remember that replacing it with a new one will run from $30 to $60.

- Inspect the monitor very carefully. You'll be looking at it all the time! Watch out for flickers, skewed or out-of-focus characters, shadows, or other abnormalities on the screen. Change the information on the screen from all characters to graphics and vice versa to make sure the monitor performs well under all circumstances. If a monitor is left on for a long time with a particular set of information on the display, the shadow of that information may be permanently burned in on the surface of the screen, which will be annoying when you use your favorite programs with different patterns on the screen. If you have to replace the monitor, remember that a new monochrome VGA monitor may cost between $100 and $150, and a color monitor may cost $250 or more.

After checking out the exterior of the PC, turn it off and wait for about 30 seconds. If the PC has a hard disk drive, it should stop making a whirring sound. Make sure there are no disks in the floppy disk drive(s). Turn the computer back on and watch the screen. The fan and the hard disk drive should start making their normal whirring sounds. The hard disk drive should be active, booting up the computer and looking for the DOS commands. However, it should not make any noticeably different sounds. After a few seconds the name of the system BIOS should appear on the top left corner of the screen. The most commonly recognized compatible BIOS brands are AMI, Award, DTK, and Phoenix. If the PC is a national name brand, it may display the PC brand name instead. Most computers also count the amount of RAM memory after displaying the BIOS. Make sure it counts up to the amount the Seller indicates is in the system. Many VGA video adapters will also show the amount of RAM on board (i.e., 256 K, 512 K, or 1 MB).

Depending on the way the seller has set up the hard disk drive, you may need to press "ENTER" a couple of times to get to the "C:>" prompt, or it may automatically get you to "C:>" or a menu. At this point, turn the computer off, wait 30 seconds, and repeat the above procedures a couple of times. If everything checks out, proceed to the next step.

Turn the computer off, place a bootable DOS disk in floppy drive A: and turn the computer back on. The computer should boot up from drive A: and after a couple of "ENTER's" you should get "A:>". Try formatting a bootable disk by typing FORMAT A:/S and then pressing "ENTER." The computer will read instructions from the DOS disk and then prompt you to put a blank disk in drive A and press "ENTER" afterwards. Follow directions and format a new bootable disk. Afterwards, turn the computer off, place the new disk in drive A:, and turn the computer back on. It should boot up the same way as with your original DOS disk. Put the original DOS disk in drive A: and type DISKCOPY A: A: and then press "ENTER" to copy the entire contents of that disk onto the other. Follow the directions on the screen to make a duplicate. Afterwards, type "DIR" to see a directory of the disk contents on the screen.

If a printer is sold with the package or is attached to the PC, turn it on and test it by holding down the "Shift" key and then pressing the "Print Screen" key. The entire contents of the screen should print on the printer. If there is any type of word processing software on the hard disk drive, try using it by typing a few lines, then having them printed.

Use your diagnostic software to check out various components. Different test programs work differently. Make sure the test program will not alter anything on the hard disk drive before using it. Ask the Seller if using your particular test program is allowed on the system. Check for the amount of memory, the capacity of floppy and hard disk drive(s), the parallel and serial ports, as well as other elements. If you don't have a diagnostic program, use the DOS command "CHKDSK/F" to find out the amount of memory and the size of the hard drive.

Check Inside the PC

After you have checked everything to your satisfaction, it's time to peek inside the PC itself. Ask the Seller if you can open up the base unit. Turn everything off and wait about 30 seconds for the hard disk drive to stop. Use the proper screwdriver to take the cover screws off. Carefully slide and/or lift off the cover. Before you touch anything inside the PC, touch the stainless steel box in the back of the PC to discharge any static electricity you may have on you. Inside the PC, look for loose parts, drives, or adapter boards. Check the memory chips and others inserted in sockets for secureness. The chips should be firmly seated in their sockets. Look at the power rating of the Power Supply. It should be at least 150 Watts. Count the total number of expansion slots and the number available. Verify that all the necessary controller boards as stated by the Seller are present inside the PC. Most PCs should have a video board, drive controller, Input/Output board for parallel and serial ports, as well other boards for extra memory, internal modem, etc.

Warranty

Most used PCs are already past their warranty periods. Some used computer exchange companies offer a warranty ranging from thirty days to one year. Usually, however, used PCs are sold as is. Therefore, adjust the value of the used PC according to how much recourse you have in case of minor or major problems. For example, a used PC purchased from a friend or co-worker may be more reliable than one purchased from a total stranger through a newspaper ad. If purchasing from a total stranger, it may be wise to pay with two separate checks: one check for about 80% of the price, and the other check post-dated 30 days for the remaining 20%.

Request a "Bill of Sale" from the Seller. It should list the date; the purchase price, the quantity and description of components; serial numbers, the name, address and phone number of the Seller; as well as any warranties or understandings that may accompany the sale.

Chapter 8. Setting Up And Fine Tuning Your PC

This chapter reviews the steps you need to take to make sure that your PC is properly set up. If you have just bought your PC with the help of this book, there is a section that shows you how to hook it up. Even if you've had your PC for a while read this section. It will help you understand what all those cable connections are for.

8.1. Creating a Safe Area for Your PC

Your PC and its peripherals represent a system that only twenty years ago required a large, specially built, chilled room and several technicians. Although you no longer have to baby-sit your computer like the old days, you can't simply treat it like a TV set, either. The environment where your PC is going to be used should be set up properly with enough space to accommodate your PC and peripherals like the printer, mouse, etc. Your desk and chair are going to be very important in determining how comfortable you'll be, using your PC. Based on the type of system you have, you probably have an idea how you'd like to set up your computer. Your comfort and convenience are the most important factors. The PC is just a machine and it can be set up anywhere you have free space. The rule of thumb is that if you are comfortable then your PC is probably comfortable too!

Power Source

Your PC and its peripherals need to be connected to a 110 volt AC power outlet. You need to make sure a wall outlet is nearby. For added safety, you should check to make sure that the outlet is properly grounded. Also make sure that the outlet is not part of a circuit used by other major appliances (e.g. copier, refrigerator, etc.).

Phone Line

If you have a modem or a Fax or plan to purchase one in the near future, you should have a phone outlet nearby. Like the power connection, make sure that you don't end up with phone wires running all over the floor.

Lighting

Proper lighting is very important to how well you will use and enjoy your PC. Make sure that the area where the PC is going to be used is well lit. Avoid light aimed directly at the monitor because the reflections on the screen are uncomfortable and will cause eye strain.

Ventilation

Components inside a PC create heat; if the heat stays inside the unit, it'll damage your system and cause malfunctions. The fan inside the power supply circulates the air inside the PC. It pulls in cooler air and moves it past the heat-generating components. It's important that the path of the air flow remain clear. The room temperature should not be less than 50 or more than 100 degrees. Otherwise, the extreme cold or heat may damage some components or cause them to shrink or expand slightly, eventually leading to failure.

8.2. Hazards You Should Avoid

Your PC is a marvel of technological innovations in all of its hundreds of components. Most components are made of solid state electronics, which means that there are no moving parts or parts that may fail easily. Under normal operating conditions, your PC should faithfully perform its duties for many trouble-free years. You should take the following steps to make sure your PC is protected from various hazards:

Power Surges

The AC power current that flows through your home or office fluctuates slightly. If several big power-consuming appliances are connected to the same circuit breaker, whenever they start or stop, they can create a surge in electricity. PCs are sensitive to receiving a fairly steady flow of electricity, and may not operate properly without it. Air conditioning units, refrigerators, dishwashers, washers, dryers, copiers and laser printers are appliances that draw a lot of current when they first start up. If your PC is connected to the same circuit breaker with one or more of these units, you may notice some irregularities in your PC's operation. You should use an outlet for your PC that does not share a breaker with one of these appliances. It's highly recommended that you use 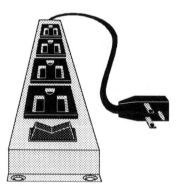 a surge protector to connect your PC and other peripherals to the wall outlet.

Static Electricity

Remember the little annoying zap you feel when you touch something, usually after walking on plush carpeting, on dry winter days? That zap is a result of the build-up of static electricity in your body. It doesn't harm you or the person you touch. However, computers are sensitive to static electricity and the results can be devastating. If you zap the case or the keyboard, the result may be that your computer will reset without any damage. On the other hand, if you zap while you are handling or touching a component inside your PC, the permanent information set by the factory in some ROM chips may be wiped clean. That could render a board or a hard disk drive totally useless. There are several precautions you should exercise to avoid both types of problems.

During normal use of your PC you can do one or more of the following to avoid static build up:

● Increase humidity in the room to above 30 percent by adding a plant to the room.

● Use an antistatic keyboard mat or floor mat.

● If you don't have a static mat, place a small 2 x 4 inch piece of aluminum foil near the case or keyboard and touch it first before touching any parts of your computer.

Magnetic Fields

Several components in and around a PC use the magnetic principle to store information. Floppy disks, the hard disk, and data storage tapes are very sensitive to magnets. You should avoid putting anything with magnets near these items or the data stored on them may be wiped clean.

Moisture and Humidity

Keep your PC away from areas with too much moisture or humidity. Similarly, keep liquids away from your PC and its keyboard. A small spill on the keyboard may cause a short circuit and damage it permanently. The same thing may happen to your PC. Eating, drinking, and smoking near your PC are not recommended.

8.3. Moving Your PC Around

Whether you just bought a new PC, or decided to move your PC across the hall, across town or across the country there are certain things that need to be done to make sure that nothing gets damaged. If you have just bought or received a new PC, the first thing to do is examine the shipping boxes for exterior damage. If you are moving your PC refer to Section 12.3 for guidelines. If you are shipping your PC, make sure that you use the original boxes and foam supports that came with it. If they are not available, use crumpled newspapers around the PC to protect it from damage.

8.4. Unpacking Your New PC

If you have just bought a new PC follow the steps outlined here for unpacking it. Instead of ripping the boxes apart to take everything out in less than 5 seconds, take your time. You should have already decided where you'd like everything to be located. The next few steps walk you through the unpacking process:

● Open the box containing the system unit (usually the largest box) and remove all the books, cables, and other unattached items inside. Carefully lift the base unit out of the box and remove the packing foam from around it. Place the base unit in the area you have already designated for it.

● Open the box containing the monitor and remove the book and other unattached items. Carefully lift the monitor out of the box and remove the packing foam from around it. Place the monitor in the area you have in mind.

● Unpack and take out the keyboard. Place it on the desk in front of the monitor.

● If you have purchased a mouse, take it out of the box and place it near the keyboard.

● If you have purchased a printer and other external devices, take them out of their respective boxes the same way and place them in their designated areas.

● Carefully check the exterior of every component to make sure there are no visible signs of dents or damage. If you notice anything, make a note of it so that you can immediately contact your supplier.

● Check the boxes to make sure there are no loose parts laying around anywhere. If you notice any parts in a box, take them out and put them next to the device they came with.

● Open the manual or accompanying paperwork with each device. In the first chapter or section you should find a list of everything you are supposed to receive in the box for that device. Compare the list with everything you have unpacked.

● Put all the packing foam and wrappers back in their respective boxes.

Keep all the boxes and packing materials for at least 30 days, preferably for a year.

8.5. Hooking Up Your PC

Hooking up a PC may seem very complicated at first. All those cables running all over the place can be intimidating. But it's much simpler than you think. Just remember that most devices need to be hooked up to an electric power source in order to work. They also need to be hooked up to the PC with another cable in order to send signals back and forth. Therefore, most devices have two cables. One is for power and the other is for transferring signals to the PC. Power cables are very obvious. Signal cables have unique shapes that makes it easy to determine what goes where.

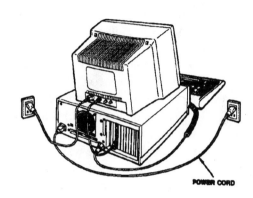

Manufacturers often try to take the guesswork out of connecting cables to the PC. Most plug connections and cables have unique shapes that mate them together. They may be an elongated "D" or a circle with a notch, etc. As you are connecting a cable to a plug, make sure that you are able to see everything clearly. Don't attempt to connect a cable to the back of the PC when you are standing in the front. The following steps, along with the guidelines in your operating manual(s), should help you connect your PC together safely:

● Locate and read the chapter on unpacking and hooking up your base unit.

● Most new PCs have labels identifying their plug connections. Your base unit should have connections for the following attachments:

    - AC Power
    - Keyboard
    - Monitor
    - Mouse

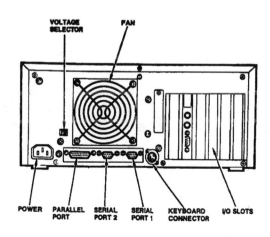

- Printer
- Serial port
- Game port (option)
- Scanner port (option)

● Locate and connect the AC power cord to the back of your PC, but don't plug it into the wall yet.

● Connect your keyboard to the appropriate plug on the PC.

● Your monitor has two cables connected to it: the AC power cord and the video cable. Leave the power cord alone for now. Connect the other cable to the back of your PC. More than likely, your video cable has an elongated "D" shape with some pins inside it. Your video connection on the back of the PC should have a similarly elongated "D" shape with some holes in it. If you look carefully, you'll notice that the cable connects to the plug only one way. Be careful not to bend the pins by forcing it.

● If you have a mouse, connect its cable to a similarly-shaped plug in the back of the PC. Mice only have one cable.

● If you have a printer, it'll have an AC power cord and a data cable. Don't connect the power cord yet. Connect one end of the data cable to the back or side of the printer and connect the other end of the cable to the back of the PC. The data cable has an elongated "D" shape at both ends, but each end is clearly identifiable from the other.

● If you have a joystick and your PC is equipped with a game port, attach its cable to the back of the PC. Joysticks have only one cable.

● If you have, as we strongly recommend, a power surge protector, plug all the power cables from the PC, monitor, and printer to the surge protector.

● Inside the floppy drive(s), you may find a square piece of cardboard; take it out and save it under the base unit. To protect the drive heads you should insert it back into the floppy drive every time you move your PC.

8.6. Preparing Your PC for Use

When you turn your PC on for the first time, depending on what components you have bought, whom you have bought it from, and what they have already done on your system, your PC will need different approaches to first time start-up.

When an IBM or compatible PC is turned on for the very first time, several activities take place. Those activities vary by the type of PC you have purchased and the preparation work already done to it. When a PC is turned on (called booting up), it will go through a self-diagnostic routine. During the self-diagnostic routine, most PCs display the amount of RAM (memory) being counted, the floppy drive(s) lights blink on momentarily and spin a little, the hard disk light blinks on, and then other devices like the tape backup and printer make some noises indicating that they are hooked up and receiving the signals. After self-diagnostic, your PC needs to find DOS (somewhere) in order to get started. It will always check the floppy drive(s) first, and if DOS is not there it will then search the hard disk drive. After reading the important parts of DOS from one of the disk drives, those DOS commands are transferred to RAM for easy access. They will remain in RAM for as long as your computer is powered up. When you turn your computer off, everything is wiped from RAM. When you turn it back on, the above process is repeated. If you don't have a hard disk drive, DOS needs to be in your floppy drive every time you boot up your PC. If you have a hard disk drive, then DOS needs to be transferred to it permanently so that your computer will always find it there and boot up from there. Therefore, depending on your system and the work done to it, you may face one of the following scenarios. If the heading of that scenario does not apply to your system, jump to the next scenario until you find one that matches your situation.

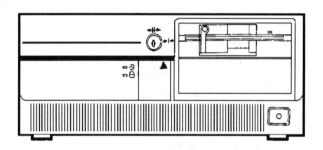

A. You only have one floppy disk drive and no hard disk drive:

    With this PC you will always need a bootable DOS disk in the floppy drive.

B. You have two floppy drives and no hard disk drive:

    With this PC you will also need a bootable DOS disk in one of the floppy drives.

C. You have one or two floppy drives and a hard disk drive:

    This is the configuration that the majority of PCs are sold. The hard disk drive will be used for boot up. However, initially it may have one of the following conditions:

1. Your supplier has already installed DOS on your hard disk

2. Your supplier has prepared your hard disk for use but has not installed DOS

3. Your hard disk is not prepared at all.

If your condition matches #1, then you can skip most of the following steps. Any of the other conditions require that you place a DOS diskette in your floppy drive before you turn it on for boot up.

8.7. Turning Your PC On for the First Time

Plug the AC power cable from the surge protector into your wall outlet. Leave the surge protector switch in the "off" position. Turn the power switches for the PC, monitor, and printer to the "on" position. Now turn on the surge protector switch.

When the power is turned on, several activities will take place within your PC. They happen within a few seconds, so you may not be able to keep up with all of them. Shortly after you turn on the switch, the monitor will show some characters. Most often you'll see the name brand of your PC on the top left corner of your screen.   Then, most computers display the amount of video RAM and a rapid count of the system RAM. Next, the indicator lights on the keyboard flash on momentarily; then the floppy drive(s) light comes on and the drive spins briefly; then the hard disk drive indicator light flashes momentarily, then the printer makes a clicking sound. This concludes the internal self-diagnostic part of your PC boot up. The computer then looks for DOS. If your condition matches #1 above, it'll start reading the hard disk drive and loads DOS into RAM. If you have put the DOS disk in your floppy drive, it will read DOS from there and load it into RAM.

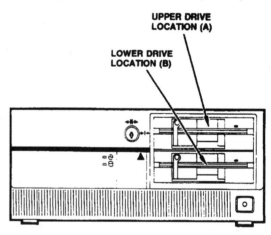

If you have one floppy drive it's called the A drive but shown as A:. If you have two floppy drives, the first one is A: and the second one is B:. If you have a hard disk drive it will be called the C: drive. Depending on which drive your PC reads DOS from, it'll show that drive's name on the screen. Drive names are followed by the point of an arrow (>) that's called the "prompt." For example, C:> is called the "C prompt," meaning that the computer is ready to use drive C: at this time. You can simply go from one drive to another by typing its name and then pressing the "ENTER" key. For example, to go from C:> to the first floppy drive, simply type A: and then press "ENTER."

8.8. Formatting Floppy Disks

One of the most important steps you need to take is to make backup copies of your important program disks. To copy disks, you need blank floppy disks that are properly prepared. Floppy disks are basically magnetic storage devices. In spite of all the quality control that goes into making the disks, parts of the magnetic surface will have some weak areas. Because computers

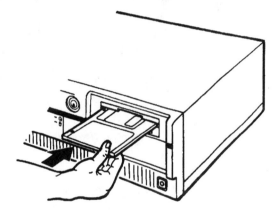

need extremely accurate data storage and retrieval, DOS needs to examine the surface of the disk to mark off the weak or defective areas. Just like your county road crew who mark around the pot holes and cracks so that they can come back and repair and resurface the road, DOS generously marks off the suspect areas and records their location. The marked-off locations are listed in a map at the beginning of the disk so that they can be avoided. This process is called formatting the disk.

Make sure you have several blank floppy disks available for making copies. At the drive prompt, type FORMAT A: and press "ENTER." The computer will look up the FORMAT command and then ask you to insert a blank disk in drive A:, and to press "ENTER." If you follow the directions you see on the screen, after about a minute the computer will come back to say "format is completed" and ask whether you want to format another disk. You can format as many disks as you wish.

8.9. Making Backup Copies of Program Disks

Programs that operate your PC or help you with various applications are sold on floppy disks. These disks are the main part of your purchase and if damaged, are not going to be replaced so easily. Novice computer users (and some veteran users as well!) may accidentally erase information from a program disk. When that happens, the entire program may be useless.

Therefore, it's important that you make a backup copy of your important program disks and then use them for installation purposes. If anything happens to one of your program copies, you can make another copy from the original.

Among the programs you should make a backup from are the operating system, the operating environment, and important and expensive application software. It only costs a few dollars per program to make backup copies, but it could save you a lot of headaches.

An important safety measure is to write-protect your disks. On 5.25" disks you need to place a small, write-protect sticker over the left notch (most disks contain a few write-protect stickers in the disk box). On 3.5" disks you need to move the small tab that opens a small write-protect window on the disk. These steps will protect your disks from accidental erasure. Three different types of DOS commands can be used for copying disks. The COPY command is used for copying one or more files at a time. It's not the most appropriate command for this purpose. The XCOPY command is used for copying one or more files and directories at a time. It's better than the COPY command, but it's still not the best command for duplicating backup disks.

The DISKCOPY command lets you copy the entire contents of one disk to another. DISKCOPY will format the backup disk and then create an identical copy of the original disk. The only limitation of DISKCOPY is that both your target disk and your source disk should be the same size and capacity. *If you use DISKCOPY, you don't need to preformat your blank disks.*

Using DISKCOPY is very simple. Place a source disk that you want to copy in drive A: and type DISKCOPY A: A: then press "ENTER." The computer responds with "Place the source disk in drive A: and press "ENTER." Follow the step-by-step instructions on the screen. After reading the contents of the source disk, it will ask you to insert the target disk in drive A: and press "ENTER." You place a blank disk in drive A: and press "ENTER." After about a minute it will ask you, "Copy another diskette (Yes/No)?" If you have several disks to make backup copies from, type "Y" for "Yes" and then press "ENTER." The whole process is repeated for every original disk. When you have completed making your backup copies, type "N" for "No" in answer to the above question. Make sure that you label your backup disks properly.

8.10. Formatting Your Hard Disk

A hard disk uses magnetics to store data just like a floppy disk. Like a floppy disk, the hard disk needs to be formatted in order to be used. In the past, most hard drives were sold to the customer without being formatted. Most newer PCs come with the hard disk already formatted and the operating system already installed. When you bought your PC, you should have found out whether the hard disk was going to be formatted by your supplier. If your hard disk is already formatted, skip the rest of this section.

Several steps are involved in formatting your hard disk . The type of hard disk drive, the controller, the capacity, and the manufacturer determine the steps needed. Because of the number of variables involved, we strongly recommend that you read the chapter in your PC User Manual that describes the formatting of the hard drive. The following descriptions are intended only to familiarize you with the procedures. Use your manual to actually format the hard drive, if necessary.

There are three steps involved in formatting a hard disk. The low-level format actually establishes some very basic and essential data on the hard disk about itself and the controller. The next step is partitioning, which is necessary for all DOS versions prior to 4.01, because they only allow up to 32 MB per drive. Some people use partitioning to divide their hard drive into several sections. The last step is the formatting itself, which searches for bad surface segments of the drive and records the mapping information at the beginning of the drive. Some manufacturers perform the low level format at the factory; if so, you may skip that step if your manual instructs you to do so.

If your hard drive is less than 32 MB capacity and uses the MFM or RLL controllers, then you can use the traditional method. That method calls for using the DEBUG, FDISK, and FORMAT C:/s commands sequentially. Newer versions of DOS (4.01 and higher) perform all the formatting processes automatically.

8.11. Preparing Your Tape Backup Drive

Most tape backup drives operate similar to a floppy drive. As a matter of fact, most of them connect to the floppy drive port of the controller inside your PC. Most tape drives don't require very much set up. Most data tapes are already preformatted at the factory. The only thing you must do is to install the tape drive software on your hard disk. To do that, you must follow the instruction in your tape drive user manual. Every brand of tape software operates differently. The tape software will automatically create a directory to store its program.

8.12. Installing DOS for the First Time

DOS (Disk Operating System) is the most important software in your computer. As you recall from earlier descriptions of DOS, it controls every aspect of your computer's operation. Most

PCs sold today include a DOS package. If your system is sold without DOS, make sure that you buy the latest version. The latest versions of MS-DOS (by Microsoft) and DR-DOS (by Digital Research), are tremendous improvements over their previous versions. Even if you presently own a PC and DOS, we highly recommend that you upgrade to one of these newer versions.

If your PC has one or two floppy drives and no hard drive, you need to have a DOS disk in drive A: to boot up your computer every time. When you need to execute most DOS commands, you must put the appropriate DOS disk in your floppy drive. There is not much setting up to do in this case.

If you have a hard drive, you need to make a directory for DOS. In the directory you will copy all your DOS files. With a properly set up hard drive (as described earlier in this chapter), you boot up your PC from the hard drive and easily access all of your DOS files on that drive. If your supplier has already formatted your hard drive and set up DOS for you, then there is nothing more to do. If, on the other hand, DOS is not installed on your hard drive, you need to follow these steps if you use DOS version 3.3 or older:

1. Boot up your computer with a DOS disk in your floppy drive A:.

2. At the A:> type "C:" and press "ENTER" to go to the C: drive.

3. At C:> type "MD\DOS" and then press "ENTER" to make a DOS directory in drive C:.

4. Type "COPY A:*.* C:\DOS" and then press "ENTER" to copy all the contents of A: into the DOS directory on C:.

5. If there is more than one DOS disk, after the computer finishes copying the first disk place the second disk in the drive and press the F3 key to repeat the command in #4 above.

6. Repeat step #5 if you have any more DOS disks.

7. Seriously consider buying the latest version of DOS and make it easier on yourself.

If you have DOS versions 4.01 or higher, the program has an installation feature which guides you step by step through the entire process. These newer versions of DOS even automatically check your system configuration and components and set up DOS so that it will take full advantage of all the power you have in your PC.

8.13. Installing Windows for the First Time

The Windows graphical user interface (GUI) acts as a graphical intermediary between DOS and you. The pictorial representations of various DOS commands help most people interact with their programs in a more consistent way. Windows installs itself automatically. It needs to be installed after DOS has been installed. Keep in mind the Windows requirements discussed in earlier Chapters.

Insert the Windows disk #1 in drive A: and type "Setup"; then press "ENTER." The setup program will walk you through Windows installation in sequence. It will automatically look at the configuration and components of your system and determine the optimum way for it to operate.

8.14. AUTOEXEC.BAT File

The autoexec.bat file contains a series of computer commands that are executed one after another when you boot up your PC. Autoexec.bat stands for "automatically executed batch file." This batch file is executed every time you start your PC or reset it by pressing the "Control-Alt-Delete" keys (called warm boot). Some of the main functions of this batch file are as follows:

- Sets the date and time that you see on the screen according to the information kept in the clock on the motherboard.

- Tells DOS how to show the prompt for the drive that you are in.

- Informs DOS where all the files are stored and what directories to access.

- Instructs DOS how to use the memory and some of the other features in the system.

If you use DOS versions 4.01 or higher, the autoexec.bat file is automatically created for you. If you use an earlier version of DOS and install Windows, it will create a batch file for you. If you simply use an earlier version of DOS, then you have to create a batch file as follows:

If you are at a different drive than the hard disk, type C: and press "ENTER" to get to C:>.

- Type "Copy Con Autoexec.bat" and press "ENTER."

- Type "Date" and press "ENTER."

- Type "Time" and press "ENTER."

- Type "Path=C:\;C:\DOS;" and press "ENTER."

- Type "Prompt=PG" and press "ENTER."

- Press the F6 key and then press "ENTER."

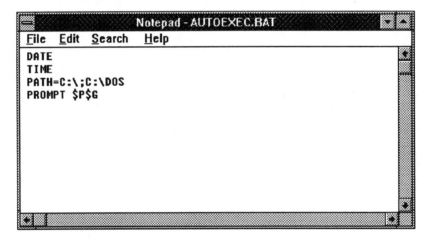

A sample screen that shows a typical Autoexec.bat file.

This will create a batch file that will show you the date, the time, and a prompt which shows which directory you are in. It also tells DOS what path to follow if it's looking for a DOS command in the DOS directory.

8.15. CONFIG.SYS File

The config.sys file is an executable batch file somewhat similar to the autoexec.bat file. It contains a series of DOS commands that are executed sequentially when the computer is turned on or the reset switch is pressed. The commands used in the config.sys file deal with system configuration and are different from those used in autoexec.bat file. Some of the main functions of this batch file are as follows:

● Tells DOS how much memory it can use as a buffer between the hard disk and the CPU.

● Tells DOS how many files can be open at the same time.

● Defines unique graphics card features not already included in your version of DOS.

● Defines other unique features or drivers for various components not in your version of DOS (drivers for disk controllers, mouse, tape drive, CD-ROM, etc.)

More recent versions of DOS (4.01 and higher) create the config.sys file for you. Windows also creates or modifies a config.sys file. If you use an earlier version of DOS by itself, you must create a config.sys file as follows:

If you are at a different drive from the hard disk, type C: and press "ENTER" to get to C:>.

● Type "Copy Con Config.sys" and press "ENTER."

● Type "Buffers=30" and press "ENTER."

● Type "Files=30" and press "ENTER."

● Press the F6 key and then press "ENTER."

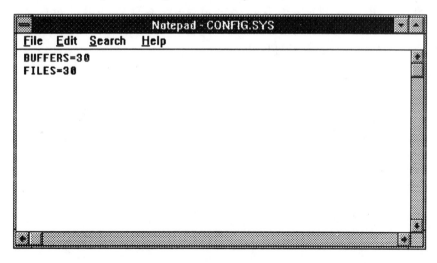

A sample screen that shows a typical Config.sys file.

This will create a config.sys file that will have up to 30 memory segments available for buffer and allows up to 30 files to be open at the same time.

8.16. Recording Your Initial Settings

At this stage, your computer is fully setup and ready to be used. Before you go any further, you should make a copy of your initial settings for backup purposes. Some of the most important information you need to record and file are as follows:

- System setup information (stored in your CMOS, i.e., drive types, video, etc.)

- DOS version

- Copies of your AUTOEXEC.BAT and CONFIG.SYS files.

8.17. Emergency Boot Disk (Everyone Should Have One)

Store the most critical information about your PC on a disk that will operate in your drive A:. This will be your emergency disk. To create this disk put a blank disk in drive A: and type FORMAT A:/S and press ENTER. This will format the disk and copy the bootable part of DOS onto it. Next, copy AUTOEXEC.BAT and CONFIG.SYS files onto the emergency disk. At C:> type COPY AUTOEXEC.BAT A: and press ENTER. Again, at C:> type COPY CONFIG.SYS A: and press ENTER. Now copy protect the disk, write emergency boot disk on the label, and store it in a safe place.

Chapter 9. Using And Enjoying Your PC

Using and enjoying your PC should always be the main reason for having a computer. If you ever find yourself not using your PC or having fun with it, then you are doing something wrong. If you've had your PC for a while and still feel uncomfortable using it, you need to clear your mind of all the apprehensions and fears that still linger in there. If you have just bought a PC or plan to buy one, remember to take it one step at a time. Keep this in mind: "You eat an elephant one bite at time!"

Most people become very comfortable using their PC within a few weeks after they unpack their system. During the first week, you should realize that, even if you make a mistake, your PC will not vanish or melt down. Shortly after that, as you use your PC, you'll begin to notice that everything is becoming more intuitive to you. Terms like "DOS," "Floppy," "Escape," "Run," etc., that once puzzled you, will start to make sense. The more you use your PC and the more you read your manuals, the more comfortable you'll become. Now you are ready to enjoy your PC and use it for what it's really intended: to entertain you, simplify your work and let you accomplish more.

After you learn how to operate your PC and use various programs, you are ready to get involved with other areas that will make using your system easier and more fun. To do that, you should be familiar with the basic uses of your PC and should be at a stage where you can troubleshoot any minor complications that may arise. That means you should have read your DOS, Windows (if installed), and application program manuals by now, so that, at the very least, you have an idea of where to look for help.

9.1. Simplifying Your Work

Like a factory-made suit or dress, computer programs are designed to be installed in a PC in their most basic formats. During or after the installation, you have the opportunity to unleash the vast features built into the program by tailoring it to your system and needs. Every program has its own way of doing things. The general ideas are often based on similar principles. Therefore, as you go from one program to another, we suggest that you allow some time to lapse between these improvements so that you can evaluate the benefits of the changes you have made.

> **AUTOEXEC.BAT**: Most programs create (if one doesn't already exist) or modify your autoexec.bat file to accommodate their specific needs and requirements. Some programs leave that option entirely up to you. Review your autoexec.bat file to make

sure the PATH contains important programs you wish to have available, as well as other components that are helpful to have.

CONFIG.SYS: Most programs create (if one doesn't already exist) or modify your config.sys file to call the necessary drivers every time you boot-up your PC.

MACROS: Most programs let you create shortcuts called "macros" to do some of the steps you use most frequently in your data entry. Certain repetitive information can be stored in the computer and used with only a couple of keystrokes every time it's needed. For example, your name and address can be stored as a macro and simply placed wherever you wish in your word processing documents.

AUTO SAVE: Some programs have a built-in feature that will automatically save your work (copy it to your hard disk drive) after a certain amount of time elapses. This is particularly helpful if you work at your computer for extended periods of time and create information that's important to preserve. For example, if you use your word processor to create a document, then after several hours of writing, your computer loses power due to a brown-out or other mishap, all the information you created since you turned the computer on will be lost. Check each of your programs as you install them to see whether they have an auto save feature that you need to activate. Some utility programs also offer that feature, which can be used in all programs. Otherwise, get into the habit of saving your work about every fifteen minutes.

9.2. On-Line Services

In the mid 1980's, as PC fever spread to millions of homes, various organizations began offering on-line computer services to the public. Some of these services have grown over the years while a few have gone out of business. These services either charge a certain fee per minute of usage, a fixed amount per month, or both. Most people living in cities or metropolitan areas have local phone numbers to call. Others may have to call a toll free 800 number or call long distance. The fees charged by these services vary, depending on the provider and the number of features you use.

The following is an alphabetical list of the most popular services available at the time this guide was prepared. To get additional information, call them at the information numbers provided below. Some services sell a membership starter kit that's available in computer stores. Other services advertise a toll free 800 number for you to call with your modem; then, using a credit card or other forms of billing, you can sign up for membership.

America Online

America Online is a service of Quantum Computer Services. It uses a graphical interface with pull down menus. You can access the service through local phone numbers in most cities and metropolitan areas. There is no charge to join; however, there is a monthly membership fee plus usage charges which, like long distance phone charges, are lowest during nights and weekends.

This service offers you news and headlines, access to a searchable encyclopedia, stock market reports and stock price checks, sports and weather, ability to download software from their software library, electronic mail access to other members, plus many other features. You can get free information by calling: (800) 227-6364

Compuserve

One of the oldest on-line services available with about two million members, Compuserve is primarily a text-based service. Consequently, the flow of information back and forth is faster than in a graphics-based environment. You can access the service through local phone numbers in most cities and metropolitan areas. You must purchase a membership kit to join, but, these kits often contain usage credits that offset the cost of your purchase. You are charged per minute of usage, with the amount varying according to the day of week and the time of day. Compuserve also offers a fixed price service.

The service offers you news and headlines, electronic mail, Fax service, bulletin boards, shopping on-line, stock market data and discount stock trading, sports and weather, airline flight schedules and on-line ticketing, plus many other features. You can get free information by calling: (800) 848-8199

Delphi

This service offers a combination of features, among them thousands of shareware programs that can be down-loaded to your computer. Usage charges are per hour and depend on the time of day and day of the week. You can get free information by calling: (800) 544-4005

Dow Jones News/Retrieval

This service offers financial news and statistics. Usage fees are somewhat complex and depend on the time of day and other criteria. The service can also be accessed through some of the other on-line services. You can get free information by calling: (800) 522-3567

GEnie

This is a service provided by General Electric Information Services. It's a text based service that offers a variety of features. You can get news and weather reports, use an on-line encyclopedia, send and receive electronic mail, check current stock closings, shop on-line, use bulletin boards, check flight schedules and book tickets, play various games on-line, etc. There are no membership fees to join. The first month of basic service is offered on a refundable, satisfaction-guaranteed basis. There are several pay-as-you-use services within GEnie. You can get free information by calling: (800) 638-9636

Internet

This service has the highest number of subscribers, estimated at over ten million. It was initially a popular network among colleges and government agencies. Now, a lot more business and individual subscribers are accessing it through other on-line services.

National Videotex

This service is based on the AT&T digital network. The basic service is offered at a low monthly rate for unlimited use. There are other pay-as-you-use interactive and transactional services available once you dial into National Videotex. You can get free information by calling: (800) 348-0069

PC MagNet

PC Magazine's online service is offered 24 hours a day. It provides utility programs offered by the magazine, an index of computer products reviewed, an exchange of opinions with the magazine editors, and access to the magazine's Computer Library and Consumer Reference Library. It can be accessed directly or through CompuServe. There are no sign up or monthly charges; you pay per minute of usage.

To join, you can go through CompuServe, if you are already a member, by entering GO PCMAG at the CompuServe "!" prompt, or you can call one of the following numbers directly: (800) 635-6225, Voice, or (800) 346-3247, Modem connection.

Prodigy

This service was started in 1988 as a joint development venture between IBM and Sears. It has about two million subscribers nationwide. Prodigy uses a graphical user interface with various pop up windows. You can access the service through local phone numbers in most cities and large metropolitan areas. There is no charge to join;

but there is a flat rate per month for unlimited use. The service is primarily supported by the advertising fees charged to various suppliers of products and services. At the bottom of every prodigy screen is a one inch wide strip of advertising.

The service offers you news and headlines, special interest clubs and bulletin boards, access to a searchable encyclopedia, stock market reports and stock price checks, on-line stock trading, sports and weather, on-line airline reservations and ticketing, on-line banking and bill paying, on-line shopping for various goods and services including groceries, electronic messaging with other members of the service, plus many other features. Starter kits with some free offers inside can be purchased from computer and software stores. You can get free information by calling: (800) 776-3552

9.3. Bulletin Board Systems

What started in the early days of the PC as a way for computer enthusiasts to exchange information has spawned tens of thousands of systems made available as bulletin boards. In the PC world, a bulletin board system (BBS) is a computer with one or more phone lines and one or more modems made available to the public. The majority of BBS's are available free of charge. The owners generally have certain interests that they would like to share with others. To offset equipment and telephone charges, some BBS's charge a nominal membership fee for the specific information they offer their members.

You can often find the name and number of local BBS's at your local computer dealers and computer stores. Some local computer periodicals print lists of the BBS's in their cities. You can call and connect with a BBS by using your modem. Once connected, the BBS will automatically inform you of the terms and conditions of using it. Then you can decide to proceed or to stop and disconnect from the service.

Often you don't know the communications protocol required for proper connection to the BBS. Therefore, set your modem software for the most commonly used parameters and if necessary change them after you are connected. The parameters are: 2400BPS speed, 8 bits, No parity, one data bit (2400, N, 8, 1).

While using a private BBS, you should exercise caution when copying files or programs to your computer. Most private BBS's serve as an exchange medium where users can copy to and from the BBS. The danger when copying from a private BBS is that the file may be infected with a computer virus. Once copied to your hard disk, the virus may harm your files and programs.

Thousands of user groups operate their own BBS, a list of some of them in major cities is included in the Appendix. For more information about bulletin boards in your area you can contact:

> BBS Press Service, Inc.
> 8125 SW 21 Street
> Topeka, Kansas 66615
> 913/478-3157

9.4. Games and Entertainment

Your PC is the key that opens the door to literally thousands of games and entertainment programs. Games cover a very broad spectrum. A great majority of new games take advantage of the more powerful microprocessors and video standards available in recent years. For these games you need at least an 80386-SX processor with color VGA graphics. These games produce arcade-quality features for hours of challenge and enjoyment for you and others in your home.

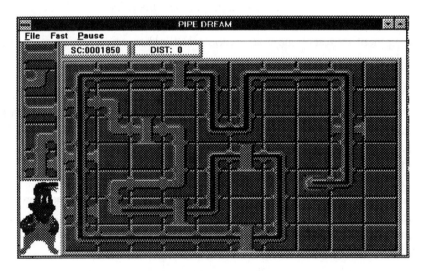

A sample arcade style video game designed for PCs.

Although most computer games usually cost less than $50, it's important to get some feedback about a game before you buy it. Sometimes the information on the outside of the package may not be enough to tell you whether or not you'll enjoy that game. Some software suppliers offer demonstrations, so you may be able to try a game before buying it.

Entertainment and special interest programs are abundant, but you have to look into a variety of sources for them. Stores carrying software may have a limited number of the best-selling programs in some categories on hand, but they, as well as mail order sources, may be able to get you other programs. The drawback to some of these programs is that they are often developed by one or more individuals with special interests in a field. They are not as readily evaluated and reviewed as other popular programs; so you may have to make your purchase based purely on a brief description or advertisement by the developer.

9.5. Shareware Software

In the late 1970's and early 1980's, a unique breed of individuals was clicking away at the keyboards of their PC. They were mostly young, idealistic pioneers in a field that was destined to change the course of civilization in a very short time. As they began to develop small programs for their PCs, they started to share those programs with other PC users. A very special culture began to develop throughout the country and, particularly, around Silicon Valley, California.

Pioneering PC users, including some of today's financial moguls, believed that software was an intellectual property that could be shared among all users and continuously enhanced through feedback from other users. They believed that software should be available at very little cost for people to evaluate. If they felt that the software was useful to them they could mail a check (usually between $5 and $50) to the developer to cover costs. Otherwise, they could simply stop using the program based on the honor system. This was the birth of what has become known as "Shareware" or "Public Domain" software.

Thousands of programs are available as Shareware. These programs are often very powerful and almost as full of features as their commercial counterparts. Their operations manuals and tutorials are often included on the program disk. You can either view the instructions on your screen or print them out on your printer. Authors of these programs may have different motivations for going through the Shareware channel. Some may believe in the original idea of sharing their intellectual property with others, and some may introduce and enhance their programs through this channel before going commercial. These programs are available at various stores or advertised in computer magazines. Although these programs are often advertised for as little as $2 apiece, if you like the program and start using it, the honor code requires that you compensate the developer properly.

9.6. Developing Programs

When the first generation PCs were introduced, no prepackaged programs were available. The pioneering users had to be programmers as well. The most popular programming language in those days was called "Basic." Early generation programming languages were not easy to use and sometimes you had to think differently to be able to interact with the machine.

Programming languages have advanced significantly in the past ten years. You no longer need to be a die-hard PC expert to develop software. Depending on the type of program and application you have in mind, several alternatives are available to you. Obviously, you need to have developed a good understanding of your PC and various programs before you try to write your own.

Most commercially available programs are based on one of the following programming languages: Basic, Turbo Basic, C, Turbo C, Pascal, Turbo Pascal, Quick Basic, Visual Basic, etc. Using a programming language means getting down to the lowest level of interaction with the machine. To use these languages, you do have to develop a high degree of expertise.

Another method for developing programs is to use an existing core program. Most of these programs are based on powerful database and spreadsheet software. You can develop what is called a "template" on top of the core program. For example, you can use a database program to create an accounting package the way you prefer it to look and operate. If you decide to sell your program, you need a special version and a license from the database developer. The special version is called "Run Time Version" and is often sold by the original program developer at a substantially lower cost than the complete package. You can develop these programs with less time and skill than those using programming languages.

9.7. Sharing the Joys and Benefits

At some point in time you will outgrow your PC at home or at work. You will buy a newer, more powerful PC and your old computer will sit idle. When that happens remember that a PC is a terrible thing to waste. You can share the joys and benefits of your PC by donating it for a good cause. A needy student or organization will be forever grateful to your generosity. If you donate your business PC, you may be able to take a tax write-off. Contact the National

Cristina Foundation, a non-profit organization, at 42 Hillcrest Drive, Pelham Manor, NY 10803, (800) 274-7846.

9.8. Sending or Receiving Data by Modem

Exchanging data between PCs by modem is very simple. Once you get a good communication software and set it up, you can send and receive information to the office computer or to friends and co-workers. If you transfer a lot of big files, you can save a lot of time by compressing the files before transferring them. They need to be decompressed at the other end.

9.9. Keeping your Hard Disk Clean

Your hard disk is like a file cabinet and you control what goes into it. Regardless of how hard you try, there will be files that end up staying there for a long time. A simple solution is to create a temporary directory every month. Call it Tempjun, Tempjul, Tempaug, etc. Store the temporary files you create every month in the appropriate directory. Every few months delete the contents of old directories.

9.10. Protecting your PC Against Theft

Make sure you record the serial numbers of your PC, monitor, and printer. If they are stolen, after you call the Police, call the American Computer Exchange (Atlanta, GA) at (800) 786-0717. They maintain a national data bank of stolen PC products.

9.11. Connecting PCs Together

Many businesses and other organizations that have more than one PC often network their machines together so that they can share programs, data, and peripherals. In a network environment, PCs are connected together by cable or, sometimes, by wireless radio wave devices. Depending on the level of access granted to each user on the network, people can access the same organization-wide data and share limited resources like printers, modems, CD-ROM, tape backup, etc. There are three types of networks: centralized, peer to peer, and zero-slot. Within each type of network, there are different ways, called protocols, by which various network programs manage the environment.

Networks are probably one of the more complex areas of the PC world. Because of the way networks interact with other programs and components, they do require installation by knowledgeable people. Depending on the type of network, they may also require periodic support and maintenance. If you decide to use a network for your organization, you should carefully evaluate the capabilities of the program as well as the amount, quality, and cost of support.

Centralized Networks

Most networks that connect a large number of PCs together are generally part of a centralized network. In this type of environment, the central computer (called file server) is usually a PC that's often faster than the rest and has a very large hard disk drive. The file server contains the programs that need to be used by the people connected to the network. PCs connected to the file server are called workstations. Like the file server, each workstation has an internal or external network adapter. Special cable is run from the file server to the workstations. The cable is connected to the adapter in each PC.

The network operating software is like an umbrella that covers the activities within the network. It manages the flow and the priority of information fed into and pulled out of the network. Some very complicated activities go on behind the scenes of a network. For example, if several people in the telemarketing department of a business are using an order entry program on a network, and one of them is entering an order being placed by customer John Doe, then another person on the network cannot make changes to John Doe's file while it's in use. Otherwise, the data might be corrupted. Network software for this type of environment is often complicated to install and needs a trained person to act as network supervisor. Depending on the number of workstations in the network, the supervisor's job may be part-time or full-time.

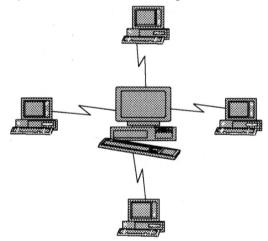

In the centralized network environment, programs are loaded into the hard drive of the file server. Programs have to be multi-user and compatible with the network software. These programs are sold either as a single package for an unlimited number of users, or one package per user.

Sharing peripherals like printers, modems, faxes, CD-ROMs, tape backups, etc., is another major reason for using networks. A few years ago, these peripherals had to be connected to the file server in order to be shared by the workstations. In recent years, network programs have made it possible to share devices connected to other workstations.

Peer to Peer Networks

An increasing number of PC networks with a few computers are using environments that allow each workstation to act as a file server. They are called "peer to peer," because all workstations are on equal footing with each other. These networks are simpler to install and maintain than those using a file server.

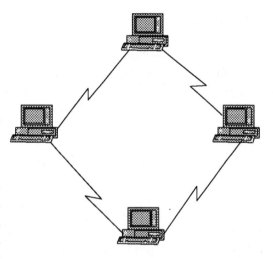

The network software acts as a traffic controller in the flow of information between the various workstations. Information can be shared among various people connected to the network. Various peripherals like printers, modems, CD-ROMs, tape backup drives, etc., can be shared as well.

In recent years, peer to peer networks have improved significantly. Some of the more powerful ones can use the same type of network adapter as centralized networks. They have also developed higher throughput speeds rivaling those of the centralized networks. In many ways, and for many organizations, these networks can be more than adequate. They are easier to install and people can be trained to use them faster. Long term, they require less support than centralized networks. These networks are more appropriate for groups of five to ten PCs. Depending on the applications used on the network, the speed of data transfer can be affected by the number of stations. For example, if a network is actively used by a business for order entry and accounting during the day, performance begins to suffer when the number of users goes beyond approximately five.

Zero-Slot Networks

These network environments are the most basic form of connecting two or three computers together to share peripheral devices or transfer files between them. They use the

computer's existing parallel or serial port instead of requiring a special adapter. Zero-slot networks usually cost less than peer-to-peer networks. They also offer less speed and fewer features. The cost of hooking up two PCs is between $100 to $200. In an office environment where one PC is the primary system and the other is used less frequently, this type of network can easily fulfill most needs.

9.12. PC Training

A PC, like an automobile, bicycle, sail boat, or even a VCR, can be used right out of the box and with little or no training. However, to get the most out of your investment, you should spend the time and the effort to be better trained in using your system and software. You have several options available to you. Obviously, the least expensive option is the material that comes with your system and software. If you need more focused training, other options are available.

Manuals and Program Tutorials

Virtually every computer system is sold with an operations manual. Name brands and those offered by most compatible manufacturers often have manuals specific to their systems. Some compatible brands that are simply assembled by the supplier include pamphlets for each component in the system. The system manual should be your first source of information about your PC. The key factor to remember is that the manual is written to familiarize you with the overall operation of your PC, as well as to provide more advanced information for expert users, and to serve as a troubleshooting guide. If you read the manual from start to finish without recognizing the broad spectrum it covers, you are bound to be overwhelmed and discouraged. We recommend that when you read the manual, review only the chapters that familiarize you with the system, without going into complicated technical areas.

The majority of software that you buy is supplied with a manual written for that specific version of software. The style and understandability of these manuals vary from one manufacturer to another, and from one program to another. Therefore, you should use the same approach to reading your software manuals as you do with the system manual. If you find your software manual too confusing (as some really are), you can look at third-party books written for that version of your program.

Many programs include a tutorial that can be operated right on your computer. The tutorials are often a combination of information written in the manual and a series of question-and-answer sessions called interactive training. You can read about the program, and then work on exercises that reinforce the material you have already read. Some tutorials are actually more effective than the manual. We strongly suggest that after installing your programs, you look at the tutorials before going over the manuals.

Shareware programs are not provided with a paper manual but many often include a manual on the disk. These manuals may be viewed on the screen or printed on your printer. Often the developer of the software offers a more complete manual after you send in a registration fee.

Computer-Based Training

Several companies offer training programs that can be viewed on your computer screen. They usually offer more features than the tutorials included in most programs. These programs are interactive; they try to give you the feeling of being in a classroom environment. The tutorial offers information about the program, then asks relevant questions and evaluates your answers. Some of these programs are text-based and others are video-based, making great use of animation and graphics.

Next to the manuals and tutorials that are included with programs, computer-based training packages are often the least expensive alternatives available. Their advantage is that they give you a closer contact with the real program than any other alternatives.

Audio or Video Training

Audio or video training programs are offered by several companies. These programs have been available for several years. Audio tape training programs are designed to be used in a cassette recorder next to your computer. The idea is to listen to the tape while exploring the program.

Training programs on video tape have remained popular among PC users over the years. Their basic advantage is that they visually illustrate the use and the features of the program. These programs often run from 30 minutes to an hour. They normally highlight the program and its features.

Classroom Training

One of the most familiar training grounds for a lot of people is the classroom. Some people feel that they can learn more in a classroom environment than they can by reading manuals, reviewing tutorials, or watching video tapes. For these people, most cities offer several choices. Some training organizations specialize in classroom-based computer training. Some dealers also offer training classes. Additionally, many colleges and universities have begun offering similar programs. Usually, local schools are less expensive than other classroom training providers. The only exception may be dealers who offer free training classes to customers who purchase computers and software from them.

When evaluating classroom training programs, you should make sure that they offer the full use of a PC per student. That way, you can follow everything the instructor does on your screen, and you can work on the exercises more efficiently.

Chapter 10. Using DOS

Do you know that one of the main reasons many people are afraid of their PCs is DOS? Some people have not even touched a PC in their life and they are afraid to get involved because of DOS! How do you feel about DOS? Are you afraid, confused, or intimidated by it? If you are, then it's about time you stopped worrying and started using your PC instead. Do you feel that you can't drive because you don't know how your transmission works? Of course not. The new versions of DOS are like your automatic transmission. As long as you know that P is for Park, D is for Drive, and R is for Reverse, you are OK. Well, believe it or not, DOS is the same way.

Today, if you use Windows, you will rarely ever use DOS. If you use DOS based programs, there are only 6 DOS commands that you may use from time to time. Those commands are: CD (change directory), COPY (copy files), DEL (delete files and directories), DIR (to see what's in a directory), DISKCOPY (to duplicate the contents of a disk), and FORMAT (to format brand new floppy disks). That's it! Yes there are many other DOS commands that you may need to use on occasion. But that's nothing to worry about. Stop worrying about DOS and read this section at your leisure. If you have an older version of DOS, we strongly recommend that you upgrade to the latest version. It's easier to use and the upgrade generally costs under $50.

Every time you turn your computer on, it goes through a self-diagnostic process. First the fan comes on, the hard disk starts spinning, and then some characters will appear on the screen. At this point, in most systems, the upper left hand side of the screen will display the name of your BIOS, the amount of video RAM and a rapid count of your system RAM. When the memory count is completed, your first floppy drive lights up and makes a sound, then the second drive repeats the sequence, and finally your hard disk drive lights up. If a printer is attached to your computer, at this point, it makes a sound indicating that it, too, is connected and ready on standby. The computer has verified the components attached to it and is ready to go to the next step. All the instructions it followed so far were being read from the ROM chips on the motherboard.

At this point, the computer needs an operating system to communicate with you through your software. DOS is the most dominant operating system for PCs. You have already read about what DOS is and, generally, what it does. The following section gives you a more detailed understanding of DOS.

10.1. Description of DOS

When your PC finishes the self-diagnostic step, it's ready to read DOS and load the necessary parts into RAM memory. DOS can be read either from a floppy disk or from your hard disk drive. If you have a hard drive and have followed the steps outlined in Chapter 8, on preparing your system, the key parts of DOS should have been copied to your hard disk. You should have also copied the rest of DOS into a directory. With DOS on your hard disk, the computer checks the floppy drives; if they are empty it will go to the hard disk to look for DOS. Once it finds DOS, it loads the internal DOS commands into your memory and proceeds to execute the instructions you have in CONFIG.SYS and AUTOEXEC.BAT files. This process is called "booting up."

DOS has two groups of commands: internal and external. Internal DOS commands are loaded into your RAM when you boot up. They can be used any time you have a DOS prompt on the screen. They don't need another file to work from. These are the most essential commands of DOS and a great deal of effort goes into making them as small as possible so they will not occupy too much of your precious conventional memory (the first 640 K). External commands on the other hand remain on the disk and are not loaded into memory automatically. They need a program file to run. To run an external DOS command, you either need to be in the DOS directory or have the DOS directory in a search path (described in Section 8.14 under AUTOEXEC.BAT). Both command types will be identified in the next section.

10.2. Important DOS Commands

Using your PC means that at some point in time you'll need to use an obscure DOS command that you've never heard of. As much as we all like to ignore things that we don't like or find particularly difficult to understand or to remember, there is a need for certain DOS commands. Here you'll learn about a few of the most important ones. If you need more information, refer to PC GUIDE for DOS or your DOS manual.

BACKUP

What does it do? Makes backup copy of one or more files and directories from one disk to another. It's primarily used to copy important files from the hard disk onto floppy disks. Backup can copy files continuously on a sequence of disks. Disks should be labeled sequentially.

How is it used? If you use MS-DOS versions 6.0 or later, you simply type MSBACKUP at the prompt and press "ENTER." An easy-to-understand backup screen appears. You simply use the arrow keys to move the highlight to where you want and then press the space bar to select it. Then follow the instructions on the screen. If on the other hand you have an older version of DOS then it gets a little more difficult! If you want to copy the entire contents of your hard disk onto floppy disks, at the DOS prompt type BACKUP C:*.* A:/S/F and press "ENTER." After you have copied the contents of your hard disk, you can use the following command to periodically backup only the files you have changed or created since your last complete backup. At the DOS prompt type BACKUP C:*.* A:/M/F and press "ENTER." To make a backup of a file (e.g., FILE.EXT) in a directory (e.g., DIRNAME) at the DOS prompt type BACKUP C:\DIRNAME\FILE.EXT A: and press "ENTER."

BUFFERS

What does it do? Allocates a certain amount of memory as buffer for hard disk access. Each buffer is 512 bytes of RAM. Because your processor is faster than your hard disk, the buffer stores data going to the hard disk and makes your processor free to do other things.

How is it used? If you use MS-DOS versions 6.0 or later, it sets up your buffers during installation. Otherwise, depending on the size of your hard disk drive, you specify the number of buffers as BUFFERS=XX in your CONFIG.SYS file. XX is the number of buffers. If your hard drive is 40 MB or less, use 20; if it's 100 MB or higher, use 40; if it is between 40 and 100 MB, use a number between 20 and 40.

CD (Change Directory)

What does it do? Is used to go in and out of a directory. It can also be expressed as CHDIR.

How is it used? If you type CD followed by the name of directory, it will change to that directory. At the DOS prompt, type CD\DIRNAME and press "ENTER." This will get you into a directory called DIRNAME. If you want to go to a sub-directory that is inside another directory, at the DOS prompt, type CD\DIRNAME1\DIRNAME2 and press "ENTER." If you want to get out of a directory and go to the root directory, you type CD\ and press "ENTER."

CHKDSK (Check Disk)

What does it do? Checks the contents of the disk or hard drive that you specify. It analyzes the integrity of the file and directory structure, the system area, the system memory, and the size of the current drive. If you specify, it converts lost sectors into files that can be recovered later.

How is it used? At the DOS prompt, if you type CHKDSK and then press "ENTER," DOS will analyze the drive name at your DOS prompt. Or, you can specify the drive name by typing CHKDSK C: and pressing "ENTER." As a precaution, always type CHKDSK/F to tell DOS to convert lost data to file.

CLS (Clear Screen)

What does it do? Clears your screen and moves the cursor to the upper left corner.

How is it used? At the DOS prompt type CLS and press "ENTER."

COPY

What does it do? Copies one or more files from one disk or directory to another disk or directory. This is a very popular DOS command.

How is it used? To copy a file from drive A: to drive C:, at the DOS prompt type COPY A:FILE.EXT C: and press "ENTER." To copy the entire contents of drive A: to drive C:, at the DOS prompt, type COPY A:*.* C: and press "ENTER." The *.* means all files. To copy a file (e.g., FILE.EXT) from one directory (e.g., DIRNAME1) to another (e.g., DIRNAME2), at the DOS prompt, type COPY C:\DIRNAME1\FILE.EXT C:\DIRNAME2 and press "ENTER."

DATE

What does it do? Displays the date kept by your PC memory and allows it to be changed if necessary.

How is it used? At the DOS prompt, type DATE and press "ENTER." The current date in the computer will appear. If it's correct, press "ENTER". If it's not correct, type the correct date in the same form as that shown on the screen, then press "ENTER." This will only change the date for this session. To change the date permanently, you need to change your PC setup.

DBLSPACE

What does it do? This command was introduced with MS-DOS version 6.0. It starts the disk compression program that nearly doubles the capacity of a disk. By using this program your disks can hold almost twice as much data as before.

How is it used? At the DOS prompt type DBLSPACE and press "ENTER". Then follow the instructions on your screen. It will be a good idea if you refer to PC GUIDE for DOS or your PC manual before installing DBLSPACE.

DEFRAG

What does it do? This command was introduced with MS-DOS 6.0. It organizes data that is scattered on your hard disk and makes them more accessible.

How is it used? Make sure that you have quit all other programs. At the prompt type DEFRAG and press "ENTER". Don't run this program while your are running Windows.

DEL (Delete or Erase)

What does it do? Deletes one or more files from a disk or directory.

How is it used? To delete a file, at the DOS prompt, type DEL FILE.EXT and press "ENTER." Use this command very carefully. When you delete a file, it may be difficult to get it back if you change your mind later.

DELTREE

What does it do? This command was introduced by MS-DOS 6.0. It deletes in one easy step, a directory and all the subdirectories and files in it. Make sure the directories you delete are not needed.

How is it used? At the prompt type DELTREE DIRNAME and press "ENTER".

DIR (Directory)

What does it do? This is a very useful and harmless DOS command. It displays all the files and directories on a disk drive.

How is it used? At the DOS prompt, type DIR and press "ENTER."

DISKCOPY

What does it do? Copies the format and the entire contents of one disk onto another of similar size and capacity.

How is it used? If you have only one floppy drive in your system and would like to create an identical copy of a disk, at the DOS prompt type DISKCOPY A: A: and press "ENTER." This command is used very often in order to make a safe copy of a program that you purchase. You can then store the original disks and work with the copy.

FDISK

What does it do? On the hard disk drive, FDISK displays, creates, or deletes partitions. It's used during low level formatting. It's only used when you first prepare your hard disk for use. It's followed by formatting the drive, which erases all the data from it. Most likely you won't have to use this command.

How is it used? After booting up your computer with a DOS disk in drive A: at the DOS prompt type FDISK and press "ENTER." A menu appears on the screen, giving you four options to create, change, delete, or display your partition(s). DOS versions before 4.01 could recognize no more than 32 MB in each drive designation. If you are using one of those earlier versions, you should divide your drive into partitions having less than 32 MB each.

FIND

What does it do? Searches for one or more words in a file.

How is it used? At the DOS prompt, type FIND "ANYWORD" FILE.EXT and press "ENTER."

FORMAT

What does it do? Performs a complete disk analysis, marks the bad areas on the disk, and prepares the disk for use. If the disk already contains data, it'll be erased.

How is it used? If you plan to format a floppy disk at the DOS prompt type FORMAT A: and press "ENTER." If you would like to format a floppy disk and make it bootable with DOS, at the DOS prompt type FORMAT A:/S and press "ENTER." Never use the FORMAT command on your hard disk without proper knowledge.

Help

What does it do? This is a very useful command. It explains various DOS commands.

How is it used? At the prompt type HELP and press "ENTER". It will show you a list of DOS commands. When you choose a command, it will give an explanation. Another way is to type HELP COMMAND.EXT and press "ENTER".

LABEL

What does it do? This command is used for creating, changing, or deleting the identification information on a disk. It's called volume label and can be up to 11 characters long

How is it used? For example, to create a new label called MyHardDisk, at the DOS prompt, type LABEL C:MyHardDisk and press "ENTER." To change or delete an existing label, at the DOS prompt, type LABEL and press "ENTER." The current volume label will appear; follow the instructions on the screen to change the label, or press "ENTER" to have no label at all.

MEMMAKER

What does it do? This command was introduced by MS-DOS 6.0. It optimizes the memory of your computer by configuring various commands, device drivers and memory resident programs in upper memory (the area between 640 K and 1 MB).

How is it used? You don't need to use this command very often. At the prompt type MEMMAKER and press "ENTER".

MORE

What does it do? Allows the display of information one page at a time. This is particularly helpful for files that are written continuously (e.g., README or HELP files that will scroll rapidly if you don't use MORE).

How is it used? At the DOS prompt, type MORE < FILE.EXT, then press "ENTER." Or, at the DOS prompt, type TYPE FILE.EXT |MORE then press "ENTER."

MSAV

What does it do? This is a great command introduced with MS-DOS 6.0. It checks your hard disk and floppy disks for viruses.

How is it used? Quit all programs. At the prompt type MSAV and press "ENTER".

PATH

What does it do? Identifies certain directories and sub-directories that should be searched for specified files even when you are in other programs or directories. For example, placing the DOS directory in the PATH will allow you to call upon external DOS commands even when you are inside another directory.

How is it used? It's used in the AUTOEXEC.BAT file. A line could contain a path to several directories (e.g., PATH=C:\; C:\DOS; C:\DIRNAME1; C:\DIRNAME2;).

PRINT

What does it do? Print is a direct command that instructs the computer to print a specified file. Most programs contain their own print commands, so PRINT is used only where there are no other alternatives.

How is it used? At the DOS prompt, type PRINT FILE.EXT and press "ENTER."

PROMPT

What does it do? The prompt is the symbol that identifies the drive your computer is currently ready to work with. For example, if the hard drive is the current drive, the prompt will look like C:>- .

How is it used? To change the prompt from one drive to another, at the current DOS prompt, type the drive letter, e.g., A: then press "ENTER."

RECOVER

What does it do? Recovers data and files that may have been corrupted by bad sectors on the floppy or hard disk drive. RECOVER examines and extracts as much data as it can from the bad sectors and reconstructs the file or the entire disk. Some data may never be recovered, and the reconstructed data may not be usable without those parts.

How is it used? At the DOS prompt, type RECOVER C:\DIRNAME1\FILE.EXT and press "ENTER."

REN (Rename)

What doe it do? Is used to change the name of a file.

How is it used? At the DOS prompt, type REN FILE.EXT NEWNAME.EXT ; then press "ENTER."

REPLACE

What does it do? It replaces the files you specify on one drive with the files on another drive. Or it reviews the files on one drive and copies the files that are not already there from another drive. This can be useful if you are updating one or more files with a newer version.

How is it used? To update a file, at the DOS prompt, type REPLACE A:FILE.EXT C:\; then press "ENTER." To search drive C: and add only the files that are not already there, at the DOS prompt, type REPLACE A:*.* C:/A ; then press "ENTER".

RESTORE

What does it do? This command works together with the BACKUP command to restore files that were backed up earlier. Disks should be restored in the same sequence they were backed up. Note that a backed-up file must be restored using the same version of DOS.

How is it used? To restore all the files from Drive A: to Drive C:, at the DOS prompt type RESTORE A: C:*.*/S then press "ENTER."

SHARE

What does it do? Allows your programs to share files, and, if you are on a network, it locks the file you are currently using to prevent others from making any changes while you are using that file. If you use a DOS version before 5.0 and have a hard disk drive larger than 32 MB, you need to use SHARE. If you are on a network, you have to use SHARE regardless of your DOS version and hard drive size.

How is it used? Load SHARE in your AUTOEXEC.BAT file.

SORT

What does it do? SORT is used for alphabetically arranging your files. It can only sort files based on one letter in the file name, and the position of that letter should be the same for all the files. For example, if you sort by the first letter of each file name, it arranges the files from A to Z, based on the first letter.

How is it used? At the DOS prompt, type DIR | SORT then press "ENTER." This will sort your directories alphabetically, based on the first letter of their names.

TIME

What does it do? It displays the current time kept by the computer, and allows you to change or delete the time.

How is it used? At the DOS prompt, type TIME then press "ENTER." The current time will be displayed. If the time is correct, just press "ENTER." If you want to change the time, simply type the correct time in the same form that appears on the screen, then press "ENTER."

TYPE

What does it do? Displays the contents of a file on the monitor. This is a very useful command for reading the contents of HELP, README, or UPDATE files that are commonly included with most programs. Some programs put their user manual on the program disk(s), and allow you to either read it on the screen or print out the contents.

How is it used? At the DOS prompt that has direct or path access to the file you are interested in, type TYPE FILE.EXT then press "ENTER." If the file is longer than one page, it will scroll quickly on the screen. To see the contents of the file one page at a time, at the DOS prompt, type TYPE FILE.EXT |MORE then press "ENTER."

VER (Version)

What does it do? This command displays the DOS version number that was used to boot up your computer.

How is it used? At the DOS prompt, type VER and then press "ENTER." The DOS version will appear. The VER command can also be inserted in the AUTOEXEC.BAT file. It will display the DOS version every time the computer is booted up.

XCOPY

What does it do? This command is used for copying files and directories. It's very similar to the COPY command, but it's capable of copying files as well as directories.

How is it used? At the DOS prompt, type XCOPY DIRNAME1 A: then press "ENTER." This will copy the contents of DIRNAME1 onto drive A:. The contents may be files and sub-directories. XCOPY, like the COPY command, is not capable of continuing onto additional floppies if the contents exceed the capacity of the first disk.

10.3. DOS Tips

There are a few things that you should know in case you need help with DOS or need to fine tune it to suit your needs better.

Getting Help with DOS

MS-DOS provides help right at your fingertips. If you need to know how to use a DOS command, simply type it followed by /? and press ENTER. It will show you exactly how to use that command for various applications.

Deleting a File

Deleting files in DOS is very easy. Simply type DEL FILENAME.EXT and press ENTER. If for some reason your file name has a blank space in the name, DOS will not recognize the blank space. You need to type a ? in place of the blank when deleting.

Memory Optimization

MS-DOS has special features that let it optimize memory usage. Most of the optimization takes place automatically when you install DOS. However, you can use MEMMAKER or manually check your CONFIG.SYS file to make sure that the necessary files are there. At C:> type EDIT CONFIG.SYS and press ENTER. This will show you the contents of your CONFIG.SYS file. You should have the following lines there:

> DEVICE=HIMEM.SYS
> DOS=HIGH,UMB
> DEVICE=EMM386.EXE RAM
> DEVICEHIGH=SMARTDRV.SYS
> STACK=0,0
> LASTDRIVE=E

Memory Utilization

MS-DOS has an easy way for you to check the status of your memory. At the prompt type MEM/C |MORE and press ENTER. This command will list the name and size of each file that occupies your conventional memory (first 640 K) and also the files that occupy the reserved and high memory (384 K above 640 and the 64 K above 1 MB). The more conventional memory you have available, the faster your PC will be able to operate.

Disk Directory

DOS has a very convenient feature called DIR which stands for directory. This command will tell your PC to display the directory of the disk you specify. For example if at C:> you type DIR and press ENTER, it will show you a list of the files and subdirectories in drive C:. If you have a lot of files on drive C:, the list will scroll in front of your eyes faster than you can read. In order to see the directory one page at a time, type DIR/P and press ENTER. This will show one page and in the bottom of the page asks you to press a key to go to the next page.

Alphabetize your Directory

Your directory builds up as you create more subdirectories and add more files. After a while searching for a specific file becomes cumbersome. DOS can easily arrange your subdirectories and files alphabetically. At the prompt type DIR/O and press ENTER.

Repeat Key

Sometimes you want to enter the same command several times. For example, if you want to copy the contents of one group of disks to another, you may type COPY A:*.* C:\TEMPNOV\ and press ENTER. Your PC copies the first disk and goes back to C:>. In order to repeat the process with the next disk, you either have to type everything over again or simply press the F3 key on the top left side of your keyboard. This will automatically type the line for you. All you have to do is press ENTER again.

Boot Errors

Occasionally, when you start your computer or reset it, you may get an error message like one of the following:

> Non-system disk
> Disk error
> Bad or missing interpreter

If you are booting up from a floppy disk, check to make sure that it's a DOS boot disk. It it's not, get a boot disk and try again. If it's a boot disk, then try another boot disk to make sure. If the second boot disk has the same problem, then something is wrong with your floppy drive. If the second disk works fine, then the first disk needs to be made bootable again. If your hard disk failed during the boot up, try booting up with a floppy disk. Then change from drive A: to drive C:. Type DIR/P and check to see if a file called COMMAND.COM is in the C: drive. If you find it there, then simply change to A: drive by typing A: and press ENTER. At A:> type SYS C: and press ENTER. This will transfer the hidden DOS files from A: to C:.

Recover a Lost or Damaged File

Occasionally you may accidentally erase a file or a file may become damaged. DOS has a couple of commands called CHKDSK/F or RECOVER that may recover your damaged or erased file. However, they are not as powerful as some of the other programs specifically designed to recover files. The most popular commercial programs are Mace Utilities (Fifth Generation), Norton Utilities (Symantec), and PC Tools Deluxe (Central Point). A couple of shareware programs called HDTest (Peter Fletcher), and ORG 2.0 (David Rifkind) can also help.

Chapter 11. Using Windows

One of the reasons you are reading this book is to become more familiar with PCs and learn to use your PC better. More than likely you are a beginner or intermediate PC user. In that case, you may be interested to know more about the Windows environment. This is more than just having little pictures to point at with your mouse. Windows creates a uniform environment where various programs work very similar to one another. Once you setup Windows for your PC and your peripherals, you don't need to worry about doing the same thing with other Windows software. As you install other programs they get the necessary information they need directly from Windows. If you are in the market to buy a new PC and software, we strongly recommend that you buy a system that works well with Windows. Carefully look at Windows software before you buy anything else. If you already have a PC, and it meets the criteria (See Chapter 6) to run Windows, you might seriously consider using Windows.

Use of graphical interfaces is becoming increasingly popular among PC users. In older PCs, all communication between the user and the computer was via text typed on the keyboard and displayed on the monitor. In the mid 1980's, the introduction of the Apple Macintosh computer divided users into two distinct groups: those who preferred the intuitive, graphic environment of the Macintosh, and those who preferred the text-based operation of the IBM and compatible systems.

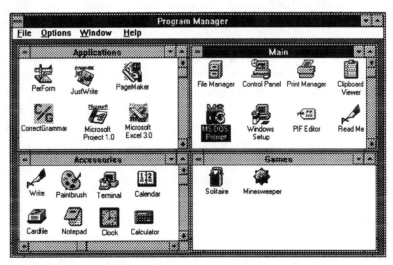

Windows Program Manager screen.

IBM and compatible systems remained popular, despite the fact that a large number of users longed for a graphical environment. The introduction of affordable 80386 SX and faster processors, coupled with the VGA video standard and Windows 3.0, broke the old barriers, and made the graphical environment a pleasant reality for millions of PC users.

If you are a new PC user, we strongly recommend that you consider using a graphical environment. You can choose either OS/2 or Windows. Since May 1990 when Windows 3.0 was introduced, it has become an accepted standard. Thousands of programs have been developed for the Windows environment. Because these programs operate within Windows, they use consistent commands and, therefore, are easier to learn and to use.

One important factor to consider is the performance requirements mandated by Windows. Although Windows will work with 80286 based PCs, or as little as 2 MB of RAM, we strongly suggest that you consider a more powerful PC in order to run Windows. As much as Windows will make it easier to use your PC, it can be very frustrating if it works slowly. The graphical interface is very demanding of your microprocessor, your memory, hard disk drive and video system.

Windows operates best with an 80386 SX or faster processor, 4 MB of memory, at least 80 MB hard drive, and a VGA monitor. You can install Windows on your computer during the initial preparation or afterwards. The installation process is very straightforward. The program searches and determines most of the components in your PC by itself. Often there is very little that you have to add or question. Once Windows is installed in your PC, Windows-based programs automatically install themselves and can be accessed like other programs.

Windows makes using your PC much easier and more versatile. The program packs a great deal of power and a significant number of features. It's intended to appeal to both novice and expert users. Because of its broad spectrum, a novice user might become overwhelmed by the various features it offers, and an expert might find the simplified beginning somewhat boring. For that reason, we recommend that if you are a novice, after installing Windows on your computer, read only the first 4 chapters of the User's Guide. Then try to use Windows for several sessions before you read any further, giving yourself an opportunity to get used to the basic features of Windows before you explore the other features.

11.1. Windows Description

The Windows environment consists of several modules, each performing certain tasks or providing some unique features. The modules and the components within them can open up like windows on your screen whenever you move your mouse-controlled cursor over an icon, and double-click a button.

Program Manager: is the central module of Microsoft Windows. Whenever you start Windows, Program Manager starts automatically and continues to operate as long as you run Windows. As the name implies, it manages various programs that are loaded into your computer and made available to Windows. Program icons appear by themselves or under the icon of a program group. When you start Windows, the Program Manager screen covers your display area. Within that screen is a smaller window that contains the icons for File Manager, Control Panel, Print Manager, Clipboard, DOS Prompt, and Windows Setup. Near the bottom of the screen are four group icons for Main, Accessories, Games, and Applications.

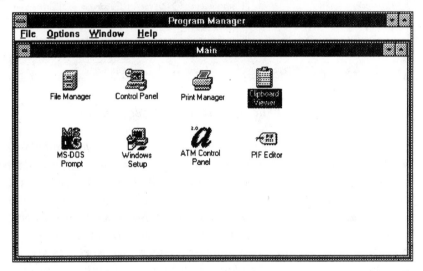

Typical main window under Program Manager.

File Manager: organizes your files and directories. It lets you view all your files and directories and arrange them the way you prefer. You can view your files in a tree structure, with directories and sub-directories visually displayed on your screen. You can also look at the contents of your directories without leaving the application you are working on, or copy files from one directory or drive to another directory or drive by simply dragging the icon from one window to another.

One of the nice features of File Manager is its ability to duplicate the entire contents of floppy disks. When you want to make backup copies of your important program disks you have to use the DISKCOPY in DOS. This requires you to insert each disk several times. Under Windows, this is done in one, easy step.

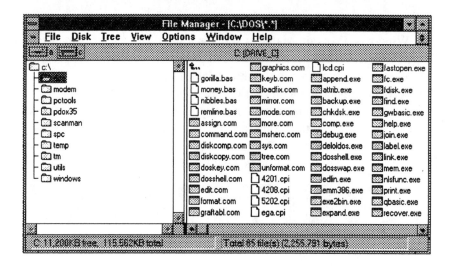

Typical File Manager screen under Windows.

Control Panel: lets you change the way your computer is configured while you use Windows. It contains several important components: *Color* lets you set the color of your Windows screen and various elements on it. *Fonts* lets you add or delete fonts for your screen and printer. *Ports* sets the communication parameters and specifications for your serial ports. *Mouse* lets you customize your mouse characteristics and set features like speed and button designations. *Desktop* lets you change the appearance and pattern of your Windows screen. *Network* lets you control your connection to a network. *Printers* lets you configure printers for use within the Windows environment. *International* lets you adjust your Windows environment for international characters, languages, etc. *Keyboard* lets you adjust the rate at which your keyboard repeats a depressed character. *Date/Time* lets you change the date and time kept by your computer. *Sound* controls the small speaker inside your computer that beeps when an error condition occurs within your computer. *386 Enhanced* is used to turn on the 386 enhanced mode, if your microprocessor is 80386 or 80486.

Print Manager: is the program that controls how you send a print task from within any program application to your printer(s). Windows Print Manager works in the background, which means that when you order a file to be printed, it's handed to Print Manager to be given to the printer in a steady flow while you continue using your computer. This is necessary, because your computer works much faster than your printer can print. Therefore, Print Manager stores the job to be printed in memory and frees your processor to do other things. If you send several print jobs to your printer,

Print Manager holds them in a queue and prints them one after another.

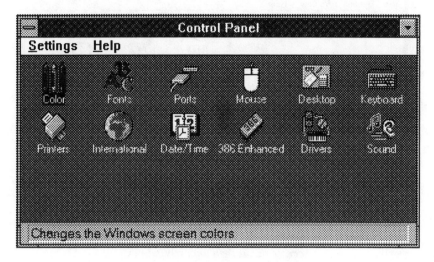

Control panel screen under Windows.

Clipboard: is a temporary storage medium that's available when you want to transfer information from one Windows application to another. For example, if you use a spreadsheet to keep track of your household budget, you can copy an expense table from there onto your clipboard, and then paste that table onto a letter you are preparing in the word processing program.

DOS Prompt: this icon lets you get out of Windows and go to the text-based DOS prompt. At the prompt you can perform whatever work you can not do within Windows. Windows stays hidden and active in the background. If you are running in the 386 Enhanced mode, you can run DOS in a window by pressing "ALT" and "ENTER." If you want to get back to Windows, at the DOS prompt, type "EXIT" then press "ENTER."

Windows Setup: displays your current settings for the processor, video standard, mouse, printer, and keyboard. You can change your settings by clicking on the item you wish to change. List of options appear for you to choose from.

Accessories: this icon group contains several useful mini programs that are an integral part of Windows. The group consists of the following programs:

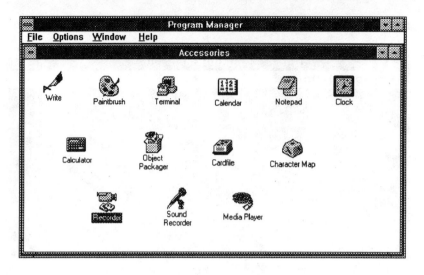

Accessories screen under Windows.

Write: is a relatively simple word processing program that has most of the basic features of a regular word processor.

Paintbrush: is an entertaining and useful program that lets you create color drawings.

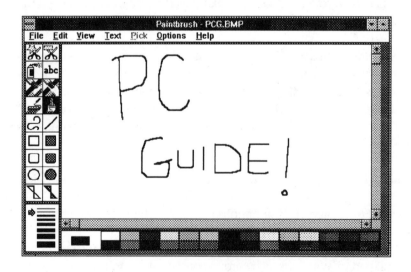

Sample screen generated by the paintbrush program supplied with Windows.

Terminal: lets you communicate with other computers using your modem and the phone line directly from within Windows. Although most modems are sold with communication software, by using Terminal you can send or receive information from within Windows application programs.

Calculator: displays the features of a standard or scientific calculator on the screen. Using your mouse or the numeric keypad, you can use the displayed calculator for all the functions you normally use a calculator for.

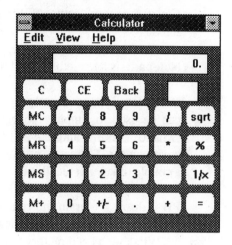

Calendar: Like having your own secretary, this feature is very useful for people who would like to keep track of their activities and appointments. The calendar displays month, week, or day. You can enter your appointments and, if you wish, you can activate an alarm that will beep to warn you of upcoming appointments.

Calendar - [Untitled]						
File Edit View Show Alarm Options Help						
1:40 PM			Saturday, July 11,			
July						
S	M	T	W	T	F	S
			1	2	3	4
5	6	7	8	9	10	11
12	13	14	15	16	17	18
19	20	21	22	23	24	25
26	27	28	29	30	31	

Sample screen showing an activity calendar.

Cardfile: is similar to a stack of index cards that you can use to store various information. You can quickly sort them or arrange them by different topics.

Clock: is a useful feature of Windows that displays an analog or digital clock on your screen.

Notepad: is a text editor used for creating or changing batch files.

Recorder: is an advanced program used for recording a sequence of key strokes that can be used to simplify your work. These sequences of key strokes are called "Macros". For example, you can record the typing of your name and address and create a macro for that. Any time you need your name and address, you simply press a couple of keys to recall it on your screen.

PIF Editor: Program Information File (PIF) is used to give Windows information about your non-Windows application programs. The editor lets you create an icon to tell Windows what directory that program is located in and what command is needed to activate it.

Games: Windows comes with two interesting and entertaining games: Solitaire and Minesweeper. They are located under the games group. You can add other games to the menu under the games group icon.

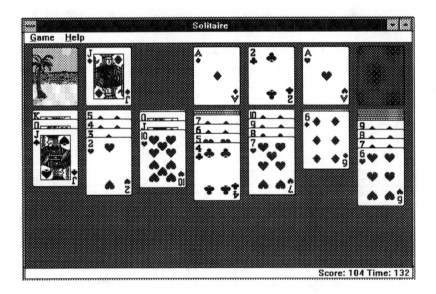

A solitaire card game that can be played on the computer screen.

Applications: this group contains Windows compatible applications programs. When you install these programs, you can choose to give them an icon in the main window or put the icon in the applications group.

11.2. Windows Tips

Windows is very easy to install and very easy to use. The Windows user manual covers a lot of grounds. Some of the tips listed here can also be found in the manual.

Speeding up Windows

Windows is a very demanding program and your hardware needs to be up to speed. There are several things you can do to speed up Windows:

● Make sure your PC has an 80386 or 80486 microprocessor.

● Have at least 4 MB of RAM in your PC.

● Create a permanent swap file on your hard disk. Make sure it's the size of your RAM. Follow the steps outlined in Chapter 14 of your Windows manual. The swap file helps Windows move files in and out of memory and onto the hard disk. A permanent swap file allocates an area on your hard disk for that purpose so that Windows doesn't have to search for available space.

● Reduce the number of icons that appear on your screen.

● Make sure that you only have the fonts that come with Windows. Some programs install additional fonts when they are installed. Unless you specifically want certain fonts, avoid loading those additional fonts. Fonts slow Windows down.

● If you don't need 256 VGA colors with your applications, reduce the number of colors to 16. That will speed up your video display and consequently speed up Windows.

Speeding Up Your Hard Disk

If you have an IDE hard disk drive, you can increase your hard disk access speed by enabling the 32 bit disk access. That's a little feature in Windows. Choose the Control

Panel and select the icon for 386 Enhanced Mode. Click on that icon then choose change for Virtual Memory. Select change and then click your mouse on 32 Bit Disk Access.

The Mighty Shift Key

When drawing lines, squares, or resizing graphics by holding down the Shift key while moving the cursor the lines become perfectly straight and the resizing proportional.

Windows-Only Programs

If you only use Windows-based programs you can save some precious RAM by removing all references to MOUSE.COM or MOUSE.SYS in your AUTOEXEC.BAT file.

The Microsoft Logo

If you have grown tired of seeing the Microsoft logo for a few seconds every time you start up Windows, getting rid of it is very simple. Next time instead of typing WIN to start Windows, type WIN : (WIN followed by space and colon) and then press ENTER. If your PC automatically comes up with Windows when you boot up, then you need to use EDIT to modify WIN in your AUTOEXEC.BAT file.

Copying Files

Windows File Manager offers a simple way for copying files. Simply grab the folder icon for the file you want and move it over to the icon for the directory or drive you want to copy it into, then release the icon.

Copying Disks

Using the DISKCOPY command to make backup copies of your program disks or data when you only have one floppy drive is a hassle. You'll have to keep putting in the source and target disks several times. This is due to a DOS limitation that can only use your conventional memory (first 640 K of RAM). Windows File Manager offers a simple way for copying disks. Simply select "Copy Disk" from the Disk menu and let Windows do everything in one, easy step.

Chapter 12. Hints and Tips You Can Use

Can you believe that using your PC is like driving your car? When you use your PC on a regular basis, it'll become second nature to you. You'll learn where everything is and how to use shortcuts. The more you use your PC, the more intuitive everything becomes to you, and the more uses you'll find for your system. The more you work with your PC, the more you'll demand from it. After a while it's easy to lose sight of the fact that only 20 years ago, the machine sitting in front you used to fit in a football field and required constant support from dozens of technicians and programmers. In this chapter we'll address a variety of helpful hints and tips which you'll be able to use.

12.1. Caring For Your Hard Disk Drive

The hard disk drive is one of the most sensitive parts of your PC. It spins at a very high speed, and the read/write heads are located extremely close to the surface of the magnetic disks. Under these conditions, the hard disk is very vulnerable to shock and other physical disturbances. While your computer is turned on, your hard drive spins rapidly, and any sudden movement of the base unit may damage it. Often a damaged hard disk may result in the loss of your data. When your PC is turned on, make sure that it does not get hit or moved.

12.2. Turning Your PC On and Off

Should you leave your computer on all the time or should you turn it on when you need it and off when you don't? Different people have different opinions. Some are speculation, some are fact, and some are based on the technology of many years ago.

When you turn your computer on, it puts a higher than usual stress on the hard drive. It also starts heating up the components inside your PC and monitor. After a short while, the hard drive reaches and stays at a constant speed. The heat inside the PC and the monitor also reach a constant level. When the computer is idle, the concern is waste of energy and wear and tear of the hard drive, the fan, and other components. When the computer is turned off, the components that were heated up and had expanded slightly, start to cool off and shrink to their original size. Either way, various components of your PC experience some change.

The solid state electronic components of PCs and monitors have a long life expectancy. You don't have to leave your system on overnight. However, you should not keep turning the system on or off during the day. We recommend that once you turn your PC on in the morning, leave it on until you are completely finished using it for the day.

12.3. Moving your Computer

Moving your computer system should be handled with care and caution. There are several steps you should follow before you move your computer:

- Turn the computer and monitor off before moving.

- Unplug all the cables from the back of the PC so it can be moved freely.

- Insert the cardboard that came in your floppy drive back in and close the drive.

- Move each piece separately and carefully.

12.4. Viruses

What started out a few years ago as humorous pranks have recently turned to vicious acts by some computer nerds. Computer viruses, like a disease, are designed to penetrate a PC from the outside and play havoc with the hard drive and other components. The damage may be quite extensive. Loss of data on the hard disk is one of the most common results.

A computer virus is usually a very small program that's hidden inside another ordinary program. Like a communicable human disease, if the infected program is passed on from someone else and installed in your system, it sneaks into your hard disk and stays there. Some viruses have a trigger, which can be a date or a word. When that date arrives or that word is used, the virus becomes active and starts whatever destruction its creator had in mind.

There are several ways to avoid viruses. The most important is to be careful about accepting programs from individuals or private bulletin boards. The other is to install virus detection software on your system to examine every program before loading it onto your hard disk. Viruses keep changing, however, and detection programs get outdated quickly. Latest versions of MS-DOS offer virus detection and elimination.

12.5. PC Publications

The personal computer field is one of the richest in terms

of the vast number of publications that cover every facet of PC products. Most of these publications are available at libraries, computer stores, supermarkets, and book stores. We strongly recommend that you look at a few of them before you buy your PC or upgrades. More importantly, you should make a point of reading at least one of these magazines every month. The informative articles, product reviews, and even advertisements in these publications help you stay abreast of the events in this exciting and constantly advancing field.

A list of some of the most popular PC publications is included in the Appendix. The subscription prices listed are the published rates. You can often subscribe through various organizations for substantially less.

12.6. Storing Floppy Disks

Floppy disks store data magnetically. They are vulnerable to dirt, magnets, finger prints, cracks, cuts, and other abuses. It's important that you take proper care of your floppy disks. There are basically two types of disks. The 5.25" disks are soft and their magnetic surface is somewhat exposed. The 3.5" disks are in a sturdy plastic enclosure and the magnetic surface is protected by a retractable metal cover. The following is a list of suggestions for protecting your disks:

- Don't touch the magnetic surface of disks.

- Keep 5.25" disks in their protective sleeves.

- Avoid using magnets around disks.

- When not in the PC, the disks should be kept in storage envelopes or boxes.

- Don't expose disks to extreme heat, sunlight, or moisture.

12.7. Backing Up Hard Disk Data

Hard disk drives have been constantly improved over the past few years. They are now significantly more reliable than their predecessors. They have fewer parts, are less expensive, and faster. However, a hard drive is still one of the most vulnerable parts of the PC. Because your hard drive stores important documents and data that you have spent a great deal of time producing, you should make regular backup copies of your data.

There are several ways to make regular backup copies of your data. You can either use the BACKUP command that's included with your DOS, use a disk backup utility program, or use a tape backup drive. The results are often the same; only the costs and the effort involved are different.

DOS has BACKUP and RESTORE commands that lets you make a copy of a single file, multiple files, directories, or the entire hard disk on floppy disks. These DOS commands often take longer than the other two alternatives and have fewer features than those two. If you only have a few critical files to backup, DOS may be adequate for you.

Hard disk backup utility programs are specifically designed to produce fast and easy backup of your important files on disk. They are often easier to learn and faster than the DOS commands. Each program has its own set of operating rules.

A tape backup drive is the most convenient method for making backup copies, but it's also the most expensive alternative. If you use your computer full time every day, you might use one tape for each day of the week and one tape for the entire week. Make a complete copy of all your important files on the weekly tape. Then set up the tape software to copy only the changes you make every day on the daily tapes. This way, you minimize your copying efforts and have a full backup if necessary.

Depending on the importance of your data, there are three methods you can use to backup your hard disk with a tape drive. The "Son" method (use one tape to make a complete backup every day), the "Father/Son" method (use 6 rotational tapes, 2 to make a complete backup on Fridays and 4 to backup only the files changed daily from Monday through Thursday), and the "Grandfather/Father/Son" method (use 10 rotational tapes, 3 to store complete monthly backups, 3 to store complete weekly backups on Fridays, and 4 to make a backup only of files changed daily from Monday through Thursday). Each method gives you a higher degree of security in case something goes wrong with your system or hard drive.

12.8. Optimizing your Hard Disk

The hard disk is one of the most important components of your computer system. After buying your PC, the hard disk is the only part that you can actually influence and improve. Think of your hard disk as a library with thousands of books or a filing cabinet with several drawers and many folders in each drawer. The way a library organizes and arranges the books directly affects how well it can service its customers. The way you organize the files and directories on your hard disk can have a similar effect on the performance of your hard disk. There are two important areas that you can improve:

Making Directories

If you appreciate the way most libraries group books by topic and then alphabetically within each topic, then you already know how that bit of logic works. On your hard disk drive, you can make directories to store files of similar topics together. For example, all the files of your word processing program can be stored in a directory. Within that directory you can make a sub-directory to store all your letters. You can make another subdirectory for your memos, etc. This will help organize all your files according to topic. When you look at a directory of your hard disk, instead of seeing hundreds of files scrolling on your screen, you'll see a number of directories. You can then go into a directory and look at the contents of that directory.

When you first install a program on your hard disk, a directory is automatically made for that program. Most programs even have provisions for making sub-directories to store the files that you make within that program. If your program does not automatically make a directory, you can do so quite easily:

- Go to the drive for which you would like to make the directory, such as C:.

- At the C:> prompt, type MD\WORDPRO then press "ENTER" to make a directory called WORDPRO.

- Type CD\WORDPRO then press "ENTER" to change into the WORDPRO directory.

- Type MD\LETTERS then press "ENTER" to make a subdirectory in WORDPRO called LETTERS.

- Type CD\LETTERS then press "ENTER" to change into the LETTERS subdirectory.

- If you want to exit a directory simply type CD\ then press "ENTER."

- If you want to go from one directory to another simply type CD\ followed by the name of that directory (i.e. DIRNAME) then press "ENTER" to change to that directory.

• Many find it much easier to use the DOS Shell to navigate between directories. DOS Shell is included in the latest versions of MS-DOS and DR-DOS.

Unfragmenting and Compacting

When you copy a file onto your hard disk for the first time, the computer tries to find a blank area to store it. As time goes on and you add more to that file, your PC stores it in other available areas but keeps track of where all the various pieces are stored. Although these files are fragmented on the hard disk, as far as you are concerned, it's totally transparent.

When you delete a file from your hard disk, the computer doesn't immediately wipe the area clear; instead it simply deletes the name from your directory and makes the area available for future use. The area made available may not be used immediately, but eventually, the computer will copy a new file over it.

The computer divides a hard disk into sectors. Each sector is 512 bytes long. When you store information on your hard disk, the computer allocates as many adjacent sectors to those files as possible. Almost invariably, the tail end of the last sectors will remain blank. When you end up with several hundred files, obviously a great deal of space is wasted. In both cases cited above, you notice that information gradually begins to become scattered on your hard disk. Eventually, having blank spaces and files scattered on your hard disk takes its toll on the performance of the drive. Your drive capacity will diminish faster and it'll take longer to read or write to the disk.

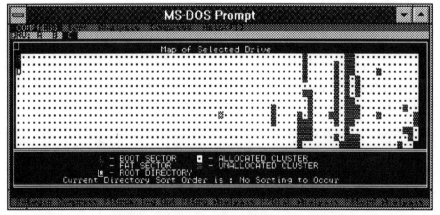

Typical hard disk unfragmentation program at work.

There are special programs in addition to MS-DOS that unfragment your hard disk. These are known as disk optimization programs. You can purchase them as a single program or as part of a utility package.

12.9. Opening up your PC

Most people spend over $15,000 for their automobiles, and many of them don't hesitate to pop open the hood to look at the engine. The same people may spend between $1,000 and $2,000 for their PCs but they are afraid to look inside the box.

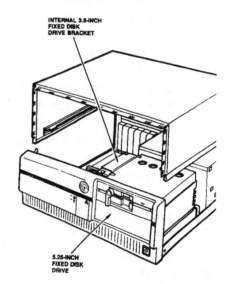

INTERNAL 3.5-INCH
FIXED DISK
DRIVE BRACKET

5.25-INCH
FIXED DISK
DRIVE

Your PC is one of the technological marvels of the twentieth century, yet it's very simple to understand its basic operating principles. The modular design of the IBM and compatible PCs makes them easy to repair and upgrade. Even if you are not technically oriented, you should take a little time to understand the basics of your PC. Knowing how to open up your PC will save you time and money when repairing and upgrading it.

There are some precautions to take and some steps to follow whenever you decide to open up your PC. Just remember that it takes only a few minutes longer to follow correct procedures than it would to carelessly jump in and possibly damage something.

● Before opening your PC, turn off the power and disconnect all the cables from the base unit. Sort the cables properly so that you can reconnect them easily.

● Make sure there is enough room on a flat surface (preferably a desk) to work on. Don't place the computer on the rug or carpet.

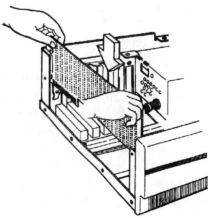

● Using the proper type of screwdriver (flat blade or Phillips), take out the screws attaching the cover to the base unit.

● Carefully and slowly pull up or pull out the cover. Some covers have a small latch inside which may catch a cable as it's pulled out.

● Before you touch anything inside the computer, locate the power supply that's usually a shining steel box in the back. Touch the power supply to discharge any static electricity that may be on you.

● If you remove any adapter boards or drives, be sure to disconnect any cable attachments necessary and then carefully remove them and place them on a flat surface without touching each other. If necessary, write down the orientation of the cable attachments (most have a unique shape or a color strip on one side). Arrange the items you take out in such a manner that you can easily put them back.

● If you have to remove the motherboard, note the orientation of the power cables and the way the board is attached to the base unit.

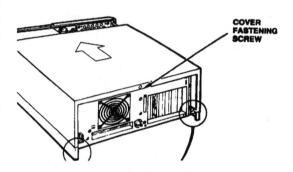

● When you start putting the system back together, simply reverse the previous steps.

12.10. Troubleshooting

One of the annoying parts of life is that everything will eventually break down. Despite their solid state electronics, PCs are no exception to the eventual break-down syndrome. With PCs there are three types of malfunctions: simple oversights (stupid mistakes!), software complications, and hardware failures. The first type is very easy to solve. The second type may require some prodding and detective work. The third type can simply be solved by swapping out the defective part(s).

In this section you'll discover that there really are no major disasters that can happen with your PC. The problems listed here are those that you may encounter after you have already set up your PC. Frequently, you can simplify solving the problem, if you can remember what changes you made before turning your computer off the last time you used it. If you call someone for help, the first question they'll ask is "What were you doing or changing before this happened?" If you can ask yourself the same question, you may also come up with the answer.

Simple Oversights

Problem: You turn the computer on and nothing happens.
Solution: Check all the cable connections and make sure the wall outlet is getting power.

Problem: The computer is on, but nothing appears on the monitor.
Solution: Check the cable connections on the back of the monitor, PC, and power outlet. Also, gradually turn the knobs on the monitor until the display appears. Double-check to make sure the video adapter connection is secure.

Problem: The computer is working, then suddenly everything goes off.
Solution: Check the wall outlet for power and a possible blown fuse.

Problem: The computer is turned on, but it stops after reading the disk inside the floppy drive, and the screen says "non-system disk."
Solution: The disk in the floppy drive does not contain the bootable portion of DOS. Either replace it with one that does, or if you have a hard disk, simply take the floppy disk out and press any key.

Software Complications

Problem: You boot up your PC and after it counts the memory and checks of the floppy drive(s), it freezes.
Solution: You may have improperly changed your AUTOEXEC.BAT or CONFIG.SYS files. Place a bootable disk in your A: drive and reboot your computer. At the A:> change to C: drive and then by using EDIT correct your last change.

Problem: You boot up the computer and everything seems to be physically on, but nothing appears on the screen.
Solution: You may have made some improper changes to your CMOS settings (settings that tell the PC what it has). Check the computer manual for the steps necessary to restart the computer and get into the CMOS, and restore it. The internal battery keeping CMOS data may have drained or died. Restart the computer using the above procedure to get into the CMOS setup screen. If the problem persists, you need to replace the battery.

Problem: You use the DOS BACKUP command to make a copy of your hard disk files on diskettes, but later you are not able to use RESTORE to put those files back on the hard disk.
Solution: The DOS BACKUP and RESTORE commands should belong to the same

version. If you backed up with one version of DOS and sometime later upgraded your DOS version, you should reboot with a bootable DOS diskette with the old version. At the A:> restore the old backups.

Hardware Failures

Problem: You turn the computer on, but the cooling fan inside the PC doesn't work.
Solution: Your power supply may have failed. It's relatively inexpensive and simple to replace.

Problem: You turn the computer on and everything works, but the monitor screen remains blank.
Solution: Double check the video cable connections. Make sure that none of the pins is bent. The connection needs to be secure. Also make sure that the brightness knob is not turned all the way down. Otherwise, the monitor may have blown a fuse or the tube may have failed. In either case, the monitor needs to be inspected and repaired by authorized technicians. **Don't try to open a monitor** and service it yourself; dangerous high voltage build-ups remain in some parts of the monitor even after it's unplugged.

Problem: The computer frequently freezes after a few hours of use.
Solution: The computer may be overheating. The fan may not be working properly, which may require a new power supply. If your computer is at least one or two years old, or is used in an unusually dusty environment, the air vents may be clogged with dust. Open the case and carefully clear away the dust and dirt. A few blasts from a can of compressed air will clean away most of the dirt. You can purchase a small can for a few dollars from most computer and office supply stores.

Problem: Some keys stick or repeat themselves.
Solution: If your keyboard is under warranty, call the supplier and arrange for repair or replacement. If the keyboard is out of warranty, turn off the system, unplug the keyboard, and use a few blasts of compressed air to clean out the dirt. If that doesn't solve the problem, turn the keyboard over and remove the screws from the back. Carefully turn the keyboard over and lift the top off. You may be able to carefully pull out the key cap. Use a cotton swab to clean around the base of the key(s) that stick.

Problem: You turn the computer on and everything looks and sounds normal, but the computer freezes after counting memory, and doesn't check the floppy and hard disk drives.

Solution: Your drive controller has probably failed. Open up your base unit and make sure that the board is properly seated in the expansion slot and the cable connections are secure.

Problem: You turn the computer on and everything is normal, but after checking the floppy and hard drives, the computer displays a "1780 Error".

Solution: Check to see if the hard drive is spinning. If it is, then make sure the signal cable between the controller and the hard drive is secure.

Problem: You turn the computer on, everything is normal but after checking the floppy drive and flickering the hard disk light for a few seconds, the computer displays a "Disk Boot Failure" message.

Solution: Your setup program for system configuration is probably lost (often due to battery failure) or altered. Run setup, and make sure the drive type information is properly set.

Problem: You turn the computer on, everything is normal but after checking the floppy and the hard drives, the "Non-system Disk" message is displayed.

Solution: Boot from a floppy drive. If you can go to your hard disk, then your hidden SYS files have been damaged. In that case from the floppy drive that you booted, type SYS C: and press "ENTER." The hidden SYS files will be copied from your floppy disk to the hard disk. If on the other hand, you cannot go from your floppy drive to the hard disk, then your hard disk partition table is probably damaged. In that case; check your user manual; you may need to run FDISK from your floppy drive to delete and then add a partition similar to the original setup.

Problem: You turn the computer on and everything is normal, but after checking the floppy and hard drives, the "Bad or Missing Command Interpreter" message is displayed.

Solution: Your COMMAND.COM file is probably damaged or missing. Boot up from a floppy drive and then copy that file from the DOS floppy disk to the hard disk. Make sure that the DOS version on the floppy disk is the same as the one on the hard disk.

12.11. Software Support

Software companies often provide free support to their customers for a certain period, usually ranging from 30 to 90 days from the date of purchase. Beyond that period, they charge a usage fee based on the number of minutes you spend on the phone with their technical support staff. Some companies use 1-(900) toll phone services for technical support beyond the free support period.

The availability of thousands of programs and their periodic upgrades make it difficult for most software retailers to offer expert support. You often have to call the software manufacturer for assistance.

12.12. Test Programs

PC owners are a lot like automobile owners. Many purchase a PC to use for their intended purpose, and are not interested in anything else. Others get into it with a special passion. They would like to have the latest and the greatest. They want to explore the inner workings of their system and fine tune it all the time. Fortunately, because of the high quality of most PCs, the first group can go on for years without worrying about their system. The second group can take comfort in knowing that there are many programs that will let them test their system, tweak it, or in some cases, correct a problem.

Test programs are available either as part of MS-DOS or as part of a utility or test package. These programs perform one or more of the following tests:

- Test, count, and map-out the memory.

- Test the CPU microprocessor and math coprocessor.

- Test the video board processor and memory.

- Test the keyboard.

- Test the parallel, serial, and game ports.

- Test the floppy and hard disk drives.

- Test the printer.

- Test the monitor.

- Test the mouse or trackball.

12.13. Regular Maintenance

Your computer system requires very little routine maintenance and, if you treat it with normal care, you'll have to do very little to ensure that your PC will last for many useful and enjoyable years. In fact, the less you tinker with your system, the fewer problems you'll have. The only useful tool you'll need is a small can of compressed air, available at most computer and office supply stores, to remove dust from the computer.

PC

Once a year, you should take the cover off of your PC and use the compressed air to blow out the dust. If you don't have access to a can of compressed air, simply use a cloth to gently wipe off the dust.

Monitor

Once a month, use a soft cloth to wipe the screen clean. You can use the same cloth to wipe the dust off the air vents on the sides or the top of the monitor.

Printer

Routine maintenance depends on the type of printer you have. If you have a dot matrix printer, you can use the compressed air to blow out the dust and paper shavings once a year. If you have a laser printer, you should use the cleaning tools that come with the printer to clean the inside elements every time you replace a cartridge.

Two of the most frequently occurring problems with dot matrix printers are caused by user negligence. Never pull on the paper as the printer is printing. It may bend one or more of the pins as it strikes the paper. Also, never turn the platten knob when the printer is on. It will damage the plastic gears inside. There are buttons on most printers for moving the paper back and forth automatically.

Peripherals

Most peripherals require little or no maintenance. If you have a mouse, you may take out the roller ball and clean it with a soft cloth once a year.

12.14. Service and Repair

Solid state electronic products have been around for more than twenty years. In the past ten years, their quality standards have reached a point where some experts claim that if a product does not fail during the first few months, it will probably last for many years. PCs, in general, have proved to be quite durable. Many original IBM and compatible systems are still working. In fact, the main reason for retiring older PCs has been technological obsolescence, rather than product failure. The concern you are most likely to have three years from now is whether your 1994 PC can do what others can do in 1997!

Hardware failure happens to a very small percentage of the millions of PCs sold every year. Most of those failures happen during the first year. Almost all systems have one or more years of parts and labor warranty; so you'll probably be covered for most equipment problems. After the warranty expires, there are several ways to have the problem corrected or the equipment repaired.

Depending on where you plan to use your PC and for what purpose, your priorities and the urgency for repairs may vary greatly. If you use your PC at home for casual applications and it fails, you probably will not be greatly inconvenienced if it takes one or two weeks for repairs. On the other hand, if you use the PC to perform important business functions like accounting, you may not be able to afford more than one day of downtime. Therefore, the level of service and repair you may need will vary according to your degree of dependence on the computer. This factor should have been one of the criteria in your selection process.

As a rule of thumb, if you are purchasing your computer for business and will be heavily dependent on it for critical daily activities, you should consider purchasing a service contract. The contract should cover both parts and labor; and its annual cost should not exceed 10% or, at most, 15% of the purchase price of the hardware. The response time should be no more than a few hours, and a loaner should be provided if your system will be unavailable more than one or two days. On the other hand, if you are purchasing the PC for home use and can be without it for a few days in case of a breakdown, a reasonably priced service contract may also be a good investment. The contract should cover both parts and labor, its annual cost should not exceed 5% to 10% of the purchase price, and your computer should not be unavailable to you longer than a specified number of days. In either case, make sure that the service contract is offered by a well established and financially solid provider.

Service During Warranty

Almost all computer systems are sold with a one year parts and labor warranty. The standard warranty usually requires that you take or ship the defective unit to the place of purchase for repair or replacement. Some manufacturers sweeten their package by offering additional benefits, like providing service at your site, or extending the warranty beyond the one year period.

If you encounter a hardware problem that can't be corrected by following some of the suggestions outlined in "Troubleshooting", then you should call your supplier for assistance. Some manufacturers have specific rules about opening up your PC during the warranty period, so read your warranty document before you get into anything. If your supplier is not local, make sure you use their toll free 800 phone number (if they have one). Frequently the technical support staff can help resolve your problem over the phone.

When you prepare your computer for shipment to the supplier for service, it's best to use the original packing materials and boxes. If you don't have the original material, use foam or crumpled newspapers to surround the unit. Make sure that you attach a label with your name, address and phone number to every item. Almost all suppliers require a photocopy of your purchase invoice. Don't send the original. Most suppliers give you a "Return Authorization Number" when you call and decide to send the unit back. The number should be written on the outside of the box as well as on the item(s) you send back.

Whether you take or ship your system back for service, always make it a point to call back after a few days to check that it was received or ship it away. Then ask when it's going to be looked at. Call back again a few days later to ask about the unit's status, and the date it'll be shipped back to you. After you receive the unit, hook it up as soon as possible and check it out carefully. Make sure that the problem has been corrected, and make sure that you have gotten everything back (even internal components). Sometimes technicians may take the system apart and forget to put everything back in. If anything is missing or not working properly, call the supplier back as soon as possible.

Service After Warranty

Once your warranty period is over, you have many choices about how and where you get your system serviced. They are primarily divided into three groups: the place where you bought your system, organizations that only provide service and repair, and last but not least, yourself. The important point to keep in mind is that your entire system is basically made up of plug-in components. Usually, if a component fails, it's less expensive to pull it out and replace it than to repair it. Another important point is that, unlike everything else, over time the prices of computer components go down. It'll often cost less than the original purchase price of an item.

Original Supplier

After the warranty period is over, your ties to the original supplier depend on the mutual relationship that may have developed between you. There are some advantages to dealing with the original supplier, especially if it's a local dealer. In many small communities, computer dealers tend to be privately held and relatively stable. They tend to become familiar with your needs and provide you with personal service.

Many mail order computer companies have set up sophisticated systems to keep in touch with their customers. Because most of them value your continued business and satisfaction, they will provide service on the systems they sell.

In spite of the advantages of going to the original supplier for service, you should not restrict yourself to that supplier alone. As mentioned earlier, computer service and repair has, in most cases, boiled down to diagnosing the problem and exchanging the malfunctioning component. You should shop around for the best price. Most local computer suppliers and service providers perform a diagnostic check for approximately $50 or less. Afterwards, you have the option of having the PC serviced by them or by another service provider.

Third Party Service

With the proliferation of personal computers in the past few years, thousands of service and repair organizations have sprung up throughout the country. The majority are privately owned and operated. There are also several nationwide organizations with branch offices in most cities and metropolitan areas. Some of the nationwide organizations are used by mail order computer companies to provide local or on-site service to their customers.

Third-party service organizations provide you with another choice for service and repair. Their rates are often consistent with those of computer sales organizations. However, as mentioned earlier, you should shop around among service providers as you did to choose your original PC supplier.

Do-It-Yourself Service

The modular design of PC components and the availability of diagnostic programs and publications have simplified the work of do-it-yourself PC owners. If you are handy with a screwdriver and can carefully read and follow directions, then you can be the best and the least expensive service provider for your PC. As you may recall from Chapter 4, there are not that many components in your system. If a hardware problem occurs, you can get the necessary tools to diagnose the problem and purchase the part(s) to replace the malfunctioning component(s) yourself. Your savings can be substantial, compared to having someone else perform the service. In most cases, you'd save the service charges as well as the mark-up on the part(s).

You don't have to be a computer technician to service your own PC, but if you are not sure of your abilities, it's safer to have someone with more expertise perform the work.

12.15. Upgrading and Expanding Your PC

Finding someone with the budget and the ability to buy a computer that can satisfy both current and future needs is rare. Moreover, every time more powerful hardware is introduced, more interesting and fascinating software is rapidly developed to utilize it. Few people can avoid the temptation to upgrade their PCs to take advantage of the newer software. That's why PCs are designed with memory sockets, expansion slots, available drive bays, and extra ports. Because of the foresight of the original designers of the IBM PC who built expandability into their computer, expanding most IBM and compatible computers is very straightforward.

From 1981 to 1987, the standards were based on the same criteria as the IBM PC, XT, and AT systems. Since then, several different memory, interface bus, and drive standards have been introduced. Upgrading your PC is still very straightforward. If you are handy with a screw-driver and have the courage to open up your PC, you may be able to reinvigorate your system every couple of years. You just have to make sure that you get the correct parts for your PC.

Before you invest in faster, larger, or more powerful components for your computer, you have to evaluate the option of buying a brand new computer. The primary factor is economy, followed by performance. If you did a good job in your selection process (as described in Chapter 6), you already have a plan for upgrading your system most economically. Therefore, you shouldn't have to replace any parts or the entire system. However, if for some reason, you face the possibility of upgrading a number of components, you should run through the selection process again. For comparison purposes go through the purchasing process in Chapter 7 to determine the cost of a totally new system with comparable components.

Before you take the plunge to upgrade or replace your PC, you have to set some limits as to how far you are willing to go. Spending over $1,000 to upgrade a PC now worth less than $500 may not be a wise move. The following sections describe the costs and the process of upgrading various components:

CPU

Every year, more powerful and more user friendly software make it easier to get the most from your PC. At the heart of all this lies the ability of your CPU to comfortably handle your requirements. If you have already been using your PC for several months, you are probably wishing that your computer was just a little faster! Most PC users start demanding more power from their system soon after they master the use of their machine. The CPU is the main source of processing power for your PC.

There are three possible upgrade paths for the CPU:

1. Replace the motherboard.

On most PCs, the CPU is installed on the motherboard, which is specifically designed for that CPU. To replace the CPU you'd have to replace the motherboard. In most cases the new motherboard doesn't have to be from the same manufacturer.

2. Replace the CPU board.

Some PCs have a versatile motherboard, often called a backplane board. These boards include the expansion slots and everything else that's not CPU dependent. The CPU is mounted on a detachable board that can be upgraded without changing the backplane board. To replace the CPU, you can simply pull out the CPU board and replace it with a new one, but you are restricted to a CPU board from the same manufacturer.

3. Add a CPU accelerator board.

The CPU accelerator board is independent of the motherboard. It contains a CPU and all the necessary chips to take over the processing inside of your PC. The board requires an open expansion slot on your motherboard.

Replacing a CPU is a little more involved than going from one processor level to the next. As you may recall from Chapter 4, there are several different processor platforms, each with different speeds. The benefits and the cost of going from one level to the next need to be carefully evaluated. If you go up within the same platform, the cost is less than jumping platforms, but the benefits may be small. For example, if you have a 16 MHZ 80386-SX system and upgrade it to a 25 MHZ 80386-SX, your cost will be less than $200, but the benefits can hardly be justified.

Replacing the Motherboard

If you are going to replace the motherboard in your PC, there are several items you should check before buying the new board:

● Check to see whether your expansion slots have 8, 16, or 32 bit buses.

● Are your existing buses ISA, EISA, Micro Channel or local bus?

● What type of memory chips do you currently have? DRAM, SIMM, SIPP?

● How many interface boards do you currently have? How many slots do you need?

● Do you currently have memory cache on the motherboard?

When you start looking for a new motherboard, you should make sure that all, or most of, your existing components can be used with the new board. Also make sure that the following conditions are met:

● The size of the new motherboard should fit your case.

● All your existing interface boards should be compatible with the new motherboard.

● If you had memory cache before, you definitely want cache on the new board.

● If your existing memory chips are the correct type and speed, you should be able to use them.

● Can you trade in your existing motherboard?

● Does the motherboard come with a warranty? Can you install it yourself?

● How much does the supplier charge to install the board and test everything?

After you buy the motherboard, if you are installing it yourself, you should follow the steps outlined below:

- Carefully read the installation manual that comes with the motherboard.

- Backup important data from your hard disk drive.

- Record the system setup information from your existing motherboard.

- Follow the instructions for "Opening up your PC" in this chapter.

- Take all the interface boards out and place them on a non-static surface.

- Unscrew and remove the existing motherboard.

- Take advantage of the opportunity to clean the inside of your PC.

- Set up the jumpers and switches on the new motherboard to closely match the settings of the old motherboard.

- Install the new motherboard and reverse the previous steps to put your PC back together.

- Place the cover back on, plug everything back into the base unit, and turn the power on.

- Perform system setup to configure your new motherboard with your peripherals.

Replacing the CPU Board or Adding An Accelerator Board

Replacing the CPU board in your PC is very similar to replacing an adapter board. However, before purchasing the board, you should follow the steps described above for motherboards. After you buy the board, if you are installing it yourself, follow these steps:

- Carefully read the installation manual that comes with the motherboard.

- Backup important data from your hard disk drive.

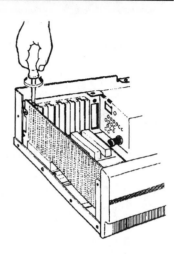

- Record the system setup information from your existing motherboard.

- Follow the instructions for "Opening up your PC" in this chapter.

- Carefully remove the screw holding the existing CPU board and pull the board out.

- Place the new CPU board into the expansion slot and gently press it down into position.

- Put the holding screw back on and reverse the above steps to put the PC back together.

- Replace the cover, plug everything back into the base unit, and turn the power on.

- Perform system setup to configure your new CPU board with your peripherals.

Memory

If you have done a good job of selecting the right type of computer for your needs, then adding memory may be one of the most common upgrades you may have to do. For most

PCs manufactured in the last couple of years, adding more memory is simply a matter of purchasing the chip modules and installing them. Since 1989, most manufacturers have designed their motherboards with enough capacity to hold at least 4 MB, and sometimes 8, 16, or as much as 32 MB of memory. For most home and business applications, 4 MB is more than adequate. However,

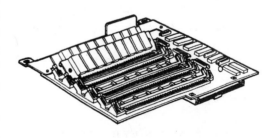

some applications require or simply work faster with more than 4 MB of memory.

Before you buy any additional memory, you should answer several questions, either by checking your PC manual, calling your supplier, or looking inside your system:

- Exactly how much RAM do you currently have?

- Are the memory chips or modules on the motherboard or on a separate memory board?

- What type of memory do the sockets on the board accept? DRAM, SIMM, SIPP?

- What's the size and speed of the memory chips you currently have?

- How many more and what type of memory chips can you add?

After you determine the answers to the above questions you can proceed to the following steps:

- Contact your supplier and determine the cost of the additional memory.

- Contact a few other sources to get comparative prices for the additional memory.

- If your existing memory has to be taken out, ask for a trade-in allowance.

- Check your new memory chips before installing them.

- Follow the instructions for "Opening up your PC" in this Chapter.

- Add the memory to the PC and adjust any necessary switches. If you are adding DRAM chips, make sure that the new chips are inserted with the same orientation of the notch as the existing chips. If you are adding SIMM or SIPP modules, make sure that they have the same orientation as the existing modules.

- Put the computer back together and modify the system configuration, if necessary.

Floppy Drive

There are two primary reasons for upgrading a floppy drive: you are either replacing a drive with a higher capacity one, or adding a different size drive. In either case, several questions need to be answered:

- What type, size, and capacity drive(s) do you currently have?

- How many and what capacity drives can your controller operate?

- How many drives can fit into the base unit?

● Do you have any more power cables for the new floppy drive?

● If the new drive is different from those described in Chapter 4, can your BIOS support it?

To answer these questions you need to refer to your PC operating manual, consult with your supplier, or open the PC to look inside. Once you have answered these questions, you can check prices with your supplier, as well as other sources. If you are replacing an existing drive, ask about trade-in allowances, as well as the cost of installation and testing. If you are somewhat handy with a screwdriver and can be careful inside a PC, you may install the drive yourself. It's not very complicated and the following steps should guide you through:

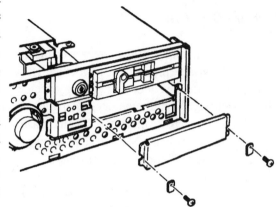

● Open your PC as explained earlier in this chapter.

● Find an empty drive bay inside the case.

● Take out the face plate in front of that empty drive bay.

● Insert the drive into the bay and tighten the screws that hold the drive inside the case. Don't use screws longer than 1/4".

● Connect a power cable from the power supply to the floppy drive. Pay attention to the cable orientation.

● Connect the data cable to the drive. Make sure the color strip on one side of the cable matches the way your existing drive is connected.

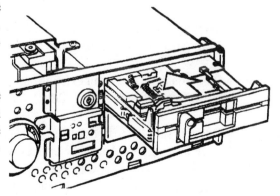

- Put the case back together and power up the computer.

- Most system configurations automatically recognize the new drive; if yours does not, add it manually.

- Test the new drive by formatting a disk and reading from a disk.

Hard Disk Drive

PC software keep getting more powerful and consequently demand more hard disk space. Even if you have properly sized your hard drive based on the guidelines described in earlier chapters, after a year or two you may decide to increase your storage capacity by adding a new drive. Next to memory, adding a hard drive is one of the more common upgrades most people make to their PCs. The increasing popularity of graphics-based software, like those that work in the Microsoft Windows or OS/2 environments, is the leading cause of the high demand for storage capacity.

Another alternative to adding a new drive is to use programs that can more than double the capacity of a hard disk. These programs are generally available for under $100. Latest versions of MS-DOS and DR-DOS include a disk doubling program. If you are going to add a hard drive, follow these steps:

- Check your manuals to determine the name and specifications of your hard disk drive (MFM, RLL or IDE).

- Check the number of drive bays still available in your base unit. If one is available, you can simply add a second hard drive. If none is available, you must replace your existing hard drive.

- Note the make, model, type, size, and speed of your existing drive. Also note whether your hard drive cable has a built-in connector for a second hard drive.

- Based on the size of your existing hard drive, the speed with which you filled it up, and your future storage needs, determine the size of the new drive.

- Call your supplier to find out the price and availability of drives in the capacity range you are looking for. Also check prices with other sources. Besides price, capacity, speed, and warranty, if you are going to install the drive yourself, you should ask what type of installation guide will be included with the drive. Drives are often sold without instructions.

After you buy your new drive, if you are installing it yourself, follow these steps to make sure the new drive is prepared and installed properly:

● Check for any installation guides, test sheets, or video guides that may be packed with the drive. Review the material carefully. Note the drive parameters, such as the number of heads, cylinders, sectors, etc.

● If you are replacing your existing hard drive, you need to make a backup copy of all important files you don't already have on floppy disk or on backup tape. If you are using the DOS BACKUP command to create your backup copies, make sure that you have a copy of the same version of DOS to prepare the new drive. DOS versions prior to 5.0, will not allow backing up with one version and restoring with another. Also write down the existing system configuration of your PC.

● Follow the instructions in "Opening up your PC" in this chapter.

● Carefully unwrap the new drive and insert it into the available drive bay. Do not drop or shake the drive. Hold the drive in position and attach it to the case with four screws. Don't use screws longer than 1/4", and don't tighten them excessively.

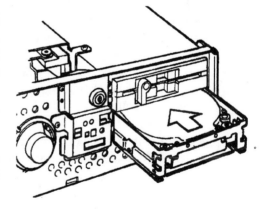

● Connect the power cable and the data cable to the back of the drive (correct orientation).

● Put the case back together and plug the cables into the PC.

● Power up your PC and go through the hard disk preparation steps outlined in your PC manual. Different systems have their own methods for preparing a hard disk for use.

Tape Backup Drive

Prices of tape drives continue to decline, thus making them more attractive to many users.

For many businesses working with crucial business data, the tape drive is an absolute necessity. It's frequently purchased with the computer. The home user, on the other hand, doesn't often buy a tape drive with the system. You may decide to buy a tape drive for the convenience of the backup or to store less frequently used programs to free up your hard disk space.

When considering the addition of a tape drive, you need to keep the following points in mind:

- Carefully evaluate the costs versus benefits of buying a tape drive. DOS as well as backup utility software let you make backup copies of important data that you routinely change or create. Although they cost relatively less than a tape drive, they do require that you be present when the backup is being made. A tape drive can operate by itself at predetermined times.

- The tape drive capacity can be the same as or less than your hard disk drive's because usually 80 percent of the data stored on the hard drive are non-changing programs. Therefore, one backup copy on one or more tapes will give you a long term backup. You can then use the tape drive to backup the remaining 20 percent that's changed or created on a regular basis.

- If you have only one floppy drive in your computer, chances are that the floppy controller can also operate the tape drive. If so, look for a tape drive that can use the existing controller.

- Check with your supplier for price and availability. Also check prices with other sources. Ask about manufacturer, model, type, capacity, transfer rate, and warranty, as well as price, and the cost of installing and testing the drive.

After you buy the drive, if you are going to install it yourself, follow basically the same procedure described earlier for a floppy drive installation. Tape drives come with special backup software which must be installed on your hard disk. Simply follow the software installation guide that comes with the drive.

CD-ROM Drive

Adding a CD drive is gradually becoming more popular as prices continue to drop, and the number of topics on CDs soars into the thousands. CD drives can be added as easily as a floppy drive. If your PC uses an SCSI controller for the hard disk drive, then the CD drive can be hooked up directly to that controller.

If you have decided to add a CD drive to your system, then simply follow the steps outlined earlier for floppy drives, hard disk drives, or tape drives. The procedure is basically the same with the following exceptions:

● Check the drive documentation to see whether it requires you to set a specific SCSI ID number for it. If it does, then set the ID number accordingly.

● Check the termination on your CD-ROM drive. If it's the last SCSI device in your SCSI chain, then it should be terminated (see your CD manual).

● Install the CD-ROM software driver.

Monitor and Graphics Adapter

If you were able to follow the purchasing guidelines described earlier in this book, you really should not have to upgrade your monitor and graphics adapter. However, if due to a very tight budget at the time of purchase or a specific need that appeared after you purchased your system, you decide that you need a better monitor, then you should find the following information:

● Find out exactly what type of monitor you have (monochrome, CGA, EGA, VGA, etc.).

● Find out what type of video adapter you have (monochrome, CGA, EGA, VGA, SVGA, etc.).

● If you plan to run some type of special purpose software, find out what type of monitor it requires.

Current video technology for most of us peaks at Enhanced Super VGA (8514/A) with 1,024x768 resolution. In this range, the monitor has 0.28 mm dot pitch and the video card has 1 MB of RAM. If your present level is well below this, then it's very easy to justify the cost of the upgrade. If, on the other hand, you have a good color VGA monitor and VGA card, you might wait a little longer and upgrade to the level above Enhanced Super VGA (8514/A). That may be a 1,280 x 1,024 resolution, 15" or 16", non-interlaced Super VGA monitor with an accelerator video board.

To upgrade from a monochrome VGA monitor to color VGA, all you have to do is buy a color VGA monitor. To upgrade from an older video standard like Monochrome, CGA, or EGA, you need to purchase a color VGA monitor as well as a VGA card. In this case, if you can afford to buy the Enhanced Super VGA, you'll be able to take advantage of newer features and the latest technology.

Upgrading Software

Like PC hardware, software is periodically enhanced and updated. As PCs become faster and the cost of RAM memory and hard disk capacity go down, software manufacturers tend to take advantage of these features to make their programs more powerful and more user friendly. They add more features, more bells and whistles, and more intuitive abilities. These features are offered in upgrades about once a year.

Since the late 1980's, PC programs have become so powerful and full of features that recent upgrades are not as revolutionary as they used to be. They are a great source of revenue for the software companies. Millions of registered users are encouraged to upgrade every time a new version is released.

You have to carefully evaluate your needs versus the capabilities of your current software version and then decide if you need the upgrade. Some upgrades offer significant improvements and can be cost justified. The wealth of features in recent PC software is so immense that they are like an iceberg. You only use a small number of the basic features, while most of the bells and whistles will often go unused.

Your PC is a wonderful tool and you should use it to its fullest potential. As you discover ways to enjoy your PC, remember that your imagination is your only limitation.

APPENDIX

A. User Groups

Alabama
Birmingham IBM PC Users
Birmingham
205/871-1939

Huntsville IBM PC Users
Huntsville
205/539-5940

Alaska
Polar PC Users Group
Fairbanks
907/452-2500

Ankor-Guide Group
Anchorage
907/349-2459

Arizona
Phoenix PC Users
Phoenix
602/943-7907

Tuscon Computer Society
Tucson
602/577-3261

The Homeport
Scottsdale
602/451-5340

Arkansas
Arkansas PC Users Group
Fort Smith
501/784-8400

Central Ark. PC Users
Little Rock
501/225-9304

Twin Lakes Computer Users
Mountain Home
501/425-9061

NW Ark. Microcomp Users
Springdale
501/361-2963

Data Point
Fayetteville
501/442-8777

California
Berkeley PC Comp Users
Berkeley
415/526-4033

Valley Computer Club
Burbank
818/842-3707

Fog Int'l Computer Users
Daly City
415/755-2000

IBM Humboldt Users
Eureka
707/442-4621

Microlink PCUG
Hacienda Height
818/917-6470

Antelope Valley Micro Users
Lancaster
805/948-5166

San Luis Obispo PC Users
Los Osos
805/528-0121

Monterey Bay Users
Monterey
408/373-6245

Napa Valley PC Users
Napa
707/255-9241

Channel Islands PC Users
Oxnard
805/983-4741

Pasadena IBM Users Group
Pasadena
818/795-2300

Riverside IBM Comp. Club
Riverside
714/685-5407

Sacramento PC Users
Sacramento
916/386-9865

Inland Empire Computer
San Bernardino
714/864-3093

San Diego Computer Society
San Diego
619/549-3787

San Francisco Comp Society
San Francisco
415/929-0252

San Francisco PC Users
San Francisco
415/221-9166

Santa Barbara PC Users
Santa Barbara
805/969-9961

Silicon Valley Comp. Society
Santa Clara
408/286-1271

North Bay Users
Vallejo
707/644-9327

Colorado
Metro Area Comp. Enthus.
Aurora
303/830-9143

Colorado Springs PC Users
Colorado Spring
719/596-6938

Mile Hi Comp. Resource Org.
Denver
303/286-7455

Windows on Rockies Users
Denver
303/733-1277

Front Range PC Users
Fort Collins
303/233-8654

Conneticut
Central CT PC Group
Coventry
203/742-6083

Bus/Pro Micro Users Group
West Hartford
203/242-6587

Delaware
PC Professional Users
Wilmington
302/656-8200

District of Columbia
IDI
Washington, DC
202/408-1163

Florida
SW Fla. PC Users Group
Ft. Meyers
813/997-0910

HogTown Hackers
Gainesville
904/392-3151

Miami PC User Group
Hollywood
305/962-8889

Jax PC Users Group
Jacksonville
904/737-6327

PB Bug
Naples
813/261-8208

Suncoast Users Group
St. Pete
813/343-2668

Sarasota IBM PC Users
Sarasota
813/924-4480

USF PC Users
Tampa
813/974-3190

Palm Beach PC Users
West Palm Beach
407/689-8841

Georgia
Atlanta PC Users
Atlanta
404/255-0258

CSRA Computer Society
Augusta
404/790-5241

Idaho
Idaho PC Users Group
Boise
208/939-9120

Illinois
N. Illinois Computer Society
Arlington Height
708/824-2650

Chicago Computer Society
Chicago
312/794-7737

Fox Valley Comp. Users
N. Aurora
708/879-6462

Peoria Computer Club
Peoria
309/685-8289

N. Illinois Computer Owners
Winfield
708/653-3416

Indiana
Anderson Computer Users
Anderson
317/646-3316

Indianapolis Comp Society
Indianapolis
317/251-2003

Iowa
Quad-Cities Computer
Society
Davenport
319/386-3484

Hawkeye PC Users
Iowa City
319/351-7462

NE Iowa PC Users
Waterloo
319/234-0654

Kansas
Topeka PC Users Club
Topeka
913/266-4505

Kentucky
Central Ky. Computer
Society
Lexington
606/266-7446

Kentucky-Indiana PC Users
Louisville
502/560-2562

Heartland Users
Paducah
502/898-2489

Louisiana
Baton Rouge Serious IBM
Users
Baton Rouge
504/924-8066

Acadiana Micro Users
Lafayette
318/235-6701

NW Louisiana PC Users
Shreveport
318/868-5950

Maine
Portland Maine IBM Users
Old Orchard Beach
207/934-5521

Maryland
Capital PC Users
Rockville
301/762-6775

Chesapeake PC Users
Annapolis
301/647-7139

Massachusetts
Boston Computer Society
Cambridge
617/252-0600

Michigan
Flint Area Comp. Enthusiasts
Flint
313/667-3183

SW Michigan PC User Group
Kalamazoo
616/349-5381

Minnesota
Twin Cities PC Users
Edina
612/888-0557

Missouri
Kansas City PC User Group
Kansas City
816/444-8709

Microcomputer Users
Kansas City
816/587-8820

St. Louis Users Group
St. Louis
314/458-9604

Nevada
Las Vegas PC Users
Las Vegas
702/431-4333

New Hampshire
Pemi-Baker Computer
Group
Plymouth
603/536-3880

New Jersey
PC Club of South Jersey
Cherry Hill
609/428-8759

New Jersey PC Users
Paramus
201/447-7111

Amateur Comp. Group of NJ
Scotch Plains
908/574-1282

New York
Buffalo IBM PC Users
Buffalo
716/695-2593

Hudson Valley PC Club
Kingston
914/657-6354

Creative Computing
New York City
212/888-3953

NY Amateur Computer Club
New York City
212/505-6021

NY Personal Computer
Group
New York City
212/686-6972

FROG Computer Society
Rochester
716/244-4038

Syracuse Microcomputer
Club
Syracuse
315/492-6437

Westchester PC Users
White Plains
914/923-1337

North Carolina
Asheville IBM PC Users
Asheville
704/274-5331

Foothills PC Users
Hickory
704/256-6924

North Dakota
Magic City IBM PC Users
Minot
701/839-6008

Ohio
Cincinnati PC Users
Cincinnati
513/745-9356

Cleveland Computer Society
Cleveland
216/781-4132

Dayton Microcomp
Associates.
Dayton
513/252-1230

Toledo PC Users
Toledo
419/471-9444

Western Res. IBM PC Assoc
Warren
216/373-2745

Oklahoma
OKC PC Users Group
Oklahoma City
405/791-0894

Tulsa Computer Society
Tulsa
918/622-3417

Oregon
Eugene PC Users
Eugene
503/484-3306

Portland PC Users
Portland
503/226-4143

Pennsylvania
Computer Users of Erie
Erie
814/454-1658

Harrisburg PC Users
Harrisburg
717/652-9097

Phil. Area Computer Society
Philadelphia
215/951-1255

Greene County PC Users
Waynesburg
412/852-1494

Rhode Island
South County Comp Users
Wakefield
401/539-6034

South Carolina
Charleston Computer Club
Charlest803/722-7445

Palmetto PC Club
Columbia
803/754-7525

Tennessee
Music City IBM PC Users
Nashville
615/662-0322

East Tenn. PC Users Group
Oak Ridge
615/435-3311

Texas
Brazos Valley PC
College Station
409/779-5050

North Texas PC Users
Dallas
214/746-4699

Ft. Worth IBM PC Users
Ft. Worth
817/656-0446

Bay Area PC Organization
Houston
713/483-4807

Dallas-Fort Worth Users
Irving
214/986-9228

Alamo PC Organization
San Antonio
512/655-1058

Utah
Utah Blue Chips
Salt Lake City
801/521-7830

Virginia
The Virginia Connection
Reston
703/648-1841

Washington
Pacific NW IBM PC Users
Bellevue
206/646-6570

Borderline PC Users
Bellingham
206/671-9113

West Virginia
Huntington PC Users
Huntington
304/529-2391

Wisconsin
Madison IBM PC Users
Madison
608/255-1205

Milwaukee Area IBM PC
Users
Milwaukee
414/679-9075

B. PC Publications

Byte
P. O. Box 552
Hightstown, NJ 08520
(12 issues/year, $29.95)

Compute
P. O. Box 3245
Harlan, IA 51537
(800) 727-6937
(12 issues/year, $19.94)

Computer Buyer's Guide
P. O. Box 318
Mt. Morris, IL 61054
(800) 877-5487
(12 issues/year, $36.00)

Computer Buying World
P. O. Box 3020
Northbrook, IL 60065
(617) 246-3800
(12 issues/year, $72.00)

Computer Shopper
P. O. Box 52568
Boulder, CO 80321
(800) 274-6384
(12 issues/year, $29.97)

Corporate Computing
One Park Ave.
New York, NY 10016
(609) 461-2100
(12 issues/year, $50 or free to
qualified applicants)

InfoWorld
P. O. Box 3014
Northbrook, IL 60065
(708) 564-0694
(52 issues/year, $110 or free
to qualified applicants)

New Media
901 Mariner's Island Blvd.
San Mateo, CA 94404
(415) 573-5170
(12 issues/year, $48 or free to
qualified applicants)

PC Computing
P. O. Box 58229
Boulder, CO 80322
(800) 365-2770
(12 issues/year, $24.97)

PC Magazine
P. O. Box 54093
Boulder, CO 80322
(800) 289-0429
(22 issues/year, $44.97)

PC Sources
P. O. Box 53298
Boulder, CO 80322
(800) 827-2078
(12 issues/year, $29.90)

PC Week
P. O. Box 1770
Riverton, NJ 08077
(609) 461-2100
(52 issues/year, $160 or free
to qualified applicants)

PC World
P. O. Box 55029
Boulder, CO 80322
(800) 234-3498
(12 issues/year, $16.97)

Windows
P.O. Box 386
Carprinteria, CA 93014
(805) 566-1282
(12 issues/year, $35.95)

C. National Service Companies

AT & T Computer Systems
One Speedwell Avenue
Morristown, NJ 07960
(800) 247-1212

Bell Atlantic Business
50 East Swedesford Road
Frazer, PA 19355
(800) 767-2876

Intelogic Trace, Inc.
Turtle Creek Tower 1
San Antonio, TX 78229
(800) 531-7186

Memorex Telex
6929 North Lakewood
Tulsa, OK 74117
(800) 331-7410

Texas Instruments
P. O. Box 202230
Austin, TX 78720
(800) 527-3500

TRW Customer Service
15 Law Drive
Fairfield, NJ 07004
(800) 922-0897

Glossary of Terms

Following is a list of the most commonly used terms relating to your PC, DOS and Windows. You don't need to read this section to simply increase your knowledge. It's a quick reference guide to the definition of various things you may run into.

286: is the abbreviated name for a family of PC microprocessors using the 80286 chip. This PC family is also called AT, which stands for Advanced Technology. PCs using the 286 chip are now considered old, outdated and slow.

386: is the abbreviated name for the 80386 family of microprocessor chips and PCs using that chip. Slightly scaled down version of these chips are called 386 SX.

386 enhanced mode: is a mode available only to 386 and newer generation PCs. In this mode Windows is able to use more of your PC memory to perform more advanced activities such as multi-tasking, etc.

486: is the abbreviated name for the 80486 family of microprocessor chips and PCs using that chip. Slightly scaled down versions of these chips are called 486 SX. Higher performance versions of these chips are known as 80486 DX2.

80X86: Intel Corporation, the inventor of the microprocessor chip began a numbering scheme using 80X86 where the X varied depending on the chip generation. The chip used in the original IBM PC in 1981, was an 8088. It was followed by 80286, 80386 and 80486. In 1993, Intel discontinued using the generic numbers for newer chips in favor of a name they could trademark. The latest generation Intel chip is called "Pentium" which would have been called 80586 under the old scheme.

Access Time: is expressed in milliseconds (one thousandth of a second) and is the length of time it takes a drive to get a certain piece of information from a disk.

Active: is a window or icon you are currently using or you have highlighted. You can only have one window or icon active at any time. When an icon is active, its name is highlighted. When a window is active, its title bar changes color.

Address: is a specific location in a computer's memory or on a disk.

Analog: is a method of data flow that is continuous, as opposed to digital, which is based on the two digits zero and one. For example, if you used a paint brush to paint a wall it would be similar to analog, and if you used a pen to place thousands of tiny dots on that wall, it would be similar to digital.

ANSI: American National Standards Institute has established a 256 character set that the computer uses to translate your keystrokes into the symbols that you see on the screen or on printed documents. The ANSI character set includes the upper and lower case letters of the alphabet, numbers, and other related characters and symbols.

Applications Software: This is a general term referring to programs written to perform particular activities such as word processing, database management, accounting, computational analysis, etc.

Application icon: is a small graphic design that represents an applications software running at the moment.

Application window: is a window which contains the applications software and its related directories. The name of the applications software appears at the top of the window.

Arrow keys: are the four keys with pointed arrows in all directions (Up, Down, Left, Right). You can use the arrow keys to move the cursor or the highlight.

ASCII: American Standard Code for Information Interchange is the code that establishes how various characters including numbers and letters of the alphabet are represented by binary numbers. Binary numbers are represented by the digits zero and one. Computers process data in ASCII format. Various programs translate your input into ASCII for the computer to understand and then translate the computer's output from ASCII to English so you can understand.

Asynchronous: is the most common form of communication between serial devices. It controls the flow of information between two devices by sending start and stop codes at the beginning and at the end of each byte of data being transmitted.

Attributes: are sets of information about a file which indicate whether the file has been changed since it was last backed up, or, if it is read-only, system or hidden file.

AUTOEXEC.BAT: is a set of instructions for the computer to execute when it is first powered up or reset. It is activated automatically.

Automatic link: is a link that is set to automatically update all the places where the object is located, every time you change it.

Background: in more powerful computers that can perform several tasks simultaneously, background refers to the program or programs that do not have the highest priority. Therefore, they may be running in the background and out of sight while the program with the highest priority is running in foreground on the screen.

Backslash: "\" is the opposite of slash "/", and it's function is entirely different from slash. It is used to identify a directory, or to move you from one directory to another. For example, \LETTERS identifies a directory called LETTERS. The backslash key is often on the top right corner of your keyboard.

Backspace key: is the key often located on the top right hand corner of your keyboard. Every time it is pressed, it moves the cursor on your screen back one space to the left. It also deletes the character or space in that location.

Basic: Beginner's Algebraic Symbolic Instruction Code is one of the oldest and most widely used

PC programming languages. Basic commands are closely related to simple English. Therefore it is one of the easiest programming languages available. But as far as you are concerned, don't worry about programming.

Batch file: is a series of DOS commands that are executed sequentially one after another when the batch file is called upon, e.g. AUTOEXEC.BAT which is activated when you power up your PC.

BAUD: Baud rate is the unit of measure indicating the number of changes in data signal per second. In modems it is used to measure the speed with which a communication link can transfer data. The higher the Baud rate the faster the modem. Baud rate is no longer used as an indicator of speed for modems. It's replaced by Bits Per Second (BPS).

Beeps: are the intermittent sounds emitted by your computer under different circumstances. The computer uses the beeps to communicate with you. Certain number of beeps when the computer is turned on or when certain events take place can tell you if the computer has a problem or is stuck. For example, if your monitor or keyboard accidentally get disconnected, the computer will emit a number of beeps which is different from the single beep that it sounds when everything is all right.

Benchmark: is a special program designed to measure the performance of certain components of your PC and compare them to others in the same category. Different benchmark programs may produce different comparative results.

Binary: is a mathematical method for representing numbers based on 2 digits instead of the 10 digits that we are used to. In our daily use of numbers we have ten digits from 0 to 9 and we use these digits to count up from 10, 11, 12, and so on. In the binary method there are only two digits 0 and 1 and the numbers following those are represented by a combination of those two digits. Computers use the binary method as electronic "on" and "off" switches to express numbers, letters of the alphabet and other characters.

BIOS: Basic Input/Output System is a software program that is stored in a microchip installed by the manufacturer on your computer's motherboard. It contains the basic instructions that tell your PC how to operate.

Bit: A bit is the smallest unit of measure in computer terminology. It represents the "on" or "off" status of a microprocessor switch.

Bitmap: is an image or graph that is stored as a series of dots.

Boot: is the act of starting the computer. There are two types of boots: cold boot and warm boot. They are both described later in this section.

BPS: Bits Per Second is a unit of measure indicating the number of bits a modem is capable of transferring in a communication link. BPS is a more accurate measure of data transmission than Baud rate. Newer modems are capable of transmitting more than one bit per data signal, therefore BPS is now the standard measure of modem transmission rate rather Baud.

Branch: is part of the directory tree in File Manager. Just like branches on a tree, a directory may contain subdirectories.

Browse: is a button in most Windows dialog boxes. It allows you to look at the contents of another box to search for files or directories.

Buffer: is a certain amount of memory between the microprocessor and another device. It temporarily holds data and feeds it to that device at a speed the device can process. Buffer can be part of the computer memory, a hard disk or an external device with built-in memory. Buffers are often built into printers, so that the printer can accept a certain number of pages, free up the PC and regulate the printing speed.

Bug: is an error or problem in computer hardware or software. It causes the PC or the software to do some strange things like freeze or mess up your data.

Bus: is a connector through which the microprocessor communicates with other devices attached to the motherboard. It is often called an expansion slot. It is an opening about 4 inches or longer, with a row of gold plated connectors on each side of the opening. Adapter boards that serve as interfaces between the motherboard and other devices have a protrusion on their bottom side that is inserted into the bus opening. A PC may have one or more expansion slots. The more unused expansion slots a PC has, the more room it has to expand.

Byte: is a unit of measure for storage of characters or numbers in the computer. Each Byte is 8 Bits. Because there are 8 positions of "on" or "off" in a Byte, there are 256 different values that can be represented by a single Byte. Size of the computer memory as well as the capacity of floppy, hard disk, tape backup and CD drives are measured by Bytes. One simple rule of thumb to relate Bytes to storage device capacity is that the average typed page contains about 2,000 Bytes. Therefore, a 40 Mega Byte (40,000,000 Bytes) hard drive can store the equivalent of 20,000 (40,000,000 divided by 2,000) pages of information.

Caps Lock: is a key usually located on the left hand side of the keyboard. When pressed, it locks the keyboard into upper case letters. Most keyboards have a small light which turns on when the Caps Lock Key is depressed. If the Caps Lock Key is pressed again, the keyboard goes into lower case letters and the light goes out.

Cascade: is one of the ways you can arrange open windows on your desktop so the title bar of each window overlaps the other and stays visible. You can make that window active by clicking on its title bar.

CD-ROM: is a new and popular way of storing and using a huge amount of information. Compact Disk-Read Only Memory means that the disk can only give you the information that was stored on it at the factory. It can not let you store information on the compact disk. CDs are capable of storing complete sets of encyclopedias, or the entire phone directories of the United States. During the 1990's, CD-ROMs will become a necessity in every PC.

Character: is a single digit, a letter of the alphabet, or a symbol.

Character set: is a group of characters that have something in common, i.e. ASCII character set

Check box: is a small box that appears in a dialog box. You can select it by clicking your mouse pointer on it. When it is selected, an X appears in the box. Like a light switch, you can turn a check box function on or off.

Chip: is brief for microchip, which is a small integrated circuit. The chip is built on a silicon crystal wafer. The tiny silicon unit is enclosed in a small plastic or ceramic case with short metallic legs. It is inserted into various printed circuit boards. Different chips are designed to perform specific functions.

Choose: is the act of picking an icon or a command with your mouse or keyboard, in order to perform a certain task.

Click: is the sound of the little buttons on your mouse. When you read or hear someone say click the left button, it means that you move your mouse until the little pointer goes over your target, then you press the left button and release it.

Clipboard: is a part of your memory and maybe hard disk space that is used as temporary storage. It is like a holding area where you move things into and out of. For example, if you cut a portion of your document, it goes into your clipboard. You can then paste that portion somewhere else.

Clock: is a special crystal that is mounted on the motherboard of your PC. The clock crystal produces a regular pulse or signal which like the human heartbeat, regulates the functions of the PC and all its components. The clock pulse is measured in Mega Hertz or millions of pulses per second.

Close: is the act of quitting an application or removing a window or dialog box. The Close command is usually located in the File Menu.

Color scheme: is a combination of colors used by Windows.

CMOS: is a special type of memory inside your PC. It keeps track of the important components that are connected to your PC. It knows your configuration, date, time, hard disk drive, floppy drives, etc. This information is maintained by a small battery that usually lasts about five years.

Cold Boot: is the process of starting the computer by turning its switch on. Because the computer was started from an off position, the computer memory starts out blank.

Command: is a special set of instructions for the computer.

Command button: is a button that represents a command action, for example: Copy, Help, etc.

Command line: is a command that you type at the DOS prompt or in a dialog box to run an application.

CONFIG.SYS: is a configuration batch file that executes various configuration commands as the computer is turned on. CONFIG.SYS is executed when the computer is turned on with a cold boot or is reset. It is stored on the hard disk or bootup floppy disk. It clears out of memory after the computer is turned off.

Confirmation message: is a message that comes up after you specify a certain course of action. It asks you if you want to continue with the action or want to cancel it.

Control key: is a special key usually located on the bottom left side of the keyboard. DOS and other software programs use it to perform specific tasks.

Conventional Memory: is the first 640 K of memory (RAM). It's used by DOS and other programs as the main area of interaction between you, the user, the programs, and various devices attached to the PC.

Copy: is a command that lets you transfer a copy of a selected text or item to the clipboard for temporary storage, before you transfer that copy to another place.

CPS: Characters Per Second is the unit of measure for printing speed. Its often established by the printer manufacturer and is usually based on somewhat ideal conditions. CPS is expressed in draft as well as enhanced or letter quality modes. Draft speed is faster than letter quality.

CPI: Characters Per Inch is a unit of measure that determines the number of characters printed per inch by a printer. Most regular correspondence is printed in 10 characters per inch. All printers except daisywheel, are capable of printing a wide range of characters per inch. Some headings may be 1 CPI, and some fine prints may be 17 CPI.

CPU: Central Processing Unit is the microprocessor chip that is the brains of your computer. It performs all data processing, interpretation, and command executions.

CRT: Cathode Ray Tube is the picture tube inside your monitor and has a conical shape. Rays of light are generated in the back of the tube and travel to the front which is the screen of the monitor. Conventional monitors that look like a TV set, use CRT's. Other types of screens used on portable computers, are flat and use a different technology called LCD (Liquid Crystal Display), similar to calculators and digital watches.

Cursor: is a blinking indicator that appears on the screen of your monitor. It shows where you are currently located. In DOS programs it's a blinking "-" dash. In Windows it looks like a pointer and is easily moved around by a mouse.

Cut: is a command that allows you to take out a selected text or item and move it to the temporary storage in clipboard.

Data: is any type of information, symbols, letters, numbers, etc. that is processed by a computer.

Database Management: is a popular type of software that can store and retrieve information quickly and easily.

Default button: is a button that is often highlighted or has a bold border. It contains the command Windows thinks you will most likely choose to use. To use it, all you have to do is press ENTER.

Default printer: is a printer that Windows considers to be active at this moment. If you want to use it, you don't need to specify it every time.

Default settings: are a set of specifications that you will most likely use in any specific file or document. You define them only once and don't have to specify them every time.

Decimal: is the numbering system we use in our daily life. It is based on the ten digits 0 to 9.

Default: is a set of predetermined numbers or rules that establish what you want your PC to do in most cases until you decide to change the rules. For example, in word processing, if you want all the lines in your letters be single spaced, make single space a default. You will no longer have to tell your PC that you want single spaced every time you type a letter.

Density: is the capacity for the amount of data that can be stored in a certain amount of space. It is primarily used for measuring the storage capacity of floppy disks. Common terms are double density or high density. Almost all newer PCs are sold with high density floppy disk drives.

Desktop: is the screen that appears in the background of your Windows. Various windows, icons, dialog boxes, etc. appear on the desktop.

Destination directory: is a directory where you plan to move or copy files to.

Device: is a component or instrument inside or outside the PC that performs a certain function.

Device driver: is a set of instructions that control how a PC communicates with a device. Device drivers for certain, popular devices are built into Windows. Others are supplied by the device manufacturer.

Dialog box: is a window that pops on your screen at certain times and asks for specific information.

Digital: is the standard for expressing information in digits. In the computer world all values are expressed by the digits 0 and 1.

Directory: is a designation or container on a floppy disk or hard disk. It may contain programs, files and other pieces of information that you would like to group together. If you think of a floppy disk or hard disk as a filing cabinet, a directory is like a drawer in that cabinet. It helps you organize various information by category or function. For example all your personal letters can be stored in a directory called: C:\Personal\Letters\

Directory icon: is a small graphic image that represents a directory.

Directory tree: is a graphical representation of the directory structure on a disk.

Disk: brief for diskette is the magnetic data storage media that comes in two sizes of 5.25 or 3.5 inches.

Disk cache: is a part of PC memory used as a temporary holding area for information frequently needed from the hard disk.

Display: refers to the screen of your PC monitor.

DOS Prompt: is the familiar C:\>- which means that your PC is ready to do whatever you tell it to do in drive C:. If your prompt shows A:\>- then it is ready to work in drive A:.

Dot Matrix: is the printing technology that creates letters, numbers, symbols and graphics by forming the shape of the characters using small dots.

Double click: is the process of rapidly clicking the mouse button twice.

DPI: Dots Per Inch is a unit of measure of how many horizontal and vertical dots can be printed per inch. The higher the two numbers, the smaller the dots, and therefore the better and crisper the printed results. For example, standard laser printers produce 300 DPI in horizontal and vertical. Their output look sharp and crisp. Dot matrix printers are usually capable of 150 to 300 DPI horizontal and 150 to 240 DPI vertical.

Dot Pitch: Computer monitors display information by forming characters made up of thousands of small dots. Dot Pitch is the distance between the display dots on a monitor. It is expressed in millimeters. The smaller the dot pitch the better the crispness of characters and the higher the price. Dot pitch ranges from 0.20 to 0.50 millimeters. A regular VGA monitor has a .42 mm dot pitch, while a Super VGA monitor is usually .28 mm.

Double Sided/Double Density: DS/DD is the description of a type of diskette. All diskettes currently in use are at least DS/DD. Earlier generation diskettes could only store data on one side of the magnetic media. They also stored data relatively sparsely on each track. As the densities increased and both sides were utilized, the DS/DD diskettes became the standard. DS/DD disk drives were used in early generation PCs and XT's that were based on the 8088 processor. The DS/DD capacity of 5.25" disks is 360 K, and for the 3.5" disks is 720 K.

Double Sided/High Density: DS/HD is the description of a type of diskette. DS/HD disks usually contain twice or four times the capacity of DS/DD disks. DS/HD disk drives are used in 80286 and higher generation PCs. The DS/HD capacity of 5.25" disks is 1.2 MB, and for the 3.5" disks is 1.4 MB.

Drag: is the process of pointing at something on the screen with your mouse, holding down the button and moving the item your mouse is holding to a different location.

DRAM: Dynamic Random Access Memory is a type of memory that holds information as long as power is supplied to the computer. Also see RAM.

DR-DOS: is the Disk Operating System developed by Digital Research Corporation. Operationally it is compatible with MS-DOS developed by Microsoft Corporation. However, it offers features that are different from MS-DOS.

Driver: is a specific program or set of commands which make a particular type of software work with a PC. Most commercially available software already incorporate drivers into their software to work with various devices. For example, most word processing programs include built in drivers for a wide variety of monitor and printer types. In case a program does not have a built-in driver for something you have on your PC, the driver may be obtained separately from the software company or the equipment manufacturer.

Duplex: is a communication standard between two devices. Full duplex allows two devices to communicate with each other simultaneously. Half duplex only allows one device to send information at a time.

EGA: Enhanced Graphics Adapter was introduced in the mid-1980's as a better means of displaying information on your PC. It was later abandoned in favor of VGA which produces better colors and sharper characters.

EEMS: Enhanced Expanded Memory Specification is an enhanced version of the EMS standard.

Embed: is the process of inserting an object from one document into another.

EMS: Expanded Memory Specification is a standard developed by Lotus, Intel, and Microsoft that lets some programs access memory above 640 K.

ENTER: is the process of submitting a certain amount of data to the microprocessor by pressing the "ENTER" (or sometimes marked RETURN) key. Pressing the "ENTER" key after you type a command or a certain amount of data, tells the computer to process that information.

Environment: is the space on your PC screen where you work. If you only use DOS, you are working in a text based environment, because everything is done by typing text into your PC, using your keyboard. If you use DOS Shell or Windows, you are using a graphical environment, because to tell your PC to execute a command you can simply point at a graphic image with your mouse.

Escape Key: is the key that lets you get out of most situations. Some programs tell you to use it if you want to quit, or go back to something else. Other programs let you use it if you get stuck.

Execute: in computer language is the process of running a program or performing a command.

Extension: every file name can have up to 8 characters. After the file name a 3 character extension allows a program or the user further identify a file by type or group. For example, your letters can all have the extension ".ltr", i.e. personal.ltr

Expanded Memory: is memory that uses the EMS or EEMS standard to access up to 32 MB of RAM.

Extended Memory: is memory above 1 MB (1,024 K) in 80286, 80386, and 80486 systems. Certain programs can take advantage of this memory to perform their functions much faster than having to use the hard disk drive. Some programs like Windows and OS/2 can use extended memory to simulate expanded memory.

External DOS command: is a command that resides in the DOS directory and is not loaded into RAM memory when the computer is powered up. To access an external command, the computer needs to read that command file from the hard disk or floppy disk where it's located.

FAT: File Allocation Table is the main map that the PC maintains on each floppy disk and hard disk to keep track of the location of files and directories. If this table is messed up or damaged, all your data on the hard disk may be lost.

FILE: is a collection of data that may be as little as a few lines of text to as big as a book. A file name is almost like the name on a folder. The folder may contain just one sheet of paper or several hundred.

Fixed Disk: is another name for the hard disk drive. It contains one or more rigid disks called platters. The platter is coated with a special magnetic material that allows it to store electronic signals similar to a cassette tape.

Floppy Disk: is a flexible data storage device used in floppy disk drives. The storage media is a thin, circular item made of paper-thin plastic and coated with special magnetic particles. It's contained in a square protective cover. There are two sizes of floppy disks 5.25 x 5.25 or 3.5 x 3.5 inches.

Flow Control: is a process that controls the flow of information from one device to another. It is found in the Control Panel and Terminal.

Font: is a set of symbols, letters or numbers that have a certain, unique design. For example, all the characters in this Glossary are the same font. Although some may be bold, or larger than others, all the "A's", or "B's", etc. look the same.

Foreground: powerful PCs that are capable of running several programs simultaneously, do so in foreground and background. Foreground refers to the program that is currently running on the screen and has the highest priority. Other program(s) with lower priority may run in the background.

FORMAT: is a definition of the way information is set up in a document. It is used for preparing a floppy disk or a hard disk for use for the first time. It is also used to completely erase everything from the disk and start as if new. Disks use magnetics to store information. The surface of the disk is specially treated and has microscopic grooves. Due to imperfections that may exist on the magnetic surface of the disk, manufacturers provide more capacity than is ultimately produced on the disk after formatting. For example a 1.4 MB floppy disk may actually have a 2.0 MB manufactured capacity, or a 40 MB hard disk may have a 45 MB manufactured capacity. The FORMAT command of DOS, analyzes the disk surface for imperfections and then marks-off all defective or suspicious areas. DOS then writes a very precise and detailed map of the areas to avoid at the beginning of the disk. Thus the controller will avoid writing any data in those areas. For consistency, DOS trims down all disks with similar manufactured capacities to a standard formatted capacity. For example, all different brands of 2.0 MB floppy disks are formatted down to 1.4 MB, regardless of the amount of defects found by formatting.

Function: is an activity performed or a role played by a command or program in order to accomplish a specific objective.

Gigabytes: is one billion bytes. Some very high capacity hard disk drives used by large organizations have gigabyte capacities. One gigabyte stores the equivalent of 500,000 typed pages of information.

Graphics mode: is a way for your PC to display graphic images in addition to text. Windows and all Windows software, always operate in a graphics mode. DOS based programs always operate in a text mode and some have a graphics mode as well.

Graphical User Interface: is also called GUI (pronounced Goo-ey). It means that instead of typing commands like DOS, you use pictures and graphics to communicate with your PC. To use GUI comfortably, you need to have a mouse.

Group: is a method of gathering certain programs or files together within the Program Manager.

Hand Shake: is a communication process between two devices through which they acknowledge the connection and determine each other's settings and operating criteria. For example when two modems are connected, the first thing they do is to exchange each other's settings so that each knows how to send and receive data.

Hard Disk: which is also called fixed disk, is a storage device that contains one or more rigid disks called platters. The platter is coated with a special magnetic material that allows it to store electronic signals similar to a cassette tape.

Hardware: refers to all the physical components of a computer.

Hidden files: are files that may reside on a floppy or hard disk drive but their names or characteristics are hidden from view. A hard disk drive, or a floppy disk that has DOS for booting up the computer, contains two hidden files created by DOS and necessary for the boot up. They are shown as a single dot and two dots. You can hide some of your own files for security reasons.

High Level Format: is a process performed on the hard disk drive after low level format. It writes essential information for DOS on the hard disk. It is performed by the FORMAT command in DOS.

High Memory Area (HMA): is the first 64 K part of your PC's memory, above 1 MB. MS-DOS versions 5 and 6, as well as Windows use this memory in order to free up more of your "Conventional Memory" (the first 640 K).

Highlight: refers to the condition of a command or icon after you have selected it. Generally, it will have a slightly different color than the other items on the screen. Once you highlight an item, it is ready to do what you want it to do.

Icon: is a small graphical representation of various items on your Windows screen.

Index line: is the bar at the top line of each index card in Card File.

Initialize: refers to the initial process of preparing a floppy disk or hard disk drive for use the first time. It encompasses activities such as formatting the disk.

Initialization file: is a file with the .INI extension. These files contain critical information about your Windows environment. Your Windows subdirectory has two very important files called WIN.INI and SYSTEM.INI. You should keep a copy of these files on a floppy disk, in a safe place.

Input: is the data that you give to the computer. It can be entered into the computer by several means such as through the keyboard, a mouse, digitizer, scanner, or modem.

I/O: Input and Output is the process of giving data to or getting data from the PC. An I/O board refers to an interface card that contains a parallel port, one or two serial ports, and a game port.

Ins key: the Insert Key is usually located on the upper right hand side of the keyboard. It's used by most programs to insert something that could be as small as a character or as large as a whole document into the position of the blinking cursor.

Interactive System: gives you immediate results and allows an interchange of information between you and the computer. It differs from the old batch system where you had to wait for packs of information to go back and forth to the main computer.

Insertion point: is a point where text or graphics is inserted into your document.

Internal DOS Command: is a command that is loaded into the RAM memory of the PC when it is first powered up. The internal commands are readily available to use instantly. They don't need to be read from a DOS floppy disk or hard disk drive.

Interface: is the interaction between two devices, like a PC and a printer.

Interpreter: is a program that acts as a translator between computer readable codes and human readable codes in a program. Since a computer is based on the binary system, the information that goes into and out of the machine is binary. However, interpreter programs translate our English commands to binary and vice versa.

KB: Kilo Bytes is a thousand bytes. That's approximately equivalent to the information on half of a typed page.

Kermit: Named after Kermit the Frog, is a popular file transfer protocol for modems. It establishes a communication link between two computers and ensures that data flows error free.

Keyboard: is the device that looks like the keys on a typewriter and is attached to the PC.

Language: is a set of communication characters, symbols and rules that allow interaction between a program and the computer. Some of the better known languages are Basic, FORTRAN, Assembly, C, Pascal, COBOL, etc.

Link: is the process of connecting together the image of an object that is placed into another file or directory instead of the whole object itself. This will take up less hard disk space. If the objects are linked for automatic update, any changes made to the main object will be reflected everywhere its image is located.

List box: is a box that appears in a window or dialog box and offers a list of available choices. For example, in your word processing file, a list box may contain a list of the files in a directory.

Load: is the process of transferring data from a floppy disk or hard disk into RAM memory so that the PC can readily access that information. Data that is in memory can be accessed much faster than on a disk.

Low Level Format: is the initial hard disk drive preparation performed by the disk controller. It defines the number of sectors per track and the interleave factor. Most hard drives that have the controller built into the drive (IDE and SCSI) are low level formatted by the drive manufacturer. IDE and SCSI drives do not need to and should not be low level formatted.

Macro: is the process of assigning a series of frequently used steps or commands to one or two keystrokes. It simplifies working with a particular program or file. For example, if in your letters you always put your name and address at a specific location, you may create a Macro for that purpose. By pressing the one or two keys for that Macro, the computer automatically types your name and address at a predesignated area.

Manual link: is a link between items placed in various places whose update is set to manual. If you change anything on the main object, its images placed in various files will not change automatically.

Math Coprocessor: is a microprocessor that only performs mathematical calculations. The math coprocessor used with 80286 and 80386 family of microprocessors is a separate chip. In 80486 chips the math coprocessor function is built into the microprocessor.

Maximize button: is a small box on the upper right corner of the title bar with a small arrow pointing up. If you click your mouse on that arrow, the window you are working on will go to its full size.

Media: is the data storage material in floppy disks, hard disks, and tapes.

Megabytes (MB): is a million bytes. It's the equivalent of approximately 500 pages of typed information. The memory in your PC as well as the storage capacity of your hard disk and floppy disks are measured in MB.

Memory: is a part of the PC which stores data while your computer is powered up. It is sometimes called RAM (Random Access Memory). Information coming in and going out of your PC is handled in memory. Data from the memory is fed to the microprocessor and output from the microprocessor is handled through memory to the screen, disk, or other devices.

Memory Resident: describes a program or programs that need to reside in your PC memory in order to operate. These programs are often relatively small and need to be within easy access.

An example is a virus detection software that's in your memory actively checking for viruses.

Menu: is like a convenient collection of commands or program names arranged in an easy-to-use manner for you to simply choose and execute. Just like the menu at a restaurant, you simply choose a meal and don't need to specify all the ingredients that go into it.

MHZ: Megahertz is a measure of computer processor speed. It's one million beats per second. That's how fast a small clock on the motherboard of the computer regulates electronic signals. The original IBM PC introduced in 1981, ran at 4.77 MHZ. Top speed of some current 80486 computers reach 66 MHZ. For comparison purposes, MHZ should be used within the same microprocessor family. For example a 33 MHZ 80386 is faster than a 25 MHZ 80386. However, the same microprocessor is not as fast as a 25 MHZ 80486.

Microchannel: Microchannel Architecture was introduced in 1987 by IBM in certain models of PS/2 computers. Microchannel is a proprietary 32 bit architecture designed to increase power and throughput rate. Motherboards with the microchannel expansion slots transfer data 32 bits at a time and only work with controller boards built with the same microchannel design.

Microprocessor: is the integrated circuit chip that is the brains of your PC. It's designed with thousands of small, electronic switches that process data and interpret various commands. The original IBM PC used the 8088 microprocessor running at 4.77 MHZ, which had 29,000 switches. A more recent microprocessor chip like the 80486-50 MHZ has 1,200,000 switches.

MIDI: stands for Musical Instrumental Digital Interface. It is a communications standard between a PC and musical instruments.

Minimize button: is a small box at the upper right corner of the title bar with a small down arrow. If you click on this arrow with your mouse, the window will be reduced to an icon.

MIPS: Million Instructions Per Second is a measure of data throughput rate in a PC.

MNP: Microcom Networking Protocol is used for error correction in high speed modems. MNP is built into the modem hardware. It compresses data and checks for error correction at both ends. There are several levels of MNP. The higher the level, the more powerful the capabilities.

Modem: Modulate/Demodulate is a communication device that uses the telephone lines to allow two computers exchange data back and forth..

Monitor: is a data display device that is used to view the information being given to the computer and the response from the computer. Most monitors look like a TV screen.

MS-DOS: Microsoft - Disk Operating System is the program developed by Microsoft Corporation. Some major computer companies purchase DOS from Microsoft and slightly modify or enhance it for their own brand of PCs. MS-DOS version 6.2 was released in October 1993.

Motherboard: is the printed circuit board that often contains the microprocessor, memory, expansion slots and other key components of the PC.

Multimedia: is the new frontier in electronic communications. It combines computer text, graphics, sound, video and animation.

Multi-tasking: is the capability of a PC to run more than one program at a time.

Multi-user: is an environment or program that can be used by more than one user at the same time. All programs are available as single user and some of them may be available as multi-user. To be multi-user, a program needs to have some built-in safeguards so that users do not alter the same information simultaneously and therefore create errors or confusion.

Network: is a group of computers connected together by cable or wireless means. They can exchange information and share certain resources.

ns: nano-second is one billionth of a second. It measures the speed of memory chips.

Numeric: is a number based character or key on the keyboard.

Num Lock Key: is usually located on the top right hand side of the keyboard. When it's pressed, a small light on the keyboard signals that it's active. It makes the numeric group of keys that are located to the right of the keyboard function strictly like the keys on a calculator. This key was necessary for the earlier generation of keyboards that had other commands on the numeric keys, therefore each key served a dual function.

Object Oriented Environment: is an operating environment whereby various commands are displayed as small, often pictorial objects. For example, the Delete command may be shown as a trash can, or a file may be displayed as a folder.

Operating System: is a program that contains various commands that control the operation of your computer. The operating system also governs how various programs interact with the PC and vice versa.

Option: is a choice or a course of action, in a dialog box.

Output: is the data produced by the computer. It can be displayed on the monitor, sent to a printer, stored on a disk or tape, or sent to another computer through a modem.

Parallel: is a predefined communication standard between two devices. It's primarily used by the majority of printers. A parallel printer needs to be connected to the parallel output of a PC by a parallel cable. The cable has 8 wires and data travels 8 bits at a time over the cable. This is significantly faster than the serial port which transfers data one bit at a time.

Paste: is the process of putting an item placed in the clipboard in a designated place in your document.

PCI Local Bus: was introduced by Intel in 1993. It is the fastest connector available. It allows various components to communicate directly with the microprocessor.

Pentium: is a microprocessor introduced by Intel in 1993. It is over a hundred times faster than the chip used in the original IBM PC.

Peripheral: is a term that encompasses a lot of devices that are internal or external to the PC and attach to it to perform specific functions. When the IBM PC was first introduced, it only contained the case, power supply, motherboard, memory, floppy drive, and keyboard. Hard disk drive, monitor, mouse, modem, tape backup, printer, etc. were added by the dealer and were called peripherals. Today's PCs often come with built-in hard disk drives, and the monitor is considered so vital that it's no longer a peripheral. Therefore, the latest reference to peripherals often encompasses printer, mouse, modem, tape backup, etc.

Pixel: computer monitors form characters on the screen by generating thousands of small dots. A pixel is derived from "Picture Element" and refers to one of those dots.

Pointer: is the name of the arrow that represents your mouse cursor on the screen.

Port: is a point of interface or connection between your PC and external devices attached to it. A video port is the connection often at the back of the PC that the monitor cable attaches to. A printer port is the parallel port which is found at the back of most PCs and the printer cable plugs into it.

Postscript: is a page description programming language for printers. It simplifies the task of transferring characters and graphics from the computer to the printer. It's primarily used as a hardware or software option with laser printers. Laser printers with postscript can print a variety of characters of different shapes, sizes and shades. Postscript laser printers cost more than comparable standard laser printers.

Power Supply: is a part of the PC that is often enclosed in a chrome plated steel box and is located at the back of the system unit. It includes a transformer that converts the 110 volt AC power into 5 and 12 volts DC power for the computer components. It also includes a small cooling fan that pulls the air in from the front and sides of the PC and blows it out the back.

Print Screen: is a key often located at the top right hand side of your keyboard. Under most circumstances, if you press this key, it will print everything that appears on your screen. However, if you are in certain programs, the PC may not respond to the command.

Processor: is another term for CPU (Central Processing Unit).

Program: is a collection of commands and instructions; written in computer language; which tell your computer how to perform certain tasks. Programs also act as interpreters between you and your PC. You interact with the program in English, and it converts that to machine language in order to communicate with your PC.

Program Information File (PIF): is a file that contains information about how Windows should use a non-Windows program.

PROMPT: is the familiar C:\>- which is also called DOS Prompt. It identifies the drive which is ready to perform what ever you tell it to do. If you have A:\>- then it's ready in floppy drive A:.

Queue: is a series of commands or tasks waiting to be processed by a device. A queue may exist for the CPU, for the printer, or other devices.

RAM: Random Access Memory is the main computer memory that becomes active when your PC is powered up. The memory is capable of storing information and passing it back and forth between the processor and other components of the PC. When power is turned off, all information in RAM is wiped clean. The role of this type of memory is very similar to the countertop of a fast food restaurant or library where items are handed back and forth on the surface of the counter.

Read-only file: is a file that can be looked at but not changed or deleted.

Reboot: is the process of resetting your computer after it has been powered up. Reboot also clears the RAM as if the computer was physically turned off and then back on. If you get stuck, rebooting your PC is better than turning it off and on.

Reduce: is the process of reducing a window to an icon by clicking on the minimize button or minimize command.

Resolution: is the sharpness of an image on your computer screen. It is defined by the number of dots that create the images on the screen. The higher the number of dots, the higher the resolution.

ROM: Read Only Memory is a type of memory chip that permanently stores certain information placed in it at the factory. Unlike RAM, if the power is turned off, the ROM chip retains the data stored in it.

Root: refers to the main part of a floppy or hard disk. The disk is like a tree with a root, trunk, and branches. In computer terminology the root is actually like the trunk of the tree with branches coming off of it. Directories which you or the software you use create on the disk, help compartmentalize special sets of information together. Those directories are like branches on the tree. For example, if you create several directories, one for DOS, one for Word Processing, Database, etc., your root directory only contains the names DOS, Word Processing, Database, etc. If you then go into the word processing directory, you may create sub-directories called Letters, Reports, etc. Sub-directories are like smaller branches off of larger ones.

RS-232: is a communication interface between the computer and other devices. It's one of the oldest standards for PCs and other computers. RS-232 is commonly called serial port or COM port and connects a modem, mouse, serial printer, etc. to the computer. There are several components within the serial port that must be defined to match the characteristics of data flowing back and forth between the PC and the serial device. In serial communication, individual bits of data are sent one at a time, sequentially and on a single wire. Other wires in the cable are used for setting up specific characteristics of the sending and receiving devices.

Run: means to start or execute a program.

Screen saver: is a small program that either blanks out your screen or creates moving images that prevent damage to your screen if it is not used for a few hours.

Scroll: is the process of having several pages of information flow upwards on your screen.

Scroll bar: is a bar that appears at the right side and the bottom of each window. Inside the bar is a scroll box. At either end of the bar are scroll arrows.

Sector: is a basic unit of storage on floppy and hard disks. It's made up of 512 Bytes. The way sectors are organized varies from one manufacturer and one drive to another.

Select: is the process of choosing an item to be the subject of your next action. This is done by moving your mouse pointer over the icon and clicking a button.

Serial: see RS-232.

Shell: is a special utility program which shows other programs in an overview format. For example a DOS shell shows various important DOS commands in an organized manner that's easier to use.

Shortcut key: is a key or key combination that is needed for performing an action or command. Most pull-down menus list the shortcut keys to the right of the command.

SIMM: Single In-line Memory Module is a small circuit board that holds several DIPP memory chips. The bottom of the board looks somewhat similar to an adapter board with gold plated fingers. The SIMM board is inserted into a SIMM socket on the motherboard or memory board. SIMM boards come in 256 K, 1 MB, or 4 MB sizes. Chip speeds often range between 60 to 80 nanoseconds.

SIPP: Single In-line Pin Package is a small circuit board very similar to a SIMM, except that the bottom of the board has a series of pins. The pins of the SIPP board are inserted into a SIPP socket with a series of corresponding pin-holes. SIPP boards come in 256 K, 1 MB, or 4 MB sizes. Chip speeds often range between 60 to 80 nanoseconds. SIPP modules are less popular than SIMM.

Source Code: is the English form of the machine language part of a program. With the source code for a specific program, a knowledgeable person can modify that program without having to know the machine language used by programmer specialists who developed that program.

Spool: is a buffering function that acts as interface between your PC and devices like printers, and modems. If the printer or modem cannot process data at the same speed as the PC, data is temporarily stored in memory or on hard disk and fed to the device at the speed the device can process. This frees up the PC to perform other functions.

String: is a series of numbers, letters, or symbols that are treated as characters.

Subdirectory: is a directory within another directory, like the branches coming off of bigger branches on a tree. For example in your word processing directory, you may create subdirectories called letters, memos, legal forms, etc.

Swap file: is a part of hard disk that is put aside as storage area by Windows. It transfers information from memory to the swap file. The file may be temporary or permanent.

Synchronous: is a form of data communication between two devices whereby the flow of data is based on a timing signal emitted between the two devices.

System.Ini file: is an important initialization file for Windows that contains specific information that tell Windows how to work with your PC hardware.

Tab: is the key that is often located on the middle left hand side of your keyboard. It's a special key that moves the cursor a certain number of spaces to the right every time it's depressed. Pressing Shift and Tab together moves the cursor back to the left.

Tape Drive: is a special drive which uses a cassette tape for data storage. It's often used to make backup copies of important data on a hard disk.

Telecommunication: is the process of transmitting data back and forth over the telephone lines via modem.

Telecommuting: is a term used for people who work at home and use their PC and telephone to communicate with the computer at their office.

Terminal: is a Windows program that allows you to communicate with other computers by using the phone lines and a modem.

Text: is the written part of a program or something you have typed into the computer. Text is different from graphics which is an image drawn by means other than the keyboard.

Terminate and Stay Resident (TSR): refers to small programs that stay resident in your memory while you are doing other things with your PC.

Tile: is a method of arranging several windows side-by-side so that they are all visible.

Title bar: is a horizontal bar at the top of every window. It contains the title of the window.

Upper memory: is the 384 K of memory above the first 640 K called Conventional Memory.

Utility: is a program that facilitates or enhances the use of another program or device.

VESA Local Bus: is a high performance expansion bus that lets various components communicate directly with the microprocessor. It works with the 80486 family of microprocessors and can go up to 66 MHZ.

Vdisk: is short for "Virtual Disk" which converts a designated amount of computer memory (RAM) to act like a disk. Data stored in the Vdisk can be accessed instantly. However, as soon as the computer is turned off all data in Vdisk will be wiped clean.

VGA: Video Graphics Array is a video standard made popular by IBM during the late 1980's. It offers high resolution and a wide assortment of colors on your screen. Practically all monitors sold since 1991 are based on the VGA standard. A higher resolution version of VGA is called Super VGA or SVGA.

Virtual Memory: is a technique that uses part of a hard disk capacity to simulate additional memory.

Warm Boot: is the process of resetting or restarting your computer by pressing the "Control-Alt-Delete" keys at the same time. It clears everything from RAM and reads the DOS commands from the boot disk in order to start over again. In case your PC locks up and no other alternatives are available, instead of turning the PC off, a warm boot restarts the computer. Warm boot causes no strain on the PC and is the recommended method of getting out of a lock-up situation.

Win.Ini file: is an important file that contains setting information needed by Windows to use various programs.

Write Protect: is a helpful feature that makes sure you don't accidentally write over an existing set of information on a disk. Floppy disks can be easily write protected. On 3.5 inch floppy disks there is a small, sliding tab on the top right hand side of the disk. If you move the tab so that a little window opens, then you can't write or delete anything on that disk.

Index

PC GUIDE Introduction - Registration Card

Thank you for buying PC GUIDE Introduction to Computers.

You have joined thousands of PC GUIDE users in the United States and throughout the world. Your feedback and comments will help us improve the quality of the PC GUIDE series and make them more useful.

Please fill out and return this card so that we may send you periodic bulletins with new information you can use.

Name: _____ Title: _____

Business Name: _____

Mailing Address: _____

City: _____ State: _____ Zip: _____

What do you think about this book? _____

_____

Why did you buy this book? _____

_____

Where did you buy this book? _____
Computer/Software Store____ Bookstore____ Discount Store____ Warehouse Club____
Office Supply Store____ Electronics Store____ Other: _____
What made you choose this book? Saw it in store____ Friend recommended____
Advertisement____ Other: _____
What parts of this book are most helpful to you? _____

_____

What parts of this book are least helpful to you? _____

_____

How would you rate this book? Excellent____ Very good____ Good____ Average____
Below Average____
Did you also buy the PC GUIDE video? Yes____ No____
What other PC GUIDE products do you have? _____
How do you think we can improve PC GUIDE to make it more useful to you? _____

_____

Other comments: _____

_____

Would you like us to use your name and quote your comments in PC GUIDE products?
If you agree, please put your initials here: _____ Phone: (   ) _____

Fold Here

Attn: PC GUIDE Registration
Inter Trade Corporation
6767-B Peachtree Industrial Blvd.
Norcross, GA 30092-3665

Tape Here